CANADIAN HOLY WAR

A Story of Clans, Tongs, Murder, and Bigotry

CANADIAN HOLY WAR

A Story of Clans, Tongs, Murder, and Bigotry

Ian Macdonald
and Betty O'Keefe

Heritage
House

CANADIAN CATALOGUING IN PUBLICATION DATA
Macdonald, Ian, 1928-
Canadian holy war

Includes index.

ISBN 1-894384-11-3

1. Vancouver (B.C.)—Race relations—History. 2. Scottish Canadians—British Columbia—Vancouver—History.* 3. Chinese Canadians—British Columbia—Vancouver—History.* 4. Vancouver (B.C.)—Social conditions. 5. Smith, Janet, d. 1924. 6. Murder—British Columbia—Vancouver. I. O'Keefe, Betty, 1930- II. Title.

FC3847.9.C5M32 2000 971.1'33004 C00-910988-9
F1089.7.C5M32 2000

First edition 2000

We acknowledge the financial assistance received from the Government of Canada through the Book Publishing Industry Development Program for our publishing activities. We also thank the British Columbia Arts Council and the British Columbia Archives.

Cover design and layout by Darlene Nickull
Edited by Audrey McClellan

HERITAGE HOUSE PUBLISHING COMPANY LTD.
Unit #108 - 17655 66 A Ave., Surrey, BC V3S 2A7

Printed in Canada

Canada

This book is dedicated to the Canadians of Asian descent who for nearly a quarter of a century suffered the injustices and indignities of the federal Asian Immigration Act. They and their descendants are now an established and integral part of the fabric of Canada and have played a large role in contributing to the prosperity of the nation and the acceptance of multiculturalism not only on the West Coast, but across the entire country.

Contents

A Note on the Cover*

The classic tartans of the clans of Scotland symbolize a culture steeped in history, pride, passion, and an unrelenting sense of self-determination. Likewise, the fourth century polished jade horse shown on the book cover and incorporated into the chapter headings represents both the sheer durability and the simple beauties of the Chinese culture. Typically, neither the origins of the jade horse nor the name of the artist who created it are known.

To the western world in general and Canada specifically, the Orient has long been a land of mystery. It was viewed simply as a source of cheap labour, and little was known about the Chinese provinces and the largely male population of "coolies" who immigrated to British Columbia during the province's first 50 years of existence. This ignorance bred suspicion.

By the beginning of the twentieth century, Canada's western cities of Vancouver and Victoria were communities where many of the founding families wore their tartan proudly. Within these conclaves of Mcs and Macs a mood of protectionism evolved, and with it came harsh attitudes toward interlopers. Their appreciation for things Chinese rarely extended beyond jade carvings and other art possessions of ancient dynasties that were displayed in museums.

*The Canadian Department of the Interior certificate pictured on the cover is sealed and signed by the Controller of Chinese Immigration and acknowledges the receipt of a $500 "head tax" paid by individual Chinese immigrants to Canada in 1913. The Chinese lettering shown below the certificate accompanies an English message on the reverse which reads: Important: It is necessary that this certificate be carefully preserved as it is of value as a means of identification.

Prologue

In the homes of many of Vancouver's oldest Chinese families, and in similar homes throughout the whole of Canada, hidden away in an upstairs closet or at the back of a drawer lies a box of papers that recount the trials and tribulations of Asian families who in the first half of the twentieth century decided to make this alien country their home. For most of that time they were not permitted to become Canadian citizens and were even threatened with having any land or property they had acquired taken away from them.

In the early part of the century they were subjected to a head tax, which grew as high as $500 per person. In 1923 the federal government passed the Asian Immigration Act, which brought an end to further immigration from the Far East until the Act was repealed in 1947, after the end of the Second World War. During the time it was in force, no Chinese were permitted to enter the country, not even wives and children of men already living here.

These severe restrictions, and the social and religious persecution that was typical of the era, created an environment where racial discrimination and prejudice flourished and where, particularly in cities like Vancouver and Victoria, the largest visible minority, the Chinese, frequently became the public scapegoat for the social and criminal wrongs of the whole community.

Chinese families suffered severe handicaps. Men who had come to this new land in order to earn enough to bring their families from China to join them had to make a difficult choice. Should they stay and send money home to their wives and children, or should they give up the chance of a new life and return to their loved ones, many of whom lived in poverty-stricken areas such as Fujian (now called Fukien)? Either choice was less than attractive.

For those who remained there were other inequities. Every Asian was required to carry a photo identification card. Birth certificates issued in Canada were stamped with a Chinese Immigration sticker.

When the Asian Immigration Act was finally repealed, Chinese people born in Canada became naturalized Canadian citizens, except for those Canadian-born women who had in the interim married Chinese-born men. They were required to reapply for citizenship.

During this period many professions were out-of-bounds to Asians simply because they could not become Canadian citizens. That is why there were no Chinese lawyers until 1953, after the Immigration Act was repealed. As soon as they were permitted to do so, young Chinese men began to study law, and five years later the first of them were called to the B.C. bar. Several had previously studied law, but they were never permitted to practise as part of the legal fraternity. The services of these essentially illegal practitioners were nevertheless much appreciated within the Chinese community for half a century.

Without the prejudice and discrimination that was so rampant during these years in Canada, and without the class structure of the past which many Britons tried to recreate in Canada during these same years, the almost immediate assumption that a young Chinese houseboy had been responsible for the death of a young Scottish girl in Vancouver in 1924 would never have occurred. The existence of that prejudice, however, made Wong Foon Sing a convenient, politically acceptable suspect and the only one that a very incompetent police department could find.

As this story reveals, the death of Janet Smith was but one of the tragedies that would unfold on Canada's West Coast after the summer of 1924.

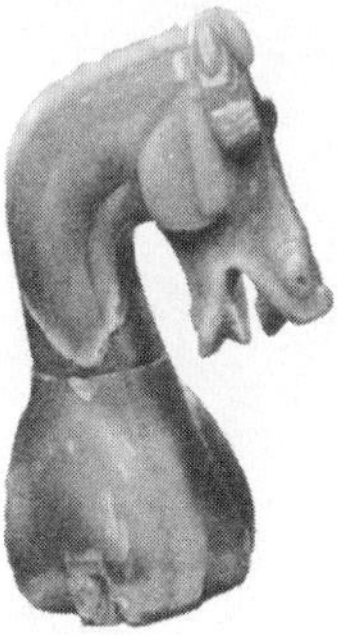

The Clans Gather

The dancers' kilts swung as the pipes skirled and the drums pounded out the beat of the old Scottish tunes, filling the air in Stanley Park. It was a cloudless sunny day at Brockton Point, the waters of Vancouver harbour sparkled, and the North Shore mountains were etched against the sky like the crags of mighty Ben Nevis in the highlands so far, far away. The multicoloured kilts of the clans made a patchwork quilt in the grassy clearing among the tall trees.

Enjoying the sights and sounds on this first day of August 1924 were some 4,000 residents of Scottish birth or with the inherited blood of Scotland still strong in their veins. They held a proud place in this young community, their numbers representing about a third of greater Vancouver's population of 250,000. They included rich entrepreneurs, professional men, merchants and their shop assistants, nursemaids and dress-makers, as well as blue-collar tradesmen and labourers who toiled in fish boats, lumber mills, and shipyards.

The social structure of the time often set the Scots apart from each other in everyday life, the wealthy seldom mixing with the working class, but on this day of celebration they were all together in Stanley Park for the eighteenth annual St. Andrew's and Caledonian Society's Highland Games. The Society was founded in 1886, the same year Vancouver was incorporated, and was the oldest Scottish organization in the city. This event was a time to honour Scots traditions and the culture brought by the pioneers to Canada. The games ensured their Canadian children would be endowed with the lore of old Caledonia, and although brought up in a new land, the next generation would not forget the ancient

Hycroft (shown here in 2000) was the magnificent mansion built in Shaughnessy between 1909 and 1913 for Major-General Alexander Duncan McRae, multi-millionaire, industrialist, Member of Parliament, and senator. He was the father of Blanche, who married Dick Baker, in whose home at 3851 Osler Avenue Janet Smith was shot to death. Hycroft was the centre for many glittering social events in the 1920s and 30s. During the Second World War the McRaes gave it to the federal government for $1 for use as a hospital. It was bought in 1962 by the University Women's Club.

legends and traditions. There was music, dancing, shouts and applause, and big, brawny men competing in centuries-old feats of strength. At one of the more popular events the competitors tossed the caber, a log almost as big as a telephone pole. They threw it incredible distances before it landed with a mighty thud that shook the ground.

One of the competing athletes was strongman John Murdoch, formerly a policeman in Glasgow and now a sergeant in the Point Grey Police Force and a prominent local amateur athlete. Among those cheering him on was Major-General Alexander Duncan McRae, one of Vancouver's richest men, who lived in splendour at Hycroft, a grand manor house on McRae Avenue. Across the field, Brigadier-General Victor Odlum also watched, keeping a distance from his rival, McRae, but anxious to pick up stories and gossip for the *Evening Star*, a two-month-old newspaper where he was the newly appointed managing editor. The two men had both served in the First World War, but Odlum resented the Major-General's promotion to the higher rank because McRae had never served in action, only from behind a desk. The two old soldiers seldom saw eye to eye on anything and were on opposing sides in politics.

Also admiring the burly muscled men tossing the caber were a host of young Scots women, many of them nursemaids enjoying a rare day off, but some with their young charges in tow. Most were in their late teens or early twenties, young women who had ventured away from Scotland with the help and encouragement of the Salvation Army to work for the well-to-do in Vancouver and perhaps to become brides for some of the many single men who lived and worked in the area. There was a great shortage of suitable, young, marriageable women in Vancouver, and the lasses from the highlands and the lowlands had high hopes of bettering themselves in this new, but still British, city by the sea. They had all taken a chance for a new life away from the bleak limitations of their Scottish homeland.

The Scots were major participants in the city's life and politics. In particular they held key roles in the administration of justice. They believed in law and order and were to be found at all levels of law enforcement: in police departments, as magistrates and lawyers in courtrooms, as judges on the bench, and in the attorney general's department at the seat of government in Victoria. Among those enjoying the games were Mr. Justice D.A. McDonald, Magistrate George McQueen, and a host of lawyers whose names began with Mc and Mac. They all cheered lustily for the Vancouver Police Pipe Band as it played in competition for the title of best in the city, their enthusiasm only slightly dampened when it placed second.

Also in the park was dour, unsmiling Rev. Duncan McDougall, a local minister who had broken away from the Presbyterian church to lead his own Highland Church congregation where he was free to express his biased, distorted view of Presbyterian Christianity and his dislike of Catholics, Jews, foreigners, and particularly Orientals, whose ways he feared and often described as evil. He ranted regularly from his pulpit on East 11th Avenue in working-class Vancouver about the sins of the foreign horde, a view lauded by some but which was an embarrassment to others. A stern, unsmiling man, he kept an eye out for human frailty and frivolity and, God forbid, any hanky-panky at the games. He also frowned on the practice, particularly common among the wealthy, of taking a swig of whiskey from a well-concealed silver flask. In McDougall's rigid, unbending world, enjoyment and the frailties of the flesh were something to be feared and avoided.

For most of the huge crowd, however, this was a happy day, and there were some in attendance without a drop of Scottish blood in their veins who came to the gathering simply to enjoy the popular annual celebration with their friends. It was a day for tall tales and gossip while everyone waited for the next major event, and in the hum of conversation that ran through the crowd on this August day in 1924, one topic dominated. The young Scots women were shocked and disturbed at the fate of one of their own, a 22-year-old lass, alone in Vancouver and far from her family. Poor Janet Smith, a Perthshire-born nursemaid, had lived in a smart Shaughnessy home with members of one of the city's best-known and respected families. Now she was dead.

There were many different views about what had actually happened to her, as well as wild rumours and speculation about the events that had transpired in that charming craftsman-style house on Osler Avenue only the week before. Some of the young people at the games had known Janet Smith, had frequented the same St. Andrew's Presbyterian Church she attended, or met her at Get Acquainted Club Saturday night dances in the Dominion Hall on West Pender Street. The opinions of the women differed as they debated what might have happened, but there was little doubt in their minds about one thing: there had been only two adults in the house with baby Rosemary the day that Janet died. One of them was Janet Smith herself and the other was houseboy Wong Foon Sing. Now the young Scottish girl was dead and the houseboy had to know what had happened to her, he had to know more than he was telling.

Dick and Blanche Baker, owners of the house on Osler Avenue where Janet Smith was shot.

Amid the more affluent Shaughnessy crowd, the girl's death was debated in whispers that would not be heard by members of the families involved. General McRae's daughter Blanche was married to one of the Baker boys, and Janet had died in their home. At the time, Blanche was vacationing in Europe with her husband, Richard, but Richard's brother and his wife, Fred and Doreen Baker, were temporarily living in the comfortable home. The dead girl had been nursemaid for their baby daughter Rosemary. At first reported as a suicide, there was now speculation as to whether Janet Smith's death was accidental, a suicide, or a murder. Most of the Scots suspected, as details were gradually revealed, that the Chinese houseboy was the killer.

Social and racial discrimination were a part of everyday life, constantly threatening to boil over in the Vancouver of 1924. It was a city rampant with supposedly God-fearing men and self-righteous women, religious fervour, Protestants, Catholics, the establishment, the working class, and the foreigners. This last group was epitomized by the largest ethnic minority: the 17,000-odd Chinese, who for the most part lived in and around Chinatown. It was nearly twenty years since the race riots of 1907, but they were still well remembered by the established communities of Scots and Chinese, who remained suspicious of each other. The language barrier prevented easy communication and thwarted understanding, so the two races who often worked together also ignored each other as much as possible.

There wasn't a wall around Chinatown, but the barriers were there, and a fortress had been built on East Pender Street near Carrall. It was five storeys high and contained living accommodation for a large number of people as well as retail space for thirteen stores on the ground level. Three- or four-room suites were available for families, and there were beds for single men, often as many as 20 or 30, who lived on one of the lower floors. The building stretched from Pender down Shanghai Alley on one side, with the other arm running along the railway tracks. One of the daily chores for Chinese children was to pick up coal spilled from railcars that shunted along the tracks behind the building. It was stored beside the stove in each suite and provided heat for the family during the winter months.

The shops on the ground level of the fortress circled Canton Alley, and iron gates leading from the Alley into Pender Street could be closed to keep out the treacherous Scots in case they again threatened Chinese lives. The Chinese had few rights and little recourse if they were cheated or beaten, so they kept to themselves and some felt safer inside the fortress.

Chinese children of this era generally attended Strathcona school during the daytime and Chinese schools from 7 to 9 p.m. Harassment was a common pastime, as white children often chased Chinese youngsters on their way to and from school. They were not the only ones to suffer from the biases and prejudices of the era, however. Protestants also harassed Catholics, and then Catholics retaliated and ganged up on Protestants. A few wary Jews kept their eyes on all of them. To youngsters of this era, perhaps fortunately, childhood was short. Everyone began work at an early age, though white children started a little later than the Chinese, who spent their summers working in the fields and vegetable gardens along the Fraser River by the time they were nine or ten.

While the majority of residents frequented the city's eight bathing beaches in summer, canoed along the shores of the harbour, played tennis, and visited dance halls and bandstands, Asians stuck to their own neighbourhood, preferring the ambience there, the food in their own restaurants, and the entertainment at the Chinese Opera to anything in the white man's world. They did not appear on the beaches nor take part in the July 1 weekend festivities, which had recently ended and had been highlighted by the appearance of two huge British

Among the many Chinese immigrants to British Columbia early in the twentieth century were the parents of Andy Joe, the first Chinese Canadian called to the B.C. bar in 1953.

warships, HMS *Hood* and HMS *Repulse*, along with the Australian cruiser HMAS *Adelaide*, which had sailed into the harbour to celebrate the Canadian holiday.

Churches were the main gathering places for a majority of residents, and on Sundays the largely Presbyterian Scots, the Anglican English, and the Catholic Irish of the community met for worship and to hear sermons advocating Christian principles and a better way of life. The great church debate underway at the time was whether to amalgamate the Congregationalist, Methodist, and Presbyterian churches, and everyone, involved or not, had a point of view. The United Church of Canada was eventually created on June 10, 1925, but only a few Presbyterian churches agreed to unite.

While the British immigrants attended their church services, the Chinese met at the Oriental Club, a brightly painted building complete with restaurant and gaming tables. It was the site of many tong society functions. One of the largest tongs, the equivalent of a Scottish clan, was the Lim Tong, sometimes called the Lam or Lum Tong. Its function was to provide social support, to loan money when members needed it, and to protect them from outsiders. Wong Foon Sing, the houseboy at the Baker home on Osler Avenue, would soon rely on the Lim Tong to hire one of the city's top lawyers to defend him. The Gee Gung Tong, or Chinese Free Masons, was a clandestine society pledged to free China from the Manchu dynasty, and its members were often feared by other Chinese, but membership in most of the tongs was based on family relationships, similar occupations, or the place of origin of its members. In Vancouver they were a support mechanism for Asians living in an alien land with few rights and no opportunity to become citizens of the country.

Some of the practices of the Chinese community particularly rankled the more strait-laced Protestants of Vancouver, who believed sin and degradation were widespread in Chinatown. Their garish gold-and-red-painted nightclubs seemed offensive to the dour Scots, and newspapers often reported that the area's mysterious, murky cabarets dealt in bootlegging and prostitution. The white population was aware that opium dens had been legal in Chinatown until 1908, and many believed that Asians condoned gambling.

The prejudice against Orientals was nationwide. A head tax of $50 had been imposed on all Chinese entering Canada in 1885. It was raised to $100 in 1901 and $500 in 1905. In 1907 many Asians were beaten and their homes destroyed when race riots raged through Vancouver's Chinatown. Things got even worse for the Chinese in 1923 when Ottawa passed the Asian Immigration Act, barring further immigration and preventing the largely male Chinese population from bringing wives and children into the country. The passage of the law added weight and a sense of respectability to the white majority's prejudice against the Chinese who lived and worked amongst them, and race relations reached a low point in the history of the country. Following implementation of the immigration act in April 1924, a regulation was introduced that required all Chinese to register with the government and carry an identification card. Also in 1924, in Regina, Saskatchewan, city council passed a by-law that prohibited white women from working in Chinese cafes.

The original Chinese Benevolent Association building on West Pender, built in 1909, remains in daily use in Vancouver's Chinatown although it is no longer headquarters for the society, which has moved to more modern premises around the corner on Main Street.

It was not long after this that the government in Victoria discussed enacting a law to prevent Chinese and Japanese from owning, selling, leasing, or renting land in B.C. or alternatively imposing conditions on their rights of ownership. Fortunately this proposal never proceeded beyond the discussion stage.

It is small wonder that the Scots and the Chinese mingled only during working hours. They did so because the Chinese provided many essential services: working in laundries, repairing shoes, and serving in the homes of the wealthy. This was an era when the iceman, the greengrocer, and the butter-and-egg man ran their regular routes in a black Ford truck or horse and cart and delivered their goods to the back doors of the city's homes. The vegetable man was almost always Chinese. In 1918 the Chinese consul made an official protest against the very high fee—$50—for the vendors licence required by vegetable peddlers. In fact, throughout the 1920s the Chinese consul found himself appealing to the attorney general for political intervention on numerous occasions when a conflict developed and threatened to lead to violence because of fragile race relations in the community. While this situation prevailed and the Chinese were banned from the rights of citizenship, the Chinese consul, the Chinese Benevolent Association, and the Chinese tongs performed an important role for the Asian population.

Following the end of the World War in 1918 there was a severe economic downturn in Vancouver and across Canada, jobs were in short supply, and new Scots immigrants arriving daily in the city found themselves in direct competition for jobs with the Chinese. Whenever there was a shortage of employment or an upsurge in crime, the Scots blamed the Chinese, who in turn felt unjustly accused and feared the Scots because of their influence with law enforcement agencies and government authorities.

Vancouver's population, white or Asian, was often enflamed into hostility or action by the daily newspapers, which were anxious to provide the news of the day and also to sell as many papers as possible. There were as many daily newspapers at this time as at any other in the city's history. Often they influenced or tried to influence public opinion, sometimes they merely reflected it, but in the case of the Janet Smith affair there is no question some newspapers had their own agenda.

Only two days after the young girl's body was found, the *Evening Star*'s managing editor, Victor Odlum, printed a headline that stated "Nurse's Death Puzzles—Suicide Theory is Not Satisfactory to Officials." The headline was not the result of hard factual news so much as personal pique. The young Scots girl's death provided Odlum with a chance to embarrass his long-time rival, McRae.

When the *Evening Star* had published its first edition only weeks earlier, on June 2, 1924, it sold for one cent per copy and its front page featured an editorial by Charles E. Campbell, the owner and publisher, who stated that the aim of the paper was the "upbuilding of Greater Vancouver and British Columbia." He emphasized that the eight pages of the daily would be the "organ of the wage earner as well as men who furnished capital." In the centre of the fairly long article was a statement of belief intended to gain new subscriptions for the *Star*. It said, "We are unalterably opposed to further invasion of B.C. by Orientals and will advocate the elimination of Asiatics from all those industries dealing with the natural resources of this province."

Vancouver was so well endowed with scenic attractions and outdoor recreational facilities that even in 1924 a total of 850,000 tourists visited the city, arriving primarily by train and ship. Many visitors would have arrived at Pier D on ships like the Empress of Australia *(right), while either the* Russia *or* Asia *is alongside the pier. The* Princess Charlotte *and possibly the* Princess Louise *are berthed on the west side of the dock.*

The statement was an indication of the level of racial discrimination that existed at the time in Vancouver, throughout B.C., and across the Dominion.

Vancouver's three dailies, the *Vancouver Daily Province*, the *Vancouver Sun,* and the *Evening Star*, were delivered to subscribers by boys on bikes or sold on street corners in the downtown area. Owners and paperboys prayed for the days when there would be an "Extra" to flog to people on the street.

By far the most outlandish and flamboyant stories appeared not in the dailies but in a weekly scandal sheet called the *Saturday Tribune*, and the most biased reporting came from the monthly *Beacon*, which was dedicated to "casting light on dark places" but rarely did so. It was produced by the aforementioned religious fanatic Rev. Duncan McDougall, who regularly expounded upon what in later years would be deemed some most unchristian thoughts. Only a few weeks after the Highland Games, this unsmiling, bigoted man told hundreds of mourning and angry Scots at a graveside service for Janet Smith that it

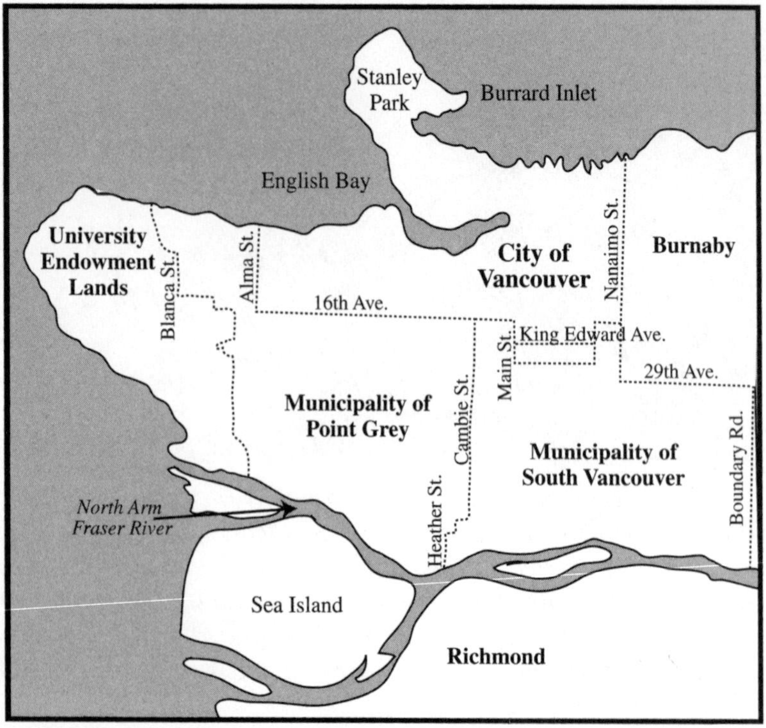

Originally centred around Gastown and the Hastings and Main area, by the mid-1920s Vancouver included, in addition to Chinatown, the residential neighbourhoods of the West End, Mount Pleasant, Kitsilano, and Fairview Heights as well as Vancouver Heights and East Vancouver, South Vancouver, and Point Grey were separate municipalities that existed from 1908 to 1929, when the three large districts amalgamated to become the City of Vancouver.

was a time of "Holy War." In his mind, the enemy was the Chinese. This statement and his other intemperate charges against Wong Foon Sing heightened the developing ugly mood.

Since 1907, Asians had subscribed to their own paper in their own language. The *Chinese Times* was published daily by the Chinese Free Masons Association and often ran between ten and twenty pages in length. It was well read and frequently provided the only source of news about events in China as well as local issues for the Chinese-speaking population of B.C. A respected publication, its coverage of local events was often more rational than that found in the English-language press.

Vancouver in the mid-1920s, despite its class structure, outlandish discriminatory practices, and attempts at sophistication, was an exciting, vital boomtown with all the attendant problems of a young city growing up very fast. Despite the Scots' concentration on law and order, policing and justice, the young city and its population had problems that concerned residents, particularly young married families with children (who made up the majority). Their concerns were reflected in the newspapers, which frequently called on the police department to clean up Chinatown. By 1924, editorial pages were full of appeals to amalgamate the police forces of Vancouver, Point Grey, and South Vancouver in order to improve the performance and crime-solving capabilities of the police in the region. (The city proper did not yet include the districts of Point Grey and South Vancouver, which were separate municipalities. Point Grey encompassed a huge area of what today includes Point Grey, Dunbar, McKenzie Heights, Kerrisdale, Shaughnessy, and Marpole. The Point Grey municipal hall and police station were located in Kerrisdale.)

The efforts of editors were rewarded in 1929 when the three communities finally joined. One of the many factors contributing to amalgamation was the death of the young Scots girl Janet Smith, and the police brutality and incompetence that characterized the ensuing investigation. A major player in the developing plot was an erratic politician, Attorney General Alex Manson, whose actual role remains clouded in legalese and evasive pronouncements, but which may have been more pivotal than anyone imagined. The involvement of individuals at all levels of the social spectrum made the death of the young girl a hot story for all the papers, as well as a major topic of conversation everywhere in the city for nearly a year. It all began on July 26, 1924.

Death on a Sunny Morning

It was a peaceful sunny morning on tree-lined Osler Avenue in Shaughnessy. Because many residents were away for the weekend or on summer vacation, there was even less traffic than usual on the boulevarded street, although there never was very much in this sedate neighbourhood.

The district of Shaughnessy was the brainchild of Canadian Pacific Railway president Thomas Shaughnessy, who lived in magnificent splendour in Montreal but built a many-splendoured summer place for himself on Angus Drive and also lent his name to the golf course, which in turn named him first honorary president when it opened on July 13, 1922. (Part of the original Shaughnessy Golf Course is now the city's famous Van Dusen Gardens.) Mr. R. Marpole, another CPR executive who gave his name to a local neighbourhood, was the first president of the prestigious Shaughnessy Golf and Country Club. The club and surrounding residential area were planned by Shaughnessy as money-making ventures for the CPR, designed as an enclave for the rich and famous on the West Coast. The homes were generally larger and more opulent than most of those built earlier in the West End and often boasted a coach house, porte-cochere, and circular drive. Many of them remain today as part of the city's affluent Shaughnessy neighbourhood.

There were still vacant lots in Shaughnessy in 1924, and the steady, muffled sound of hammering could be heard on that day as two men worked to build a new home they hoped to complete before the autumn rains set in. They were working next door to 3851 Osler Avenue, which was a relatively small house, dwarfed by some of its more stately neighbours across the street or down the road. The house, built in what was then the relatively new craftsman style, was almost entirely constructed of wood and featured two tall stone chimneys, a gabled roof, and a wide covered veranda. There was a small stone wall in front with an iron gate. The house was not built of huge stone blocks or adorned with towering pillars like some of its neighbours, the massive mansions of McRae Avenue, Angus Drive, Hudson, or The Crescent. There were a few residents of the area who had summer places along the coast or tucked away in mountain valleys that were comparable to the home built at 3851 Osler.

Sometimes neighbours wondered why Blanche Baker, the daughter of General McRae, didn't live in something grander. Her father presided at Hycroft, one of the grandest homes in the city. Built between 1909 and 1913 it contained 30 rooms on three floors: ten rooms on the main level, twelve on the second floor, and eight upstairs, which were the servants' quarters.

McRae was born in Glencoe, Ontario, and went to the United States, where he opened an insurance business. Several years later he sold it, returning to Winnipeg with an investment of $50,000, which he soon parlayed into a fortune through land purchases and sales. By 1909 he was reported to have amassed $9 million. In British Columbia his fortune multiplied through investments in land, forestry, fisheries, and coal mining.

McRae's daughter Blanche married Richard Baker at a quiet ceremony in July 1922 in Minneapolis. The wedding took place at St. Clement's Roman Catholic Church and was followed by a small reception at the home of her grandmother, Mrs. Howe, who was in poor health. The newlyweds visited Winnipeg, Banff, and then cruised B.C.'s Sunshine Coast on their honeymoon. Blanche and her husband now resided in the modest Osler Avenue home, just a short walk from the McRae manor.

Although at this time not a wealthy man, Richard Baker was well connected and had an enviable war record. His aunt, the extremely wealthy Lily Lefevre, was on a social par with General McRae. Mrs. Lefevre was the widow of Dr. John Lefevre, CPR physician and dealer in Vancouver real estate. He had purchased land on the far side of False Creek just before the first bridge was built across it. Mrs. Lefevre's business acumen and stock dealings had more than doubled the fortune left by her husband when he died. She was an artist, writer, and patron of the arts, a doyenne of society. With no children of her own, Mrs. Lefevre had taken a particular interest in her sister's three youngsters, Richard, Frederick, and Nanno Baker, influencing their education and upbringing, and often inviting them to her elegant home in the West End and later to Langaravine, a beautiful estate she had built far out in Point Grey at 6106 Northwest Marine Drive. It had a commanding view of the North Shore and Howe Sound.

The Baker children had been born at Donald, in eastern B.C., where their father worked for the CPR. Under their aunt's guidance in Vancouver, they began to live the good life, mixing with all the right people, attending the elegant balls and country club events that were part of early Vancouver society life for the wealthy. They were bright, privileged young people, born into a shining new twentieth century, living in their own sheltered world in the days before the First World War.

Richard began his career in commerce and was positioned as a bottom-of-the-ladder Bank of Montreal clerk to gain experience, while Fred articled with a law firm as a future barrister. In an affected oft-practised British way, the Baker brothers were often referred to by their initials; Richard Plunkett was R.P. and his brother Frederick Lefevre was F.L. Their sister Nanno learned the art of entertaining under Aunt Lily's tutelage. But Europe's guns of August in 1914 changed everybody's world. A year later the Baker boys enlisted with the infantry and marched off to war, soon transferring to the Royal Flying Corps to serve with a group of volunteers who took on one of the war's most dangerous roles, with a deadly casualty rate. Both of them lasted about six months in the Royal Flying Corps before being shot down. Miraculously, both survived. Dick Baker had the dubious honour of being the 40th recorded kill for Manfred von Richthofen, the Red Baron. He managed to land his plane, was captured by the Germans, and held as a prisoner of war. He returned to Vancouver a hero and shortly thereafter married Blanche, General McRae's oldest daughter. Fred, on the other hand, was shot down near Lens in France, wounded, and spent some time in hospital in England before returning to Canada. Back in Vancouver, he was restless in civilian life and returned to London where he became a partner in a small import-export business dealing in pharmaceuticals. His partner in the firm of Baker, Golwynne and Company was Henry Golwynne, an English businessman with whom he had become acquainted. During a visit to Vancouver in 1921, Fred met a Victoria girl, Doreen Marie Smith. They were married in the capital city on January 19, 1922, in St. Andrew's Roman Catholic Cathedral. The *Victoria Colonist* noted that their "Pretty Wedding Was Quietly Solemnized." Doreen had only one attendant, her sister Mary, and Herbert Wilson was the best man. Following the ceremony the couple left the capital by boat for Seattle en route to London, England, where they lived for about a year

Fred and Doreen's first child, Rosemary, was born there in November 1922, and Doreen interviewed a number of young women seeking positions as nursemaids before finding a young Scots girl named Janet Smith, whom she hired in January 1923. In the spring, a business associate of Baker's firm was arrested for suspected illicit dealings in drugs, and Baker decided to liquidate his holdings on the continent. As a result, the family moved to France in April. Janet Smith went along and was soon taking French lessons in her spare time, revelling at the chance to live on the continent. The decision to stay with the Bakers when they moved on to Vancouver in the fall of 1923 was more difficult, but in the end Janet, a lively, happy blonde, decided it might be an exciting new adventure.

Richard and Blanche Baker departed in the spring of 1924 for an extended trip to Europe. The couple left their home in Shaughnessy in the care of brother Fred and Doreen, who moved in temporarily from a house on Nelson Street in the West End that they shared with Fred's mother. With the Osler Avenue home came houseboy Wong Foon Sing, who cleaned, cooked, and polished for the family, sleeping in the "Chinaman's room" in the basement. Wong was 27, a handsome, well-dressed man with an athletic build and, at 5' 8", taller than the average Chinese. He had arrived in Vancouver several years earlier and obtained

The house at 3851 Osler is not much changed externally today from what it was in 1924 when Janet Smith was shot to death in the basement. Only a few hours before her death, the 22-year-old nursemaid brought baby Rosemary to the outside iron gate to wave goodbye to her parents as they left for downtown. It was the last time her employers, Fred and Doreen Baker, were to see alive the Scottish girl they had brought with them from Europe to Vancouver.

the job with the Richard Bakers through a recommendation from his uncle, who worked for a prominent Vancouver lawyer. Fred and Doreen, with baby Rosemary and nursemaid Janet Smith, took up residence at 3851 Osler in May 1924.

On Saturday, July 26, the Bakers left the house early in the morning, Fred going to his import-export company office and Doreen heading for the shops and to do some family errands. The nursemaid brought Rosemary down to the garden gate to wave goodbye to her parents. The infant then was returned to her upstairs nursery for a morning nap, and Janet Smith began the laundry and ironing in preparation for the family's return to Nelson Street, which was scheduled for Monday when the Richard Bakers were due home. The houseboy cleared up the breakfast dishes and turned to his other regular chores. Rosemary's parents were expected home for lunch, and just before noon Wong began to peel potatoes. Before he finished he was startled by a loud bang that sounded like a car backfiring. He looked outside but could see nothing unusual in the street. He was puzzled by the noise, not sure what had caused it. All was quiet in the basement where he had last seen Janet Smith. She usually sang at her work, but now there was only silence as Wong hurried downstairs to check on her.

He cried out at what he found. Janet Smith was lying flat on her back on the laundry room floor, broken glasses beside her. There was a hole in her temple above her right eye. Blood had stained her thick, blonde hair and was now forming a pool on the concrete floor. A large revolver lay near her outstretched hand, and the hot iron, its cord pulled from a plug in the ceiling, lay on the floor beside her body. Her head was almost under the laundry tub and her legs were under the ironing board on which the baby's clothes were neatly piled.

Wong, horrified and frightened, knelt beside her and tried to raise her head. His hands and his apron became covered with blood and he wiped them with a towel. Realizing he could do nothing to help he dashed upstairs and phoned Fred Baker to tell him of the terrible tragedy he had discovered. Near panic, he excitedly stammered that something had happened to "Nursie." Baker said he would be home immediately. While he waited, Wong Foon Sing called his uncle, Wong Ling Sai Jack, the long-time servant of leading city lawyer Harry Senkler. He then went into the garden to wait for Fred Baker, who arrived within a few minutes and dashed upstairs to check on Rosemary. Assuring himself that she slept peacefully, he descended to the laundry room, knelt beside the young girl's body, and tried to put some water to her lips. He checked for a heartbeat but found none and realized she must be dead. Baker phoned the Point Grey police, who arrived within ten or fifteen minutes, accompanied by a doctor.

The mystery of Janet Smith's death was beginning to unfold. It was a tragedy that was to affect the reputations and lives of many people in the next eighteen months, but none more than Wong Foon Sing.

Hasty Inquest

An inquest was called within two days of Janet Smith's death. It was a routine inquiry into the demise of a domestic servant in a Shaughnessy home. Point Grey police had decided her death was a suicide. Young girls of this era often took their own lives when things went wrong rather than face the shame and embarrassment of public scorn, and it provided a convenient explanation for the somewhat ill-equipped and ill-trained men of the Point Grey detachment.

Victor Odlum's *Evening Star* pounced quickly on the story and began extensive coverage of the girl's death. The first headline on Monday, July 28, stated, "Janet Smith, 23-year-old Nurse Girl Shot in Right Temple."

The inquest was straightforward and proceeded quickly. No lawyers had been hired to represent anyone, and there were no challenges or questions asked as testimony was presented. Coroner Dr. W.D. Brydone-Jack was brisk and matter of fact, keeping the details of the case to a minimum.

Chief Hiram Simpson of the Point Grey police and two constables gave their versions of events and their investigations and stated they believed Janet Smith had taken her own life. None of the evidence they presented actually pointed to this possibility, but their minds were made up and they were adamant she had committed suicide.

Fred Baker testified that he believed she must have been examining the gun out of curiosity and somehow it discharged. It was his, he said, and he had put it in a haversack, which he hung on a peg in the hallway when he and his family moved into the house in May. Smith's employer said the gun was loaded but jammed, and houseboy Wong Foon Sing had put it away in the attic a few days after they moved in. Baker said he and Constable James Green both handled the gun after the policeman picked it up and tried to unload it. The weapon was once again jammed and defied their joint efforts to loosen it.

Baker offered his view that the .45 went off while Smith was "playing with the gun." It seems unlikely she would have done this while in the midst of the ironing, but nobody challenged the suggestion. Baker said his nursemaid was a happy person and he knew of no reason why she would have taken her own life. He acknowledged that one of the first questions Green asked him was if there had been any trouble between Smith and Wong Foon Sing. He replied that there was none.

Dr. Archibald Hunter, who carried out the autopsy, said the girl was five feet one inch tall, weighed 125 pounds, and had been in good health. He then raised an issue that dogged the investigation from the beginning and was never resolved. He found no powder burns on Smith's forehead. With no burns, he said, the shot must have been fired from more than ten inches away, and it would have been very difficult for the young woman to hold the heavy revolver that far away, point the barrel at an angle, and then pull the trigger. This information contradicted the suicide theory, but the point was not explored by Brydone-Jack or anyone else. It almost appeared as if the participants had agreed on the verdict before the inquest was held.

Dr. Hunter and Dr. R.H. Mullen, who also examined the body, were puzzled by the amount of skull damage, wondering how it could have been inflicted by a single bullet. Mullen said he had never seen so many fractures made by one bullet, and Hunter commented that the major skull fracture was more than six inches long. Baker suggested that in falling, the woman must have hit her head on the laundry tub.

When Wong Foon Sing took the stand, he was cautioned that whatever he said would be taken down in writing and could be used at any further proceedings. The *Daily Province* reported, "The Oriental willingly gave his evidence through an interpreter." The houseboy said he spoke "working" English, which wasn't good enough for testimony in a legal situation, and an interpreter was required. Wong repeated the story he had told the police earlier. He explained that his hands and his apron were covered in blood because he had lifted Janet's head off the floor. It had been an automatic reaction, he said, an attempt to help her if she was still alive. The six-man jury listened attentively to his evidence but had no questions.

Sitting grimly in the small courtroom was an increasingly angry friend of Janet Smith, a fellow domestic servant. Cissie Jones displayed mounting aggravation and annoyance with the testimony. When later called as a witness, she seemed self-possessed and confident, stating that Janet was a happy young woman who would never kill herself. Jones had her own agenda and very carefully planted the seed that she hoped would grow into a major issue. She said that her friend "Nettie" was afraid of being alone in the Osler house with Wong. Jones stressed that Smith had lived in fear and was apprehensive of the houseboy. The jurors listened to her evidence, but again asked no questions. Whether or not they believed Cissie's testimony was a moot point. She had managed to turn the spotlight of suspicion on Wong Foon Sing.

Janet Smith had left two small diaries that were entered as exhibits, but nothing was read from them. It took the jurors less than fifteen minutes to reach a verdict of accidental death, but there were a mounting number of unanswered questions that came to the minds of those who attended the hearing. Coroner Brydone-Jack nonetheless accepted the jury's finding, so it seemed the story of Janet Smith's life and death was closed. Chief Simpson told reporters that there had been nothing in the evidence to suggest foul play and there was nothing else to be done in light of the jury's verdict.

The following day the *Star*'s reporter, anxious to keep the story on the front page, dug a little deeper and suggested something other than accidental death. The headline read, "City Scots to Probe Death of Nurse, Jury's Verdict Unsatisfactory." Other sub-headlines proclaimed, "President J.M. Ross of Caledonian Society Wants Private Investigation. Janet Fell on Top of Gun, Was Burned on Right Breast and Arm. Fracture of Skull All the Way to the Crown." The story reported that inquest doctor Mullen "had never seen so many fractures from a bullet," and his associate Hunter stated she must have been shot from more than six inches away because there were no powder burns.

The *Vancouver Sun*'s story on the inquest was brief and could easily have been missed. It appeared on page thirteen, under a heading that read, "No Suggestions Of Foul Play In Girl's Death." It quoted Baker as stating he had tried to unload the gun a few weeks earlier but it was jammed, and Wong testifying that he and Smith had first seen the gun about the same time, shortly after the Fred Baker family moved to the Osler Avenue home.

The newspaper stories generated enough talk to prompt Police Chief Simpson to take another look at the basement where Smith's death occurred. He went there with his trusty constables James Green and Fred Fish to reconfirm the details. This visit turned into one of the more outlandish happenings in the Keystone-Cops-style history of Point Grey's finest. Lying on the basement floor in full view was a .45 calibre bullet, which the police now presumed to be the one that tore through Janet Smith's head. How they came to miss it during their first investigation and how it remained undamaged after travelling through her skull was never explained.

The police had earlier recovered the gun, but their handling of it had wiped out any chance of identifying fingerprints on the weapon. Also, if the gun was jammed earlier and jammed again after the girl's death, could it actually be the murder weapon? Few observers disagreed with a plaintive plea for understanding that came a few weeks later from Point Grey reeve and police commissioner G.A. Walkem, who said his men were not trained investigators but they had done their best. Their best was, however, awful, and their bungling from the start compounded the mystery of Janet Smith's death.

Her burial, like the inquest, was short and simple. She was laid to rest in Mountain View Cemetery, far from her home and family in Scotland and England. The ceremony was conducted without fanfare by the Rev. James Henderson of St. Andrew's Presbyterian Church, which she had attended regularly. There were only a few on hand to watch as her casket was lowered into the ground. Among them was her employer, Fred Baker. As earth covered the simple coffin, there were those with ulterior motives who began to set the wheels of unrest in motion. Janet Smith would not lie in peace for long.

Cissie Jones Cries Murder

Within hours of her friend's burial, the vengeful Cissie Jones called on the Rev. Duncan McDougall and poured out her angry suspicions about the Chinese houseboy. She was convinced he had killed Janet.

Cissie Jones knew Rev. McDougall's reputation well because of his public diatribes against foreigners and the Shaughnessy establishment, made from the pulpit in his church and in meeting halls where he addressed young Scottish immigrants. One of his favourite topics was the exploitation by the wealthy of working girls from Britain, particularly Scottish girls. Both Cissie Jones and Janet Smith were typical of many young immigrants of the period who represented the downtrodden from the British Isles. Cissie felt strongly that the rich misused the serving class, who were badly treated and underpaid. Janet Smith had received $20 a month plus room and board, probably considerably more than Cissie herself was paid as housemaid in the home of John Rose.

Jones shared her convictions about Janet's death with Rev. McDougall, who as part of his ministry supported a variety of radical causes, including the Ku Klux Klan. He revelled in controversy. Cissie Jones received a sympathetic hearing from the minister, and McDougall quickly agreed with her. His interest was further whetted when she explained that the event had transpired in the Bakers' home and they were a Catholic family. McDougall promised Jones he would convey her fears immediately to people he knew within the United Council of Scottish Societies, which coordinated the activities of some twenty Scots organizations ranging from the Burns Society to the Daughters of Scotland and the St. Andrew's and Caledonian Society. The Council regarded itself as the guardian of all Scots, particularly young immigrants.

The minister's representations, however, got a cold reception from leading members of the Council, who knew well his extremist views and wanted as little as possible to do with him. McDougall then tried another approach, as he did have some support within the Council. He talked to some of the members individually, and he found ready listeners whenever he stressed Cissie Jones' suspicions about houseboy Wong Foon Sing. As he gained support, McDougall went further afield, approaching groups outside the Council that he knew shared some of his views.

The Scots continued to follow stories in the papers and discussed in particular comments made by John Lake, a longshoreman and close friend of Janet Smith, who had taken her to a Get Acquainted Club dance while her fiancé was out of town and had also escorted her to a picnic on Bowen Island. Her ticket on the *Lady Alexandra* cost him a dollar. Lake talked to a reporter at the *Daily Province*, explaining that he had given information to the police but they had not followed it up. Lake said he last met Smith at a dance two days before her death and had walked with her from the dance hall to a streetcar. He said he had always found her vivacious, attractive, cheerful, and fun-loving, but he explained that when he thought back on their conversation that night, he was disturbed by some of the things she told him. His misgivings were not disclosed in precise detail in the newspaper story, but emerging from it was the tantalizing hint of an affair between the young white woman and the Chinese houseboy. Among his statements was one that indicated Smith had told him that Wong Foon Sing "bothered her and tried to act smart on frequent occasions."

There were some who wondered about Lake's objectives. Janet Smith, on the spur of the moment, had become engaged to Arthur Dawson, a recent immigrant from England and a widower in his early 30s. Lake apparently escorted Smith whenever Dawson was out of town and had also proposed to her, but she had turned him down. Her friends suggested Janet fell in and out of love very quickly. The Scots began to wonder if she had had an affair with Wong or if Lake was a rejected, angry suitor with his own motive.

Another news story carried a statement from Arthur Dawson and appeared shortly after he arrived in Vancouver from Roberts Creek on the Sechelt Peninsula, where he was homesteading and working at a lumber mill. He was building a house for his bride-to-be, whom he had first met some seven months earlier. He went to the police and was shown his late fiancée's diaries. Dawson thumbed through them and later told reporters he was "satisfied." It appeared that he accepted the police version of what had happened and the jury's inconclusive finding of accidental death.

On July 29, only three days after Smith's death, the *Vancouver Sun* went on a law-and-order crusade and ran a story stating that a branch of the Ku Klux Klan had been organized in Vancouver and officers had been appointed. No names were mentioned and the story was skimpy on facts, but the Klan at the time was making inroads in Canada and across North America. The B.C. headquarters of the organization was listed in 1925 as Glen Brae at 1690 Matthews Avenue in Shaughnessy, the home of William Tait. There was also a branch in Toronto. The *Sun*, anxious to push its campaign for amalgamation of area police departments—especially those in Vancouver, South Vancouver, Point Grey, and Burnaby—used Smith's mysterious death, along with the reported rise of the KKK in the city, as fodder to support its cause. One editorial was headed "Metropolitan Detective Service Needed." It stated that despite Chief Simpson's contentions, not all the facts had been brought out in the Smith woman's death. In honeyed tones, the paper asserted that this didn't mean Point Grey hadn't brought out all the facts it had uncovered and hadn't taken every possible step "within their competence to elucidate the mystery," but that they still needed help. The *Sun* argued that the ham-fisted amateurism underlined the need for a "metropolitan police force with a trained detective department." The paper's final comment was that it was not derogatory to suggest such a trained detective department had made discoveries the Point Grey investigators had missed.

The law enforcement agencies in Greater Vancouver were a long way from Scotland Yard. The two requirements for a policeman were that he be big and tough. Vancouver police had a slight edge over their Point Grey colleagues in capability, but not much. Training was almost nonexistent. A veteran who joined the city force shortly after the Smith affair recalled, almost 70 years later, that he walked into the Vancouver headquarters and inquired about a job as a policeman. The officer behind the desk asked a few questions and said, "Alright, you're from good stock and you're big enough." Long after his retirement he said, "And there I was next day out on the street in a uniform with a billy, handcuffs, and a gun. I had never fired a gun in my life."

The man with responsibility for provincial law enforcement at this time was a lawyer and Liberal politician, Alexander Malcolm Manson, who held the position of attorney general from 1922 until 1926. He did not possess the characteristics expected in the province's top legal authority, and early in his political career he was described by the *Sun* as "a bigot with a hatred of all Orientals." In an editorial the newspaper pointed out that "curious anomalies and inconsistencies appear in the careers of public men. Mr. Manson has more than his share." It must be admitted that *Sun* publisher Robert Cromie, a staunch Liberal, belonged to an influential group inside the party that could not abide Manson, and his paper often exposed the owner's concerns to the populace. Cromie himself wrote articles for the newspaper, saying that he found Manson arbitrary, arrogant, querulous, and egotistical, with the characteristics of a bully.

Another newspaperman, Russell R. Walker, who covered provincial politics for daily and weekly papers during the 1920s, saw Manson in a slightly different light. He described him as a man "geared for speed … sometimes the impetus of his drive might cause him to stumble but he seldom lost his political feet." Walker said Manson wore down his opponents with an avalanche of facts and figures that seldom could be countered and was well versed in the details of other ministers' portfolios. His long-winded, convoluted arguments could be terribly boring, wrote Walker in his book *Politicians of a Pioneering Province*. He also noted that when Manson became attorney general he erected a wall between himself and all callers, ensuring no information about his sensitive department was divulged until he could announce it on the floor of the House himself.

Attorney General Manson favoured the amalgamation of police departments in the Vancouver area, but his ideas on the final format were far different from *Sun* publisher Cromie's. He wanted a provincewide force headed by the government. An existing small provincial force was tightly controlled by the politicians, and an extension of its power and influence was something Manson wanted but most municipalities shunned. Cromie thought Manson's suggested plan for the province would be worse than the status quo.

While Manson infuriated some, he had a goodly share of followers who saw the articulate 42-year-old lawyer as a potential premier. He was a forceful orator, a handsome, ambitious man, more Scottish than Braveheart and Bonnie Prince Charlie combined, but he had a secret that he guarded closely. He had not been born in Canada but wished ardently that others believed he had been. Manson was born in St. Louis, Missouri, on October 17, 1883, of Scottish immigrant parents. Following the death of his mother when he was only a child, he moved to Canada to live with his grandparents in 1889. From that day forward he considered himself Canadian. Manson occasionally visited his father in Missouri until the latter's death late in the 1920s. He attended Niagara Falls Collegiate and graduated with a BA from Osgoode Hall at the University of Toronto. He read law with Smith, Rae, Greer, O'Brien and Henderson in Toronto and was called to the Ontario bar in June 1908 and the B.C. bar in Victoria in July 1908. He began work as a young lawyer in Prince Rupert, a principal with the firm of Williams, Manson, and Gonzales. Despite his birthplace, he had a hearty dislike of the United States and frequently warned Canadians to beware of the American eagle.

Manson often attended public functions wearing his kilt and sang Scottish songs at every possible opportunity. He was proud of his British heritage and invoked the finer qualities of British justice, fair play, tradition, and history as his ideals, using the federal Liberal election slogan from 1912, "Let us be British," as a motto. Manson ruled his department like a chieftain, accepting no criticism, crushing all foes, and confidently handling his portfolio. With such an attorney general, the Council of Scottish Societies felt it had a stout friend who would support its view of justice, and he was the man it turned to in the case of Janet Smith.

Many Scots were becoming convinced, whether by Rev. McDougall's representations or by their own suspicions, that their clanswoman had been brutally murdered by a slant-eyed foreigner. They were not to be appeased with vague assurances that there was an ongoing investigation, and they totally mistrusted, not without reason, the efforts of the Point Grey force to solve the case. The Council held a meeting and its members unanimously agreed to send a wire to Manson voicing their displeasure with the "apparent improper investigation" conducted by the police and the Coroner. They demanded an "immediate and full investigation by your department, free of the Point Grey police." Vancouver City police also began to take an interest in the Smith case although technically it was outside their jurisdiction.

Political colleagues in Victoria began to pressure Manson as well, because there was now talk of a cover-up of events at Osler Avenue. (The name was changed from Avenue to Street late in 1924.) Rumours began to fly, a particularly vicious one maintaining that Smith had been an unwilling participant in an orgy that took place upstairs in the home and was attended by several of the city's prominent men. Politics played a large part in personal life in the mid-1920s, and elected members constantly sniffed the wind for traces of trouble and suspicions of errant behaviour that could be voiced about rivals or enemies. They knew that while the B.C. Provincial Police was less than superlative—the bungling Point Grey Constable James Green for years had been one of its chief investigators—the politicians themselves retained complete control of the 150-man force. Its intervention in the case would please the large number of voting Scots and those of Scots descent among the electorate, and the government would control the whole procedure. Manson had decided to act even before he got the Council's demand by wire. The case was turned over to Inspector Forbes Cruickshank of the B.C. Provincial Police as soon as Manson felt the pressure building, heard the sweeping speculation, and read the transcript of the inquest. He initially believed Janet Smith had committed suicide, deciding that accidental death was highly improbable.

Cruickshank's appointment, as predicted, went over well with the Scottish community, which hoped for an early arrest of Wong Foon Sing. Cruickshank had credibility as a former policeman from Aberdeen, who had served with the Royal Canadian Mounted Police after immigrating to Canada. He was more competent and experienced than most of his colleagues, but he also followed policing methods of the times, and often during the 1920s that meant rough justice prevailed. Cruickshank sat in on the first conversations Point Grey municipal leaders had with Arthur Dawson when he arrived in town. This upset the elected officials, who saw Cruickshank's presence as an infringement of their jurisdiction and an attack on the investigative methods and competency of their police force. A *Sun* headline quoted Point Grey Chief Simpson—"Provincial Police Are Just Curious"—but community leaders were unhappy despite his statement to reporters that "important developments are expected within days." The chief had discarded his earlier position that nothing more could be done in the case following the jury's verdict of accidental death. Hauled over the coals by Reeve G.A. Walkem, Simpson claimed the provincial intervention wasn't a reflection on his force and had been prompted only by loose newspaper talk and wild speculation.

The spotlight of suspicion once again glared down on Wong when a *Province* headline on August 12 contended "What Diary Has Disclosed, Her Fear of Chinese." Somebody had leaked information from the diary to the newspaper. It reported that her writing "disclosed that the Chinaman paid marked attention to her" and gave her gifts. The headline was an exaggeration. Janet Smith never wrote of any fear of the Chinese houseboy, but expressed her amusement that he seemed fond of her and had given her several gifts, which she accepted. The *Province* also told its readers, "The carefully kept little book gives an insight into her life." The entries showed she was of a "sunny and carefree disposition" and told of her love of dances and of the young men she met. The paper stressed, however, that Janet

Smith was not "wanton," noting that "her conduct as exemplified in the diary entries bears out the assertions of her friends that Janet was a good, happy and likeable girl filled with the joy of living." The maintenance of an unsullied reputation for Rosemary's nanny was a preoccupation of the *Province.*

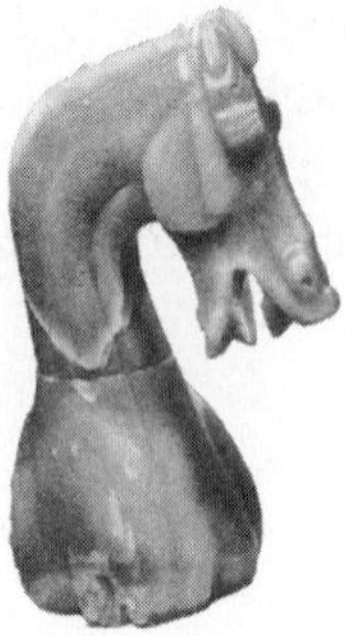

Canadian Detective Bureau Strikes

About this time Wong Foon Sing was visited at the Osler house by a man named Wong Foon Sien, who claimed he was speaking for a Chinese group seeking information about Janet Smith. Suspicious of the visitor because he provided no details about whom he supposedly represented, the houseboy said little. He was on edge anyway because he had noticed a man driving a large white car that parked on Osler and seemed to have the house under surveillance. On several occasions he felt sure he had been followed.

The same night, August 12, that the *Province* story about the Smith diary appeared in the evening edition, Wong took a streetcar to Chinatown to meet two friends. As he joined them at the corner of Cordova and Carrall, a car pulled up beside them, and two men jumped out and bundled the protesting houseboy into the vehicle before it sped off.

Wong had been snatched by the Canadian Detective Bureau, led by a burly man named Oscar Robinson, who was acting on instructions from Inspector Cruickshank. This was an era when the police often hired freelance detectives to do their dirty work. Suspects were roughed up in order to obtain information, particularly if they were downtrodden, defenceless, or Asian. Inspector Cruickshank didn't shy away from these methods, but in this instance he apparently decided to act carefully. The high profile of the Smith case and the possible involvement of influential families made him cautious. Turning part of the investigation over to a private operator wasn't a principled practice, but this was a rough-and-tumble era and Vancouver had not yet shaken off all the traces of its earlier years as a frontier town way out west.

Robinson often handled cases involving Chinese people and had several Asian operatives working for him. He wasn't concerned that most were minor criminals, so long as they did the job required. One of his employees was Wong Foon Sien, reputed to be involved in both drug peddling and prostitution, who had earlier visited Wong Foon Sing on Osler. Wong Foon Sien's knowledge of English often gained him employment as a court interpreter, and in addition to his assignments with Robinson he did translation work for the police. These connections made him especially useful to all concerned.

After being grabbed off the street, Wong Foon Sing was driven to what he thought was the police station, but which was in reality the premises of Robinson's detective bureau in the Empire Building on Hastings Street near police headquarters. It was a scruffy, two-room office that looked like the down-at-heels hangout of a disreputable private eye—which it was. Wong was forced into a chair in a dimly lit room. Among the several men present he recognized Wong Foon Sien. He later identified the others present as Robinson, Inspector Cruickshank, and two provincial policemen, Sam North and James Hannah. There were also several Chinese in the room who he didn't recognize.

It was about 8 p.m. when Wong was nabbed from the street, and for the next several hours the frightened houseboy was roughly interrogated by his captors. They didn't accuse him of murdering Smith, but they did want him to tell them who had done it. They wanted to know if he had been bribed to keep his mouth shut. Wong insisted he didn't know any more than he had already told the police.

An angry and exasperated Robinson suddenly hit Wong on the side of the head, knocking him out of the chair and onto the floor. During the long evening hours Robinson hit him several times, but the blows seemed meant to intimidate rather than to injure. Cruickshank would have had a difficult explanation on his hands had word got out that he watched while the houseboy was battered and bruised.

When a statement in English was thrust in his face, Wong refused to sign because he didn't know what it said. Robinson told him he would go to jail if he didn't sign. Under continuing threats, he finally put his name on the document. This satisfied his captors, who then took him in a police car back to Osler Avenue.

Dick Baker had been told by Wong Foon Sing's friends about the abduction. He phoned several of the police departments before he was finally told that Wong was being held in custody, he was "all right," and would soon be sent home. Baker was at the door in the middle of the night when the houseboy returned.

A few hours later the public learned of the incident in a story that also revealed the latest development in the Smith case. A *Sun* headline screamed "Smith Girl Murdered." It stated that the attorney general's department in Victoria, after studying the evidence presented to it, had concluded that her death was neither accidental nor a suicide. It was murder. The attorney general's department also revealed that Wong had been taken in for "a severe grilling," but didn't disclose what had actually occurred. The official line was that Wong had been taken to police headquarters, when in fact he had been in Robinson's office. Quizzed about the houseboy getting the "third degree," a police spokesman told reporters that "he was taken for examination when he was ready for examination and no force or coercion of any kind was used." That wasn't how Wong Foon Sing saw it, but he wasn't asked and he had no injuries bad enough to prove otherwise.

The *Province* was unhappy with the outcome. It noted that though "the Chinaman was grilled from every angle by the police he stuck to his little story throughout telling it in the same way as he did at the inquest." The papers said nothing about Oscar Robinson, although it is hard to believe that reporters covering the police beat weren't aware of him. They were familiar with police methods and obviously accepted them as routine.

Robinson's involvement was noted in Chinatown, however. Immediately following the August 12 abduction the *Chinese Times* began to take a larger interest in the case. The paper told its readers that Wong Foon Sing had been beaten by the "police" to try to force a confession from him.

With the spotlight of suspicion shining on the houseboy, the Point Grey police tried some primitive experiments in their station house basement to learn about powder burns. They rigged up a piece of white canvas and fired shots at it from a .45 revolver similar to the one found at the scene. Not surprisingly, they came up with confusing results that proved nothing.

On August 22, *Vancouver Sun* readers learned that the "fog" had lifted in the Smith case and the provincial police had uncovered a significant clue. The paper stated that it was a breakthrough that would lead to police action within 48 hours and possibly a murder charge against Wong. Two days later nothing new was reported and the "fog" was as thick as ever.

Scots' Anger Grows

The implacable Scots were fast losing faith in all the law enforcement agencies and decided to ask Attorney General Manson to look into the possibility that something other than a bullet caused some of the injuries to Janet Smith. Council president David Paterson told reporters that he believed Manson would agree to the request in light of the startling nature of facts that had been brought to his attention. Paterson gave no hint of the nature of the startling facts, but his statement to the press created wild speculation. He said he would be part of a four-member committee that would be in charge of the Scots' own investigations and would represent the Council in all aspects of the affair. Paterson added that a prominent Vancouver lawyer would act in the interests of the organized Scots people in the city, who were "determined to see the investigation through to the finish" and discover who killed Janet Smith. While the Chinese community appeared quiet on the surface, the tongs were mounting a similar effort to investigate the case, again using privately hired sleuths.

The need for new, more detailed information about the girl's death resulted in calls to have her body exhumed. Dr. G.F. Curtis, a Vancouver physician with considerable experience in post mortems, and a friend of the Scots societies, was named as the likely candidate to perform the new autopsy. The *Province* reported that Smith might have been killed in another part of the house and her body carried down to the basement. One story suggested she had been hit with a blunt instrument and taken to the basement, where a bullet was fired into her head as she lay on the floor. This, according to the paper, was done in a bid to draw attention away from hints of a party or upstairs orgy. Newspaper readers were told that statements implicating several prominent men had been made and that private investigators claimed there would be an early arrest. The paper concluded, "Several of the hitherto baffling links in the chain of circumstances have been joined."

Police contended that statements from various unidentified spokesmen were hampering their investigations and wasting their time. However, they still maintained that despite these difficulties they were getting reliable information and piecing the mystery together.

With mounting anger the Scots asked lawyer Alex Henderson to press Manson for a second inquest. Henderson, an old colleague and fellow Liberal who was fearful of the party becoming involved in a major scandal, persuaded Manson to order an exhumation, a second autopsy, and another inquest. In an effort to placate the clans, Manson told Henderson that the Scots could have legal representation at the second inquest, an offer he didn't extend to the Chinese.

But the Scots wanted more. They demanded that Coroner Dr. Brydone-Jack be excluded from the hearing and replaced because they were convinced that he had bungled the first inquest and had been too ready to agree that Smith's death was accidental. Among the gossip gaining currency were allegations about the coroner's role in what seemed to be the unusually hasty embalming of Smith's body before a full medical examination had been completed. Manson refused the demand for Brydone-Jack's exclusion, and the unhappy Scots were forced to accept his decision.

Smith's Body Exhumed

Manson announced on August 25 that he would approach the Supreme Court for permission to hold the second inquest. Asked if he had submitted to pressure in seeking the order, the attorney general told reporters, "In fairness to all concerned I may say that no representations whatever have been made to me or officials of the department in this connection. Such a thing would be ridiculous and if any one made such a move it would only give us an opportunity to pick up additional clues. I have appointed Mr. C.W. Craig counsel for the department to assist the Provincial Police so that everything possible might be done to solve the mystery."

This statement was untrue. Manson had been hounded by the Scots, visited by their lawyer Henderson, and pressured by his political colleagues. The next day in Supreme Court chambers, Mr. Justice D.A. McDonald gave permission for the new inquest.

The *Province* reported that the Chinese community was planning an intervention on behalf of Wong, although it had not been invited to do so by Manson. The headline stated, "Chinese Tong Leaders Initiate Probe in Effort to Solve Mystery," and the paper reported, "Prominent Chinamen in the city have suddenly realized that the connection of Wong Foon Sing with the tragedy is bringing the Chinese race to the attention of the public in an unwelcome manner and they have decided to probe the matter themselves in order to ascertain the facts as they can reach them." The paper noted that most Chinese in the city gave their allegiance to the tongs, which were often referred to as secret, sinister, or threatening. The fact that most were largely family or regional groupings, not unlike the Scottish clans, was ignored.

While the reporting of the city's main English-language press generally whipped up emotions with extensive coverage and the wildest exaggeration concerning Smith's slaying—the *Province* in particular never let up on its racist viewpoints—the reporting in the leading Chinese-language newspaper, the *Chinese Times,* kept to the facts, using moderate language.

The public finally learned that the police had tried to "draw out" the houseboy, but there was no reference in the newspapers to a punch in the head and other blows. The *Province* reported that the police didn't believe his story at all, but were unable to make him change it in any particular. The paper noted, "Since that time, however, it is believed the China boy has made other statements and it is these that have caused the attorney general to ask for an order to re-exhume the body. The tongs will do nothing to usurp the authority of the police but will help them, it is claimed by the Chinese, and the interrogation of Wong will be the principal effort." This story stopped just short of saying Wong was guilty when it pointed out that while the police investigation admittedly was "a rather bad bumble, new and amazing facts have been obtained from him." A half-hearted attempt to be fair only compounded suspicion about the houseboy when the paper noted, "The police, it is understood, do not credit rumours that the Chinese had anything to do with the crime although the officers believe that the Oriental has not been frank and complete in his explanation of what occurred."

Coroner Dr. Brydone-Jack carried through with his promise of fast action on the second inquest, and on August 28 Janet Smith's grave at Mountain View Cemetery was opened and her coffin removed. Among the reporters and others watching at graveside was Council of Scottish Societies president Paterson. Desperate not to make any more mistakes, Brydone-Jack ordered that the coffin lid be slid off immediately in order to ensure it was Janet Smith's body that had been recovered. Her remains were then taken to Vancouver General Hospital and a second autopsy began at 11 a.m. with a battery of doctors in attendance. In addition to Brydone-Jack, the Scots insisted that Drs. G.E. Gillies and B.D. Gillies be present. Also present were Drs. G.F. Curtis, the autopsy specialist, W.F. Baird, W.F. Kennedy, and

Archibald Hunter. The latter had conducted the first examination and raised the matter of an absence of powder burns on Smith's forehead.

While the press speculated that the findings of the second autopsy would be different from the first and probably lead to a finding that Smith had been murdered and not killed accidentally, more information appeared in print, leaked from the unfortunate victim's two diaries. "Woman Maybe Killer, Jealousy Behind Janet Smith Tragedy" was the *Sun*'s front-page headline on August 30. The story stated that entries in the notebooks showed "she was fond of the company of the opposite sex." The paper also reworked the possibility that she had been struck down before the bullet was fired into her head. A spokesman for the Council of Scottish Societies added to the speculation by announcing more "evidence" had been found and that new information and letters were in the hands of Henderson, the Scots' lawyer, but again there was no detail. The statement further clouded the situation.

The anger of the Scots had swelled rather than abated. It was as though a burning cross, the blazing symbol that runners carried across the moors and into the mountains to summon the clans to action in old Scotland, had been sent through Vancouver's streets. The clans were gathering outside Vancouver's courthouse for the second inquest.

Tension Mounts at Second Inquest

Hours before the second inquest opened on Thursday morning, September 4, a seething mass of humanity had gathered outside Vancouver's Georgia Street courthouse, pushing and shoving, trying to get into the small room where the hearing was scheduled to take place. The clamouring crowd was made up largely of young domestics eager to learn what had happened to one of their own, members of clan societies determined to see justice done, and well-dressed women from Shaughnessy agog to learn more about the rumoured orgies on Osler Avenue, which might involve men they knew. The crowd spilled onto the street, where it was joined by curious onlookers who swelled its ranks even more.

Hats were lost and clothes torn as women jostled and shoved their way toward the entrance of the building. When the main courthouse doors finally opened at 9:30 a.m., hundreds poured through them into the marble hallways of the stately old building, charging towards the locked inquest room that would hold only 50 of them at most. During the ensuing bedlam, a veteran court attendant sniffed to reporters caught up in the crowd that it was "the most disgraceful display I have ever seen." One newspaper reported in its evening edition that "unhealthy rumours and vicious whisperings" had raised the level of excitement.

Among those pushing to get in was a harassed-looking Coroner Dr. Brydone-Jack; impeccable, debonair Harry Senkler, the hot-tempered city lawyer hired by Chinese interests to represent Wong Foon Sing; and the normally controlled, sedate Crown attorney Charles Craig, appointed by Attorney General Alex Manson. The coroner was tense, knowing the Scots wanted him dumped because he had been a key player in the controversial, supposedly premature embalming of Janet Smith.

He was presiding nevertheless, and he must have approached his position at the front of the room with some misgivings, although nothing showed on his face.

With some difficulty court officials escorted the six-man jury, selected the preceding day, through the crowd. Before proceedings got underway, the panel posed in a group for press photographers. The coroner asked who had been chosen as foreman of the jury, and James Wilson stepped forward. He was a former Liverpool policeman who now operated a bicycle repair shop. In the days to come he would ask some of the more pertinent and perceptive questions that surfaced during the inquest—the kind of questions, newspaper reporters pointed out, that had been missing from the first inquest held under the jurisdiction of the original Point Grey investigators.

During the picture-taking episode the crowd remained outside the courtroom, and a constant hammering noise grew louder as women pounded on the door, demanding to be let in and asking what was being hidden from them. The growing crescendo added to the general hubbub of excited voices and stamping feet. As the time approached for the inquest to begin, one loud voice insisted, "This is not Russia."

Brydone-Jack addressed the jury before the public was admitted, telling members they would first visit the city morgue to inspect Smith's body. As a result they were forced to shove their way back out through the crowd to Georgia Street. The coroner told officials to unlock the doors and let some of those waiting into the inquest room. One reporter, amazed at the yelling, bruising stampede that followed, noted it was accompanied by some very unladylike language. When the seats were filled, some of the women sat on the floor and had to be persuaded that they could not remain there. The more persistent actually had to be shoved back into the main hall. A press count showed 40 women and 10 men had obtained seats in the small room, all of them prepared to sit for hours if need be until the jury returned and proceedings commenced. It was said that in the city's history, "no case had stirred up such excitement and interest."

At the morgue, the jurors peered closely at the young body lying on the slab, the only evidence of injury the hole in her right temple above her eye. Dr. Curtis drew a small piece of wire along the path taken by the heavy bullet as it tore through Smith's skull. From the angle of entry he deduced that the girl's head had been level with the gun when the shot was fired; it was pointed neither up nor down. The jury was provided with a list of other medical facts repeated from the first inquest. The entire group then left the morgue and proceeded to the scene of the crime in Shaughnessy.

Wong Foon Sing didn't know the jury was to visit Osler Avenue and, ironically, he was in the basement ironing when the entourage arrived. The iron he held was similar to the one that Janet Smith had been using, which had been found beside her body.

The basement laundry room was soon crowded with officials, jurors, lawyers, doctors, police, and reporters. Brydone-Jack set the scene for the jury by explaining that the houseboy was in the kitchen, heard a loud noise, later identified as a gunshot, and then hurried downstairs. The coroner asked the young man to take the role of Smith. Readers of the *Sun* were told that "Mr. Brydone-Jack commanded the Chinaman to lie down in the position in which he found the body." Obviously not relishing the role, Wong surprised the men assembled in the basement by refusing the coroner's orders. This was not how houseboys were expected to act, particularly when confronted by authority. The reporter noted that his reluctance was partly due to the fact that he was wearing a clean shirt and collar, and "the houseboy always was a well-dressed bit of a dandy but he was finally persuaded to do so." The hot iron he had been using was wrapped in a towel and placed where the original one had been found beside Smith's body. Then Chief Simpson took out his own gun and with a dramatic flourish put it near the houseboy's hand, in the position where Constable James Green had found the supposed murder weapon. The Scots' lawyer, Henderson, then drew the jury's attention to three small indentations, two on the floor and one in the wall, that he suggested could have been made by gunfire. Much time was taken in the next few days and weeks discussing these marks, but in the end it was generally accepted that they were not made by bullets. What caused the marks was never disclosed, and as a result some felt to the end that there had been repeated gunfire in the basement room.

Back in the Vancouver courthouse, the fortunate few who had shoved their way into the inquest room waited patiently, discussing the tragedy, some eating the lunches they had brought with them. No one was willing to give up a seat to go out for a meal. When Brydone-Jack and the jury finally returned, they repeated their difficult route to the courtroom, pushing through the crowd of people outside who were still hoping they might at the last moment have a chance to watch the drama unfold inside.

For the next few days the jurors heard an incredible story of incompetence. They learned how badly the initial investigation had been botched, heard there had been an order for an embalming before a full forensic examination was complete, listened to witnesses who contradicted each other about the results of primitive ballistics tests, and tried to understand the details of various alternative medical theories. They also heard an intimate and naively innocent tale of romance read from a young woman's diaries and learned the details of upstairs-downstairs life in the attractive Osler Avenue home. There was only one outstanding consistency as the unbelievable story unfolded, and that was the unshakeable, unswerving account of events told by the man on the spot, Wong Foon Sing.

On the table in front of the coroner were the exhibits. They were vivid, poignant reminders of a young life that ended suddenly on a sunny summer Saturday morning. Beside Janet Smith's blood-stained denim dress, apron, and broken glasses lay the diaries, the revolver, and the iron found beside her at the scene. As the items were placed on the table, some spectators observing the proceedings from the back of the room stood on their chairs to get a better view.

The dislike some clanswomen held for the bungling Point Grey police had been growing in the weeks since Janet Smith's death until it now bordered on hatred. Their feelings were evident on their faces and there was an audible sharp intake of breath when the first witness took the stand. He was Constable Green, the man who had labelled Smith's death a suicide. A rumpled man in his 50s, he looked grey and bedraggled, his stoic face reflecting his awareness of the animosity in the room. The women hung on his every word, many convinced he knew a lot more than he was telling and others, with more vivid imaginations, sure he had been bribed to keep quiet, to tell only part of what he knew.

Crown counsel Craig questioned James Green, leading him carefully through the sequence of events as they had occurred on July 26. The policeman said his initial conclusion was that Smith's wound was self-inflicted, and he added he didn't know whether it was intentional or accidental. He later became convinced it was suicide, he said, although he denied making a statement to Chief Simpson that it was the most obvious case of suicide he had seen in the 46 such deaths he had investigated during his long police career. Green tried to explain the inconclusive experiments made at the Point Grey station when shots were fired from a .45 revolver at a white sheet to try to determine at what range powder burns would be seen. He admitted that at the same range, sometimes there were burns and sometimes there were none. Green also recalled a previously confirmed suicide he had investigated when a gun was used at close range and there were no traces of burns.

There were disbelieving looks and grumbling noises from the court audience when he maintained that he didn't find the bullet lying on the basement floor when he first arrived at the scene because there were too many people about. Yet the evidence showed there were only two or, at the most, three others in the basement when Green arrived. How not one of them had seen a bullet, later found lying in full view, was one of the inconsistencies that obviously perplexed the puzzled jury. Green told Craig he did not believe the theory being pushed by newspapers that Smith had been killed late in the night elsewhere in the house, her body carried to the basement, and a gun fired at the corpse's head in an attempt to cover up the upstairs crime.

This story had persisted, frequently recurring in newspaper accounts, and so was embedded in many minds as part of the evidence. The scenario was, however, refuted by Dr. Bertie Blackwood, the first doctor at the scene, whose testimony should have laid this suggestion to rest. He was probably a more credible witness than Green and testified that when he arrived at the house shortly before noon on July 26, Smith's body was still warm and he estimated she had died about an hour earlier.

Various doctors who attended the autopsy had published conflicting statements concerning the cause of death, and opinions differed as to the reason for the massive damage to the inside of the victim's skull. One doctor contended that Janet Smith could have been bludgeoned with a heavy instrument before the shot was fired. The team of doctors who made the more detailed examination at the second autopsy, however, generally concluded that a heavy .45 bullet fired at close range inflicted all the damage. Dr. Archibald Hunter graphically demonstrated the team's findings when he hauled a human skull out of a bag to show the jury how the bullet travelled through Smith's head. Dr. Curtis, the chief examiner, was the most conclusive witness when he stated, "After that examination I am of the opinion that the bullet caused all the wounds in the girl's head."

The absence of powder burns still remained an intriguing question. The doctors testified that they manipulated Smith's arm to try to determine if she could have held the heavy weapon at a distance from her head and in a position to kill herself that would have left no powder burns. Their conclusion was it was virtually impossible. Dr. Curtis explained, "We made measurements and found the greatest distance the girl herself could have held the weapon from her head was ten-and-a-half inches." The muzzle of the gun, however, would have been several inches closer to her head. The jury already had been shown pieces of skin from the head of a pig used in ballistics experiments. At close range of about six inches, the tough skin showed burns.

The courtroom hushed and waited expectantly as Crown counsel Craig asked the doctor, "What would you have to say as to the probability or possibility of this girl inflicting this wound upon herself?

"I would consider it highly improbable," answered Dr. Curtis, a response the Scots had been waiting for, conclusive proof to them that Janet Smith had not killed herself. They voiced open support of the answer, nodding and murmuring, "Hear, hear."

Craig continued, "What were your reasons?"

Curtis responded, "I would expect to find more epicules of powder and perhaps some burning."

Craig then asked, "If a person intended to kill himself, would you expect him to hold it [the gun] as far as possible from his body?"

Curtis replied, "No, I would not. I would expect him to place it as closely as possible to the body."

The medical witnesses testified they thought Smith likely would have fallen forward if she were shot, rather than backward, and would not have been found flat on her back. Jury foreman Wilson, the former policeman, wondered if the woman might have staggered about after being shot. "You don't think she would be lying in the composed or semi-composed state in which the body was found unless she was put there?" he asked. This matter apparently had never been discussed by the investigators. After consideration, Dr. Curtis answered in the negative, although the position in which Smith's body was found remained another question that was never truly resolved. Apparently no one thought to ask Wong Foon Sing if he had placed the girl's body the way it was found after he first discovered it in the basement and tried to lift her head.

Dr. Curtis disagreed with some colleagues about how burns found on Smith's arm and shoulder were caused. He said she fell on the hot iron after it slipped from her fingers when the cord pulled away from the plug. Some believed she could have suffered the burns through her clothing without the cloth itself being scorched, while others felt that this was impossible. This was another point never satisfactorily explained.

One of the more serious questions that was never pursued was why no brain tissue was found on the floor or walls at the scene of the girl's death when the police first arrived. This would have been expected. Green and his Point Grey colleagues had managed to miss seeing the bullet on the floor and had destroyed evidence by handling the gun, and this additional point was without doubt another detail they failed to look into during their initial investigation.

The interest of society matrons peaked when the poised, dapper Fred Baker took the stand. He had the handsome, smooth good looks of a matinee idol and he was central to the rumours persisting about a bohemian lifestyle at Osler Avenue. There also had been speculation about his dealings in the pharmaceutical business in Europe. Rumours abounded at country club affairs and Shaughnessy cocktail parties about the possibility that his business went beyond pink pills and Epsom salts into the criminal world of hard drugs and their illegal uses.

Baker repeated the story he told at the first inquest, that he was at his office Saturday morning when he received a phone call from Wong Foon Sing stating something had happened to "Nursie," the houseboy's name for Smith. Baker rushed home, found Wong waiting for him in the garden, checked his daughter upstairs, and then went down to the basement. Smith was lying on the floor. He splashed water on the woman's face and tried to put some through her lips, but there was no sign of life, so he phoned the Point Grey police. Baker told the jury that Smith's face was composed, with no sign of fear or apprehension. There was only the hole in her forehead and blood in her hair and on the floor.

The witness said the gun found lying nearby was his. It had been issued to him during the war and he had brought it home as a souvenir. When Fred and his family moved temporarily to his brother's house on Osler, he had brought the gun with him. It was left for several days in a haversack hanging on a peg in the hallway. This struck many as an odd place to leave a loaded weapon, even if it seemed to be jammed. The fact that he even had a weapon was unusual, but would have been excused as he was a returned veteran. Baker said that three or four days after the family moved to Osler Avenue he noticed the haversack was gone. When he asked Wong about it, he was told it had been put away in the attic. The question of exactly who knew the gun was in the house and where it was kept was a major point that for unknown reasons escaped detailed examination by any of the lawyers.

Baker's view of events hadn't changed. He said Smith knew the revolver was upstairs, and he believed that out of curiosity she might have taken it downstairs to examine it. Then somehow the gun went off accidentally. It was possible, but no more believable than another theory making the rounds that the woman was so afraid of the houseboy, or maybe of a jealous lover, that she had taken the weapon downstairs to the laundry room for her own protection.

Asked what kind of girl Janet Smith was, Baker said, "She was a good girl of sunny disposition, and she was always cheerful, especially so that morning. She was not the type to kill herself." The first time he saw her that day was when she brought the baby to the garden gate to wave goodbye as he and his wife left for town.

Reporters and the public were intrigued by the fashion parade put on by some of the spectators and the expensive clothes worn by the wealthy. One young woman sitting quietly in the public benches attracted considerable attention with her scarlet dress, hardly the midday colour choice of the times. The fashion plates were all upstaged, however, when Doreen Baker, Fred's very attractive wife, the mother of twenty-month-old Rosemary, now pregnant with her second child, took the stand. The *Sun* reporter wrote, "It was a dainty little figure that tripped along behind the barristers' table, young, pretty of face, attractively gowned." In flowery, social-page style, readers were told that "Mrs. Baker, costumed becomingly in a black dress, black silk overdrape, black hat and black satin shoes, with a white fur neck lining on her cape and tight grey stockings, was a striking figure in the dock."

She told the jury that she had gone downtown shopping that morning, asking Janet Smith to wash and iron some of the baby's clothes before she returned at noon. The *Sun* noted that Mrs. Baker was calm, poised, and spoke, as her husband did, with a low, drawling voice, which was considered an upper-class accent. It was claimed later that she also had a fierce temper, but it didn't show in any of her court appearances. She stated that "as servants," Smith and Wong Foon Sing seemed to get on well together. She agreed with her husband's description of the nursemaid, whom she obviously liked because the girl had been taken with the family to Paris and then to Vancouver. Mrs. Baker said Janet Smith never indicated any fear of the Chinese houseboy during the weeks they lived in her brother-in-law's home. She assured the inquest "the woman would have complained if she was upset, but she never said a word." Mrs. Baker also testified that Smith was never left alone in the house in the evening with Wong. They took the nursemaid and the baby to Fred Baker's mother's house on Nelson Street whenever they went out at night and were going to be home late.

The jury was intrigued by the evidence of two men who might have been the last to see Smith alive on that sunny morning—except for her killer, if indeed she was murdered. George Williamson, a contractor, and Albert Hicks were working on the house about 150 yards from the Baker residence, with trees to some extent screening their view. During the week they had heard Smith's singing several times and had dubbed her "The Nightingale." Williamson testified that at about 10:30 a.m. that Saturday he heard someone singing and saw a woman at a window of the house. He wasn't absolutely sure it was Smith because he couldn't make positive identification from so far away, but it sounded like her. Hicks also saw the woman and heard the voice. He was fairly sure it was the same one he had heard all week, but could not be absolutely certain. Neither heard the fatal shot. Their evidence was enough for the *Province* to produce a headline that stated, without equivocation, "Met Death With Song On Lips," but it was not enough to lay to rest the rumours of a drunken orgy.

Again it was jury foreman Wilson who made one of the more astute comments about the testimony. He made the point that if Janet Smith sang at her work, and possibly was doing so very shortly before she died, it hardly indicated that she was living in fear of Wong. He emphasized that the two were alone in the house that morning except for the baby.

This second inquest was indeed a difficult time for the coroner, who looked tense and uncomfortable when evidence about the embalming of Smith's body was introduced. The Scots watched his reaction to every bit of testimony and were sure he was trying to cover up something. Undertaker John Edwards testified that one of the officers at the scene, he wasn't sure which one, told him to embalm the body. Edwards said that later in the day he telephoned Brydone-Jack to confirm the order. The undertaker said the coroner told him to proceed.

Realizing he was in trouble, the coroner interrupted to ask Edwards, "Didn't I say 'Wait a little time'?" The witness said "No." The Brydone-Jack confrontation with Edwards was a stand-off, with the coroner contending he hadn't given permission and

Edwards, equally adamant, saying that he had. When lawyer Henderson pressed the witness on the question of the hasty embalming undertaken before a full forensic examination was completed, Edwards responded that the decision came from two sources, the Point Grey police, although he couldn't identify the actual officer, and Brydone-Jack after a check-up call.

Jury foreman Wilson once again put the matter succinctly. He had a keen mind, and his involvement in the Smith case had his investigative juices running. The inquest was obviously much more exciting for him than working in the bicycle shop. He asked Edwards, "Have you ever before removed a body in a case of violent death and embalmed it before it had been viewed by the coroner or his deputy?" The witness said, "No."

Wilson asked, "This is unique and the first time you ever heard or saw it being done?" Edwards replied it was. There was more of who-said-what-to-whom about the issue, including a statement from Chief Simpson that if he had known all the facts at the time he would not have permitted the embalming. There seems no doubt he was the officer who gave Edwards permission to proceed, or he had told one of his men to do so. Simpson added that when he gave consent, he had accepted Green's conclusion that Smith's death was accidental and there was no indication she might have been murdered.

Brydone-Jack looked far from guiltless in the exchange, but there were other vital issues that took precedence and he escaped censure. The paranoid among the Scots were sure the coroner had intentionally tampered with medical evidence and that this was part of a planned cover-up to hide the actual reasons for the killing as well as the identity of the killer.

The fiery Harry Senkler had been unusually quiet during most of the hearing, asking few questions and complaining only mildly about some of the Crown's questioning and its relevance. Wong's lawyer was happy with the contradictions being presented, hopeful that it would lead to another finding of accidental death, letting his client off the hook. Senkler also knew Smith's two diaries would in due course speak loudly for the defence.

The jury heard next from Janet Smith's friends and fellow domestics, Annie Kendall, Jean Taylor, Dora Harper, Jean Brown Haddowe, and Martha Baron, all of whom testified that

Smith had told them of her fear or apprehension at living in the same house with Wong. Mrs. Mary Field, the owner of a Jarvis Street shop frequented by Smith, repeated the same assertion. Senkler asked her if she knew that while Smith was engaged to Dawson she had at least one other beau. There were "titters in court" from the public when Mrs. Field said, "Yes," adding she didn't think it unusual for a girl to go out with another man under those circumstances.

Another witness, Mrs. William Parker, testified that she knew Janet Smith because they met at the Girls' Friendly Society, a social organization favoured by domestics, which met on Tuesday evenings at 1267 Robson Street and often sponsored Saturday night dances in the Dominion Hall. She said that "all new members arriving in the city were cordially welcomed." Mrs Parker added the girl had asked for advice and at the last meeting had seemed upset. "She said he was very hard to keep in his place … I told her to keep the Chinese in his place," said Mrs. Parker.

Cissie Jones was the last of Smith's friends to testify, but as she was handed one of Smith's diaries to identify she began to cry and swayed unsteadily in the box. She was given a glass of water, but it didn't seem to help and she suddenly fainted, crumpling to the floor. Court officials rushed to her aid, helping to bring her back to consciousness. Coroner Brydone-Jack had now had enough and adjourned the inquest for the weekend.

The evidence of Smith's friends, all stressing her fear of Wong, was powerful and didn't augur well for the houseboy. One newspaper headline declared, "Witnesses Tell Of Janet Smith's Fear Of Chinese Servant." The evidence also created criticism for the Point Grey police, who were blasted again in a *Sun* editorial headlined "Tanktown Police Work." There was now a growing public awareness of poor police performance, which leant new impetus to the argument for amalgamation. The editorial maintained Chief Simpson had refused to consider the possibility of murder because of the cost involved in a more extensive investigation and because he was also short of manpower. The editorial contended that in trying to maintain a reputation for departmental efficiency, Simpson had downplayed the fact that Point Grey had a growing rate of crime.

The paper maintained that if nothing were done, the area would "become the sanctuary of every blackleg and crook on the Pacific coast." It said Simpson was a man of sterling character but no Sherlock Holmes, nor could he be expected to be because Point Grey had outgrown small-town methods.

Stung by criticism and by the mob scene that had marked the opening of the inquest, Brydone-Jack and his officials moved the hearing into larger premises when proceedings resumed on Monday morning. This alternate room held about 100, but it was far from large enough for the huge crowd that showed up. It was more orderly than the earlier one, but there was still considerable pushing and shoving to get seats near the front. This time when the seats filled, dozens of spectators were allowed to stand at the back, although many still remained outside. It was a warm September day and the hot, stuffy atmosphere did nothing to cool the tempers of Smith's supporters. They were once again very vocal in their criticism when they heard statements they didn't like.

A no-holds-barred battle developed almost immediately between Harry Senkler and a determined, now implacable Cissie Jones, who had those in the crowded, sweaty, public benches enthralled by her story. Encouraged by the fact that their applauding, hissing, and hooting had not been silenced earlier, the Scottish women in the chamber now turned on Senkler as the enemy. He was frequently abrasive during his questioning, and to them he became a despicable figure, defender of Wong Foon Sing, the obviously guilty killer of Janet Smith.

The Scots viewed Cissie Jones as a humble seeker of justice, bravely resisting another fainting spell as her emotions brought her sorrow and pain. To her supporters she was a simple immigrant girl, overworked and underpaid, battling against a powerful lawyer who was well paid with money from the Chinese community. Jones was, however, anything but humble. She told Crown counsel Craig that the day before Smith died she had confessed to Jones that for three days she had been afraid to go into the kitchen when Wong was there. Jones said Smith had described how the houseboy looked longingly at her, but gave no specific examples or details of any other treatment. Emerging from the testimony was the suggestion that Wong had developed some affection for Janet Smith and perhaps had a crush on her. It was a situation that concerned the young girl just a little, but she seemed more amused by it than frightened.

Cissie Jones faced John Harold Senkler, a prominent, wealthy member of the city's elite establishment, a well-known lawyer, married to the daughter of a former B.C. lieutenant-governor, Albert Norton Richards (for whom Vancouver's Richards Street was named). Senkler and his wife Margaret lived at Horningtoft, a comfortable home near Stanley Park, where they and their six children were often seen riding on horseback.

Senkler's strategy was to portray Smith as a confused young woman with a vivid imagination and an involved love life that was the basis for jealous grievances, broken affairs, and angry arguments. Senkler suggested two alternatives. Was she emotionally unstable and capable of taking her own life, or was her death an unexplained accident as the first jury ruled? Senkler argued that murder hadn't been proven and so no charge should be laid against Wong Foon Sing.

Senkler knew Cissie Jones would be a handful, and almost immediately she confirmed she was no meek, uncertain servant girl overwhelmed by events, as some might have thought after her initial fainting spell. Cissie Jones' working-class convictions had toughened her over the years. She rebelled at class distinctions and she believed young women like herself were being exploited by Shaughnessy employers. She was a dominant force among the many domestics who worked in the area and who met and socialized during their brief off hours, and she proved to be the lawyer's match. She was not prepared to give an inch in trying to prove Wong Foon Sing was a murderer. She was hailed by the press for her spunk and for her refusal to buckle under the questioning of an experienced and skilful lawyer.

The keys to the defence were two small, inexpensive paperback books in which Janet Smith had recorded entries that the defence lawyer argued refuted the contentions of her friends. Instead of being afraid of Wong Foon Sing, Senkler claimed, the scant references to him in the diaries showed the pair had been getting along well during the two-month period they had known each other.

Probably intended for no eyes but her own, the diaries were the emotional revelations of a young woman, and they laid bare her soul. Her words exposed her thoughts and feelings, the chaste and innocent sexuality of a girl far from home, bright, perceptive, working at a job that was well below her intellectual capabilities and talents. Janet Smith's entries were well written, thoughtful, and often light-hearted, but her heartfelt outpourings could be subject to many different interpretations. The newspapers jumped immediately on some of the possibilities. "Diary Bares Flirtations" was the headline in the *Sun*, and flirtatious was the best word to describe Janet Smith's lifestyle in Vancouver in the mid-1920s, when there were many more young men than women and a pretty girl had many choices for dating and numerous options for choosing a husband. From the moment her body was discovered, many wondered if sex had been the motive for murder, though the papers of the time didn't use the word sex or rape—ravishment was the preferred terminology. This possibility titillated some of the women waiting expectantly for the facts to unfold. Reporters handled the issue carefully, and Senkler was equally cautious, hoping that the diaries' disclosures would speak for themselves.

The young women of the city were eager for answers to many perplexing questions. Had Janet Smith lost her life while fighting for her honour in the basement at Osler Avenue? Had Wong Foon Sing ravished the woman and then killed her to cover his crime? Would the diaries reveal scandalous details of sexual relationships with the men she seemed to pick up in a casual way and with whom she fell in and out of love, one after the other? Would her words explain how she rationalized being engaged to one man, who was building a home for the two of them, while she continued going out with others?

While embalming had affected her internal organs, medical evidence indicated that Janet Smith was a virgin when she died. This supported the contention that she hadn't been ravished, nor had she hopped in and out of bed frequently, if ever. This information had been revealed in testimony before Senkler turned to the dead girl's diaries.

The more conservative women in the benches openly voiced disapproval when Senkler opened the little notebooks. They felt the innermost thoughts of the young woman should not have been exposed to the public. Most of the entries had been written in the months immediately preceding her death. She had not made entries on a daily basis, but only when she had concerns or emotions of importance to express. Almost all her comments dealt with affairs of the heart.

The first entry in the first diary was from December 1923, about six months before the family moved to Osler Avenue. It seems her charms found her companionship even when she went to church on Sunday. She recounted meeting one young man before the service and being escorted home by another when it was over. Not much later, Smith wrote of meeting four young Englishmen in Stanley Park while she was feeding the bears. In the group was her future fiancé, Arthur Dawson, as well as the longshoreman John Lake. Another man of her acquaintance was named Carl, and she had several dates with him. Writing two months later, she said her fascination with Carl had died.

She readily accepted small gifts from men. She said John gave her candy, and another man named Steve presented her with a powder box. Janet liked John but wrote, "I am feeling disturbed today as I feel I must let John go. He wants me to marry him. He is good and steady but there ought to be more than that to matrimony." Presumably she was referring to the same John Lake when she later recorded, "Waiting in miserable anticipation of John's reproaches. He told me he would not keep me bound so tightly that I could not go out with any other man."

Janet knew well the art of flirting. She penned, "Met Morrison again. I know by my symptoms that I am in love again. I'll try different methods. I'll use the freezing method in his case." She didn't describe what this chilly approach was, but the public benches listened in fascination as Senkler read on. Even those who disapproved of the disclosures were intrigued by the feelings expressed by the young woman before her death. It was hardly the stuff of today's tabloids or drugstore magazines, but it was racy material for the time. As Senkler read from Smith's diaries, a defiant and infuriated Cissie Jones glared daggers at him. She curtly told the lawyer she knew some of the men mentioned by Smith but not all.

Janet had her down times, writing once, "I think I have a rotten disposition and wish I were dead." Senkler didn't try to link this to any thought of suicide, appreciating that it was the kind of statement many people made when life, for one reason or another, became difficult, even when they had no intention of killing themselves. "I feel as if I could throw things around. I get so bored here," Smith wrote of life at Osler Avenue in another blue period.

Janet loved dancing and went to dance halls at every opportunity. In Vancouver in this era there were many halls frequented by young people, as well as more expensive private establishments, tennis and golf clubs, and major hotels visited by the wealthy. Dancing was one of the most popular forms of entertainment in the 1920s, and there were commercial halls that held to all the proprieties and generally were seen as respectable, although some religious groups said they were depraved and evil traps for young women. It was not, however, regarded as wanton for single women to frequent such establishments.

One night of dancing produced this entry about Paul: "When we dance Paul holds me tight and kisses my hair. This makes Annie jealous." Another item spoke of Paul kissing her hair again and her hoping that Mary would not be jealous. Entries like these may have inspired the *Sun* headline, just before the inquest, which contended, "Woman Maybe Killer, Jealousy Behind Janet Smith Tragedy." Nobody took the suggestion seriously, but the story may have sold a few papers. Cissie Jones said she didn't know the Paul or Annie referred to and spit out a denial to Senkler's probing that she was the Mary mentioned by Smith. Mary was Cissie's proper name.

Dancing sometimes got Janet into trouble with her employers. She wrote, "I danced until I was exhausted. Got into a row when I got home, but was too exhausted to retaliate." In 1920s Vancouver, employers had strict rules for domestics who lived in their homes.

There was no question that Janet Smith was flirtatious and seldom turned down an invitation. On one occasion she wrote, "Met nicest man and walked in the park with him." She also noted that one day she got several phone calls from various men, commenting, "Mistress doesn't like it, but I do."

While Arthur Dawson was working out of town, northwest of Vancouver on the scenic but at the time sparsely populated Sechelt Peninsula, Smith dated John Lake. On one of Dawson's visits to town, a nasty scene was narrowly avoided when he found his fiancé in a dance hall with Lake. He apparently was very forgiving and made no fuss. Janet Smith undoubtedly did not tell Arthur that John had also asked her to marry him. One of the many mysteries was the fact that police did not look very deeply into John Lake's possible role in the affair.

Smith was guarded when writing about her relationship with Dawson. She went with him to see a play entitled *Three Weeks*. His actions when saying goodnight must have gone a little beyond a goodnight kiss, which surprised her as she wrote that she thought he was level-headed and incorruptible. She may have forgotten that he was considerably older than she was and that he had been married before. Her comment was philosophical: "I suppose I will always play with fire. I expect it is what the fortune teller means when she says I have the girdle of Venus."

Smith made it clear in one entry not long before she died that her engagement to Dawson was on its last legs, writing, "I know my love has cooled. I will just see how long now until the end. My heart used to almost stop when he telephoned but now I just feel bored." She was unhappy with herself. "I think I am a mean little wretch. I don't want Arthur for keeps and I don't want him to have someone else. I have a rotten disposition and I wish I was dead"—again a petulant observation more than a true death wish.

It wasn't possible to tell from the entries if she dated all the men she named, but she certainly was popular. "Had tea in Teddy Forrester's flat with all the boys," was one item. In another entry she commented, "I think all men are like sheep and just chase other chaps' girls."

The atmosphere became electric and sparks flew between Senkler and Jones when he turned to the entries concerning Wong Foon Sing. These comments challenged Jones' claims that Smith lived in fear of the houseboy. In the first entry Smith wrote that she had helped Wong preserve a large quantity of strawberries. Only a few days later she commented, "Poor Wong he must be in love. He gave me a silk nightie and two camisoles." Senkler read the final entry about Wong, dated July 23, three days before Smith's death: "Sing is awfully devoted; gave me two rolls of film for my camera also sweets, and does all my washing and ironing."

Senkler asked, "Does that suggest she was afraid of the Chinaman?"

Jones replied, "Yes, I would have done the same myself. She was afraid of him."

Women in the crowd broke into applause at Jones' angry response. Coroner Brydone-Jack this time threatened to clear the court if there was another disturbance. "This is an inquiry to get at the truth," he stated.

Jones testified that she had picked up photographs that her friend had taken, possibly with the two rolls of film given to her by the houseboy. There were some of Wong with Rosemary, the Bakers' baby. The houseboy was said to have a daughter about the same age in China. Asked what happened to the pictures, Jones vehemently responded that she had torn them up "because I knew how he had treated her." Her anger boiled over and she added, "I felt I could have torn him up if I had had him there." Her strident voice trembled as she attacked the Chinese man.

Asked by the Scots' lawyer, Henderson, if the contents of the diaries had changed her feelings about Smith, the witness replied, "No, I don't take any notice of it. She didn't run after men." The entries indicated the opposite, but Jones was loyal and ignored anything that didn't fit with her way of thinking. When asked, she emphasized that she didn't keep a diary, adding, "No, it's too bad she did or that she didn't take it with her."

Senkler questioned Jones again, asking why, if Smith were afraid of the Chinese, she would not have mentioned it several times in her diary. Jones replied, "Suppose she did not have time. If she had known she was going to die she would have written more about the Chinaman. It is too bad she didn't write more." Jones didn't budge in her conviction that he was guilty of much more than was known. She was a favourite with the Scots women present, who gave her their praise and congratulations as she left the witness box.

Possibly the words penned by Janet Smith in a short entry one night at Osler Avenue best summed up the emotions of the young woman who was sometimes lonely despite all the men mentioned in her diary: "Heavenly night, enormous moon and nobody nice to love me."

The fiery exchanges of the Senkler-Jones confrontation and the revelations in the diaries had stirred the imagination of nearly everyone in Vancouver, their individual interpretation of events ranging from steamy sexual encounters to harmless flirtations and a young woman's romantic musings. The diaries in particular had whetted public interest in the details of the case, and excitement soared when it was Wong's turn to testify.

The Chinese houseboy was calm, apparently undisturbed by all the eyes glued on him in the stuffy courtroom. He had obviously been well briefed by Senkler on what to expect of the largely hostile crowd when he took the stand late on Monday. He was prepared to be examined exhaustively by Charles Craig and to have his story dissected by Alex Henderson in a search for inconsistencies and contradictions.

Wong's "working English" again was inadequate for something as serious and detailed as an inquest. The houseboy's demeanour didn't change, but he must have been surprised and dismayed to see that the court-appointed interpreter was none other than Wong Foon Sien, the man who had visited him on Osler Avenue and had been present in Robinson's detective offices when he was snatched from the street, questioned, and beaten.

There was an unexpected delay in the proceedings when Henderson intervened, explaining to Coroner Brydone-Jack that for "certain reasons" he wanted Wong Foon Sing to swear an oath other than the fire oath taken at the first inquest. The lawyer wanted him sworn in using the chicken oath, a demand that left the courtroom wondering what on earth he was talking about.

The *Province* told its readers, "The fire oath calls for the destruction of the soul of the man in fire. This terrifying pledge was not deemed sufficient in this instance and the crown [actually Henderson] demanded that not only should Wong Foon Sing place his own immortality in the balance but that of his children and his children's children. It is an awful oath."

The demand did not appear to upset either the witness or his lawyer, and the *Sun* reported, "The most sacred oath is the chicken oath. The coroner, the jury, police officials, counsel and newspapermen left the room and went to the areaway between the two buildings and there the oath was administered. A block of wood was set up on end and beside it were two incense candles and a bundle of joss sticks. These were lighted and then the Chinese affixed his signature to the oath written on yellow paper. The oath was then set afire, the head of the chicken was laid on the block, and while the oath was still burning Wong Foon Sing chopped the chicken's head off." This detailed description of a Chinese rite no doubt further established in some Scots' minds the heathen nature of the Chinese community.

Chinatown's *Chinese Times* also reported that the prosecutor had insisted Wong Foon Sing be required to take the chicken oath, pointing out that this was the most serious in the Chinese culture. The paper explained in detail the legal arguments between Wong's lawyer and Alex Henderson, representing the Scots. In another edition the *Times* stressed that the Scottish community had raised money to pay for its own investigation into Smith's death. The paper was supporting moves in the Chinese community to raise funds for Wong Foon Sing's defence, and it offered a reward for information leading to the identity of Smith's killer. Posters appeared on Chinatown streets outlining the houseboy's plight and urging that donations be made. Like the white community, the residents of Chinatown had their own interpretation of events that were widely discussed on the streets and in club rooms.

Crown counsel Craig put the witness through his story slowly and carefully, while Henderson pressed some points in meticulous detail. It was slow going, the houseboy saying a few words that were then translated by Wong Foon Sien. Wong had just one advantage and that was the delay between the time the question was asked and the time the translation was provided. His English was limited, but Wong was able to grasp most of the questions, so the translation delay gave him time to consider each question carefully before answering it.

Some of Craig's questions were picayune and repetitious, but if they were designed to confuse the houseboy and produce contradictory statements, they were unsuccessful. In the two days he testified, the only slip he made was in the number of times he had gone to the basement that morning in the course of his duties. This time he said there was one more trip than he had stated originally, but it was before he heard the shot. It was a meaningless point of no significance.

Wong repeated that the Bakers left the house that morning and that the baby was in her room upstairs. He heard Smith working on the top floor and later saw her hanging out washing and then taking a bundle of clothing downstairs to the basement for ironing. Typical of the questioning was Craig's desire to know if, when Smith went downstairs, she had used the inside stairs or gone through a door from outside. Wong said he didn't know.

The houseboy described his chores during the morning: clearing the breakfast table, polishing the brasswork on the door, throwing out dead flowers, washing the kitchen floor, and going down to the basement from time to time for a smoke. It wasn't electrifying evidence, just the everyday duties of a Shaughnessy servant, but the courtroom hung on every word. Craig never relented, probing for details on every point as he had with the question about the stairs. During one of the growing, unusually long delays in the narration, Senkler talked to his client. He then told Brydone-Jack that the houseboy was having trouble fully understanding Wong Foon Sien's dialect. The coroner ruled that the interpreter would continue in the case until they could find another man to do the job. It could have meant they were receiving wrong information until the new man arrived, but nobody seemed concerned, not even Senkler.

Wong testified that it was sometime after 11 a.m. and he was peeling potatoes for lunch when he heard the gun go off.

Craig questioned him, "When you were peeling potatoes you heard a shot?"

Wong answered, "Yes."

"Did you know it was a revolver shot?" asked Craig.

Wong replied, "When I heard the report I thought it was some kind of gun. I didn't know."

Craig then asked, "What did you do?"

Carefully Wong explained, "I looked through the window and then went down below." The witness said he found the doors to the basement open, first the one leading to the outside and then the other one into the laundry room.

"What did you find?" asked the prosecutor.

"I found her lying down," stated the accused.

"Did you think she was hurt?" queried Craig.

"I saw she was bleeding," Wong replied.

"Did you think she was dead?"

Wong said, "I thought she was not dead." He said Smith was lying on her back, her eyes open and staring. He told the jury that her mouth twitched once. He said he was horrified and scared, but he kept his composure in the box. He said he put his hands under Smith's head and raised it up slightly in an effort to help her if she was still alive.

Craig never let up with his questioning and asked, "Was there blood on her face?"

Remembering it all as he relived it, Wong replied, "Whether there was blood on her face I did not notice. I lifted her head up and was very frightened."

Craig continued to press for details. "There was more blood at her back than on her face?"

And Wong's answer came, "I do not know. I was very frightened."

Still Craig persisted. "Was there more blood after you lifted her?"

Painfully Wong answered, "I put her down and my hands were covered with blood." The houseboy said he wiped the blood from his hands with his apron. He told Craig that he did not move the position of the body—"I just moved her head. I did not touch any other part of her body"—although in earlier testimony he had said that when he first saw her and touched her head he made an effort to lift her but quickly stopped.

Despite the seeming contradiction, Craig did not make a major issue of the response to his repeated questions about the position of the body and the possibility it had been moved. Wong Foon Sing did not even remember seeing her broken glasses, later found by Dr. Blackwood, lying on the floor.

The witness said he ran upstairs and phoned Baker. He then called his uncle, Wong Ling Sai Jack, to tell him what had occurred. His uncle told him to phone Baker but he had already done so.

Wong told Henderson that he initially refused to wash the bloodstains from the basement floor but did so on the Wednesday after the shooting at the request of Dick Baker. The older Baker brother had returned from his European trip to find his home the scene of a violent death and the centre of a police investigation. He nonetheless moved back in immediately. The request that the blood be cleaned from the floor came initially from General McRae, who didn't want his daughter to be upset by the reminder of what had occurred in the basement of her home. Fred and Doreen Baker, along with baby Rosemary, had moved from Osler two days after the shooting, returning to his mother's home on Nelson Street in the West End.

Wong was in the witness box for about eight hours spread over Monday and Tuesday, the third and fourth days of the inquest. There was some surprise when Craig and Henderson stated they had no more questions. Observers had thought they would hammer away much longer, trying to shake Wong's story. When it became obvious that they were not getting anything new from him, they quite suddenly gave up. The Scots were unhappy that more hadn't been extracted from the houseboy. They had hoped for incriminating statements that pointed to his guilt.

Senkler kept a relatively low profile during the questioning of his client, his hot temper under control, his experience telling him that Craig and Henderson were not getting far in trying to impress the jury. Before his client left the box, however, Senkler brought up his abduction from the street and asked him who did it. Without hesitation Wong identified Robinson, who was standing at the back of the room with Constable Hannah of the Point Grey police.

A *Sun* reporter assessed the houseboy's testimony, stating that he bore up well, although the ordeal had not lasted as long as expected, and he had not wavered under questioning. It was racial stereotyping, but the writer stated that he was "the imperturbable Oriental who so readily answered the questions put to him." He added that Wong seemed unconcerned under the grilling, his only sign of nervousness an occasional tapping with his clenched fist on the witness box railing.

In a final effort to unearth new information, the Crown suddenly and inexplicably became concerned about the movements of the Bakers on the morning of the shooting. Perhaps the lawyers were reacting to newspaper stories that suggested the Bakers were somehow involved in the girl's death. In any case, the questioning indicated that the Crown wanted to know if the Bakers had had any opportunity to return home during the morning hours. The sudden interest was short-lived and revealed nothing new, but it did bring an angry response from the family's lawyer, J.L.G. Abbott, who insisted on calling more witnesses to verify the whereabouts of the Bakers during the morning.

Before the jurors retired to reach their verdict, Coroner Brydone-Jack reminded them the objective of his court was to aid the law by fixing on the guilty in the case of a crime or saving the innocent from unjust suspicion by ascertaining if a death was accidental or not. He added that it was essential for those involved in such investigations to exercise great care to ensure that nothing was overlooked. It didn't have to be said, or even suggested, that the Point Grey police had completely blown the investigation.

Foreman Wilson and his five colleagues retired at 11:20 a.m. on the fifth day. A half-hour later they asked that the revolver and ammunition and a floor plan of the basement from the exhibits be sent in to them for study. They astutely broke for lunch on the Crown at 1 p.m. before returning to a still packed and expectant courtroom with their decision at 2:05 p.m. One reporter wrote, "Nothing that preceded it could be compared with the thrill which the crowd experienced in waiting for the verdict of the jury." Considering the mass of contradictory and confusing evidence they had listened to, it hadn't taken them long to reach a decision—just 2 hours and 45 minutes, less an hour for lunch.

In response to Brydone-Jack's question if they had reached a verdict, Foreman Wilson began reading from a sheet of paper. "We find that Janet K. Smith was on July 26 wilfully murdered in the course of her employment in the laundry in the basement of F.L. Baker's home by being shot through the head, but by whom we do not know."

The courtroom burst into roars of approval, cheers, and applause. None were louder than the Scots, who were led by Council president David Paterson and secretary Mrs. Jessie Stratton, both members of the committee that set up the private investigation into their countrywoman's death.

Wilson had more to add, but he had to wait until calls from the coroner and court officials for silence quietened the excited room. The foreman then attacked the Point Grey police. "The want of any proper investigation when the tragedy was discovered was responsible for the protracted inquiry, causing great suffering to innocent persons and probably shielding guilt," he stated. Wilson then added a jury conclusion that not many people agreed with: "We exonerate Chief Simpson and Constable Fish entirely." This dumped all the blame on hapless Constable James Green, who probably was the worst offender but didn't deserve to carry the load all on his own.

Senkler also was criticized for having read the excerpts from Smith's diaries, though it was obvious he had to do it in order to offset the evidence of her friends' claims that she was terrified of Wong and helpless in the houseboy's hands. Wilson read the jury's rebuke, "It is regrettable that the reading of picked extracts from the deceased's diary tended to defame her pure and unsullied memory." Apparently it was wrong to defame the character of Janet Smith, but defaming Wong Foon Sing was something else entirely. Senkler was unrepentant

The headline of a *Province* special, rushed into the streets and grabbed up quickly from newsboys yelling out the verdict, summed up the situation: "Janet Smith Murdered By Unknown Persons, Want Of Proper Investigation Is Condemned, Chief Simpson Is Exonerated."

The cheering of the Scots had hardly died away before they were planning their next move. The second inquest had reversed the finding that Smith had committed suicide or died accidentally. She had been murdered, but by whom? The clansmen and women were convinced there was no need to look further than Wong Foon Sing, despite the fact that the hearing had underlined the absence of any real evidence against him. For good reasons they still challenged the competence of the police investigation and insisted their own probing was necessary. It was generally assumed that their planned fundraising was to pay a private detective agency—there were others in town similar to Robinson's.

Point Grey Police Chief Simpson commented to reporters that he was glad the jury had seen fit to clear his name and emphasized he had acted "conscientiously and properly" on the advice of Constable Green. Another incredible oversight of the Point Grey force surfaced the following day, however, to contradict Simpson's words.

On Friday morning, two days after the jury's murder verdict, Inspector Cruickshank, acting on a hunch that the police from Point Grey might have missed something else, took a small group of provincial and Vancouver police to Osler Avenue for a thorough search of the premises. By this time the basement had been thoroughly cleaned. Despite this, in the laundry room, only a few feet from where the body of Janet Smith had been found, one of the men pulled open the furnace door and was startled to find clothing in the coal cinder box. There lay the burned remains of a woman's corset and a man's handkerchief. Both items were stained with red streaks that the policemen construed could be blood. News of the find electrified newspaper reporters, who expanded on their own theories and rumours about the case. Followers of the story began to wonder if the hapless initial investigators had searched the premises at all. How could the force have missed first the bullet and now this?

The clothing was sent to the city laboratory for analysis, and again Wong Foon Sing was questioned. He said he knew nothing about the clothes. The *Province* reported, "It is known, of course, that the question of the arrest of the Chinaman has been considered."

Four days later all speculation died. Tests showed that the stains on the corset were rust from the garment's metal stays, as were some of the spots on the handkerchief, although others could have been tiny stains from a pricked finger. It was also discovered that the furnace had not been used since early July. Who owned the corset and who put it in the furnace was never revealed.

With a reversal of his previous praise of Constable Green, Chief Simpson suspended the investigator until the Point Grey Police Commission had time to study the situation. With a quick look and a fast vote, the Commission gave Green a slap on the wrist and reinstated him with pay. There was, however, at least one dissenting commissioner. H.P. McRaney, a Scot, disagreed with the decision and made his opinion known, as did Councillor H.O. McDonald, who stated that it was "the worst bit of bungling of police work in Canada."

Prominent Chinese Man Gunned Down

The United Council of Scottish Societies became increasingly critical of the police investigation into Smith's death and objected to the attitude taken by Attorney General Manson. Following a rancorous meeting of the executive, the Council made a call for funds to all member organizations so that a $1,000 reward for information about the Smith affair could be offered and other money made available to mount a separate, private investigation of all the evidence.

Many Scottish women felt an empathy with the dead girl and were influenced by the views of the Council. They became vehement in their belief that Wong was a murderer. Others argued there was no proof. Manson had his own doubts about Wong's guilt, but the persistent criticism from the Scots was beginning to worry the haughty attorney general, who had been riding high in political popularity and had a blinding ambition to rise still higher, possibly to the post of premier. To Manson, the Chinese houseboy became the best suspect regardless of the facts, and he was anxious to please the Scottish voters. He favoured what was known at the time as a "fishing trip," which involved laying a charge to bring pressure to bear on a suspect with the hope that new or incriminating evidence might surface during the proceedings.

Manson then announced publicly that the investigation had initially been botched, and in his strongest statement to that time he declared that some of the oversights of the Point Grey police and the coroner's office bordered on the criminal. He asserted that because of the bungling, many avenues of investigation had been closed off prematurely. As a result, further probing into the cause of Janet Smith's death was difficult, almost impossible. Manson charged that since the girl's death there had been an avalanche of rumours and many "wild imaginings" that had complicated the whole investigation. The attorney general then announced that the provincial government would outdo the Scottish Council by putting up a $2,000 reward for information leading to a resolution of the case.

The public had become frustrated and angry with law enforcement agencies at all levels. As the impasse in the Smith case continued, some disgruntled Vancouverites turned their animosity toward the city's Chinese. There was a growing belief that these people who had come from far across the Pacific Ocean, from what was viewed as a heathen alien world, represented a violent challenge to the law and order of this new land. Tension mounted dramatically, feeding the fear and anxiety that was already widespread, when four shots rang out in Chinatown just eight weeks after the death of the young girl in Shaughnessy. With racially stressed emotion running rampant, a gangland-style slaying was seen as further evidence of the threat that a crime-ridden, murderous Chinese inner city posed to the whole community.

On September 24, 1924, 40-year-old Lew Hun-Chang was gunned down as he left a restaurant with a friend. Also known as "Davie" Lew, this intriguing man was a key link between the Chinese community and the rest of the city. He filled a role that probably cost him his life. There wasn't much he didn't know about events in Chinatown, either on the streets or in the tongs, and he was reportedly involved with various gambling organizations. Lew had offices on the fourth floor of the Holden Building on East Hastings Street. He drove a big car and was described as a Chinese broker and "confidential agent." He had been in trouble with some of the tongs operating in Cumberland, Nanaimo, and Victoria on Vancouver Island and had recently won a suit for slander against one of them. In the weeks immediately prior to his death he had been preparing a report for the Chinese community on the treatment of Wong Foon Sing.

Police admitted he had also lately provided them with information about a bootleg liquor case involving a woman who was the mistress of a tong leader, as well as helping them uncover immigrant smuggling operations. Perhaps some of his compatriots felt he knew too much and was too close to white authorities. Suspicion that he was an informant could have been enough to earmark him for death. There were large amounts of money involved in people smuggling, gambling, and drugs.

His slaying wasn't a botched robbery, vengeance resulting from a love triangle, or the result of a sudden quarrel. It was an assassination. Davie Lew had been stalked to the Pekin Chop Suey House, on the second floor of a building at the corner of Pender and Carrall. He took four bullets in the back as he descended the stairs from the restaurant to the street on the evening of September 24. He died on the spot in the doorway. His death looked like a gangland killing, and extravagant newspaper coverage further disturbed a city still caught up in the tragedy of the "Nightingale." This was Chinese against Chinese, possibly one tong against another, and one news story stated the killing threw "Chinatown into the greatest state of excitement in the history of the Oriental quarter."

On September 25, colourful red-and-yellow posters appeared in Chinatown offering $6,000 reward for information leading to the identity of the killer. The money was provided by the powerful tong to which Lew belonged, and the size of the reward was an indication of his position in the community. A few weeks later the Lew family offered another $1,000 reward.

Lew had been brought to Vancouver as a nine-year-old by his father, a prominent builder and businessman in the city, who had retired to his place of birth and now lived in Canton. His son remained in Canada and was educated at schools in Vancouver and New Westminster. Lew studied law at the University of B.C. but did not sit for final exams, knowing that no matter how well he did, he would never be admitted to the B.C. bar. He could not practise legally because he could not become a Canadian citizen.

His knowledge of the law, however, and his fluent, unaccented English, relatively unusual at this time, opened many business opportunities for him in 1920s Vancouver. He was the go-between for many members of the Chinese community in legal matters, and because he had grown up in the community he was well aware of all the activities that took place there, be they legal or a part of the underworld. He became a court interpreter, the assistant consul for China in western Canada, and an important contact for the Chinese community with the broader world of Canadian business.

The police ran into their usual problems investigating Chinatown crime. There was the ever-present language barrier, and the insular Asian community would not soon forget the violent treatment it often received, nor the kidnapping and interrogation to which Wong Foon Sing had so recently been subjected by local law enforcers. They viewed local police with considerable suspicion, and a veil of silence descended on the Lew assassination case.

Facing a civic election in December, Mayor W.R. Owen stated on October 2, as civic leader and chairman of the Vancouver Police Commission, that he would clean up the situation in Chinatown. A *Province* headline stated, "Declare War on Chinatown Underworld, Statement by Mayor Owen." The mayor told reporters, "Gambling must be stopped in Chinatown; the selling of narcotics must cease; tong activity must be curbed to remove the threat to public safety; the sale of liquor in chop suey houses and blind pigs [a term that generally referred to bootleggers but sometimes included people running bookmaking operations] must be suppressed and civic bylaws must be rigorously enforced." The mayor said the city's good name was being besmirched and the deaths of Smith and now Lew were making headlines in many places outside of the province.

Mayor Owen used the animosity towards the Chinese as he campaigned for re-election. "The persistence of rumours about the trafficking of tong leaders in slave girls suggests that there may be some foundation in truth to the stories," he said in an irresponsible statement that only helped to heighten racial tension. The suggestion, however, played to the biases and prejudices of many voters and probably gained him votes. The effects of his statements on the Chinese were of no concern because they couldn't vote.

During his campaign, the mayor added something new to the investigation of the Lew murder. "We do know on the night of his death, Mr. Lew was to give the police information in connection with a fracas which was said to have its origin in a gaming house war," said Owen. The statement for the first time publicly raised the possibility that Lew was a police informant. This was the only reference ever made to this evidence, but as chairman of the police commission, Owen obviously had access to a great deal of information that was not general knowledge.

Tension mounted in Chinatown in the weeks following Lew's murder, and police braced for trouble from his supporters and his opponents. The statements by Mayor Owen did nothing to cool the prevailing atmosphere. The *Province* summed up the situation when it stated, "Probably no local Chinese was better hated by a certain section of the Oriental community than Lew Hun-Chang." Stories blossomed about the young man, whom the paper described as "debonair, slight and fast-moving." Many of the details were unsubstantiated, but the *Province* said Lew's life had been threatened on numerous occasions and he was known to have carried a gun. It was alleged that his apartment had been set on fire by an arsonist in a previous bid to kill him.

There were several delays in scheduling Lew's funeral, which was complicated because of the time needed for members of his large extended family to travel from around the world to Vancouver for the service and burial. The papers anticipated it would be one of the largest events in recent Chinatown history, with much pomp and ceremony. One incongruous headline stated that a "Pompous" funeral was expected. Police plans for a quiet show of strength, which included the calling out of all reserve constables, were ready when the date of the funeral was finally announced for October 25, more than a month after his death.

When the day dawned, police fears of trouble were confirmed quickly by an axe-wielding assault. Fortunately, it proved to be an isolated attack by one man on another, with no bearing on the Lew murder.

Hundreds of Chinese and whites jammed the chapel at the Nunn and Thompson Funeral Home, and a large crowd gathered outside on the street, waiting for the service to conclude and a parade to wend its way through Chinatown. Presbyterian minister Rev. R.G. McBeth conducted a service in English. It was followed by one in Chinese.

When the services were over, two Chinese bands wailed as the procession moved through the community. There were a great many police on hand who chose to be inconspicuous, although they were ready to move quickly in the event that violence erupted anywhere along the route. The crowd of thousands—men, women, and many children—watched in silence from the sidewalks and the windows of buildings. There was no trouble as the bands played and the cars carrying Lew's relatives moved slowly by. A fleet of taxis followed the hearse to Mountain View Cemetery where Lew was laid to rest. Fate had extinguished one of the leading lights in the Chinese community, a man of many parts, well known and respected, but some of whose activities were wrapped in mystery. The police hunt for the killer went on.

The funeral did nothing to halt the mayor's campaign, and he now maintained his demand for a crackdown had the support of "every decent citizen." The *Sun* reported that the police were given a "free hand to go the limit. They were to raid a premises a dozen times a day if need be." Within hours they had moved, in one raid arresting 21 people who were said to be playing "um gow" or "pi gow." In another swoop, 45 were carted off.

Garbage collection and disposal in Chinatown, where a high concentration of restaurants were located within a relatively small area, became the next target in the mayor's drive for re-election. Inspectors were sent to check for spilled garbage as well as violations of electrical or plumbing by-laws, conditions that were not at all difficult to find. The public was told that gambling, bootlegging, drug dealing, and other crimes "nest in dark alleys and unsanitary conditions, which are the breeding ground for drug addicts." Within days Vancouver's medical health officer, Dr. F.T. Underhill, said the cleanup was going well. A police department claim that gambling was all but wiped out was more difficult for Vancouverites to believe.

The RCMP became involved in the drug crackdown, sending a squad aboard the *Empress of Asia* when the Canadian Pacific liner docked in Vancouver from Hong Kong. They found quantities of opium hidden on the ship and arrested several members of the crew for illegal drug possession.

The *Sun* continued its criticism of the police in its crusade for an amalgamated Vancouver force, while challenging Alex Manson's wish for a government-controlled, provincewide force. One editorial maintained this latter arrangement would lead to rampant crime in the city, "checked only by the feeble efforts of a few political hangers-on who have attained sleuthdom by a patronage route." The paper stated it wasn't necessary to go as far back as czarist Russia "to see how utterly damnable a politically controlled police force can become."

As well as suffering newspaper attacks and increasingly loud complaints from the Scots about lack of action in the Janet Smith case, which seemed to have reached a dead end, the attorney general came under criticism in the legislature in Victoria. The opposition smelled blood, and Manson became involved in an angry debate that boiled over into racist diatribes on the floor of the House.

T.G. Coventry, a former RCMP officer, now a Conservative MLA, wanted to know how many police forces were involved in the Janet Smith investigation. A week later he demanded immediate intervention by the RCMP because neither provincial nor municipal police "have succeeded in running the criminal to earth." Coventry threw more fuel on the fiery debate when he said "higher ups in the dope trade" were responsible for Smith's killing, although he admitted he had no facts to support the assertion. As a former member of the RCMP, however, he may have seen reports emanating from London and Hong Kong relating to dope-smuggling investigations undertaken against business associates of Fred Baker. Coventry is reported to have said on November 24, 1924: "When the man or woman responsible for the murder of Janet Smith is brought into court, you will find the real centre and kernel of the dope trade of this province."

Manson was immediately on his feet in the House, trying to divert as much blame as possible away from his own department. Without directly addressing Coventry's accusations, he said Smith's embalming was not done by "ordinary measures." It hadn't been established who exactly gave the order for the embalming, although Coroner Brydone-Jack was the likely candidate, but there had been nothing mentioned up to this time to suggest the embalming method was unusual.

The attorney general also maintained that he had been phoned by a newspaperman who claimed that all the facts in the case had not yet come out. The caller was not identified, but it likely was John Sedgwick Cowper, eccentric reporter and editor of the *Saturday Tribune*, who knew Manson well and would soon become a key figure in the case.

Newspapers capitalized on the House debate, playing up the developing racist uproar. They even found another story that produced a headline spotlighting two minority groups at the same time: "Chinese Sold Dope to Hindu."

In a wide-ranging speech filled with eloquent phrases, Manson defended himself and his department in the legislature, playing on the emotions of his audience when he said everything possible had been done and the province of B.C. had a "heart" for a girl from the old country. As usual, he took the opportunity to criticize Point Grey, saying the district's police force had not acted "as wisely as they might, resulting in the destruction of evidence and hampering the inquiry." His argument was strong enough to counteract the petition presented by Coventry, in which he had recommended the RCMP be called in immediately. The MLA finally agreed to drop it.

Committed to a new public posture he felt sure would gain him support in Vancouver, where most of the voting public lived, Manson announced that the Smith killing supported the belief that Orientals had a greater influence for evil on white girls than others, a statement that was, of course, outrageous coming from the province's chief law enforcement officer. It was obviously made to point the finger of guilt towards Wong Foon Sing. The statement was also made in support of the new Asian Immigration Act passed by the federal Liberal government in 1923.

The Vancouver police countered Manson's suggestion when they announced that in the previous year not a single case of a Chinese assaulting a woman had been reported. The police department analysis showed that the number of offences against women in the city was up, however, with the main culprits being of Irish, English, and Scots nationality. As Scots were prominent in the department's upper ranks, it was a surprising and frank admission that their fellow clansmen were responsible for some of the attacks, but not the Chinese.

In spite of police department statistics, Mrs. Mary Ellen Smith supported Manson's view. She was the Liberal MLA for Vancouver, the first woman ever elected to the B.C. legislature, and, in fact, the first woman in the British Empire to hold such an office. She told the House she would move to ban Orientals and white girls working together in B.C. homes as an amendment to a general Women and Girls Protection Act that she had proposed earlier as a private member's bill. Smith, who was not related to the slain Janet Smith, said she had collected the names of 28 girls who were prepared to quit working as housemaids in "fashionable homes" because of the killing and the young women's fear of the Chinese men in their households. An official in Victoria said Smith's legislation had little chance of passing because of constitutional rules. It ultimately did not pass, but it did bring a sizeable response. One reaction was a hurried statement from Chinese Consul Dr. Lin Pao Heng, who contacted Premier John Oliver and said that any move to segregate employees by race would be a "gross discrimination and not justified by conditions in Vancouver." Japanese Consul Isago Gomyo told reporters that while there were not many Japanese domestics in the city, they were protected by a 1911 treaty signed by Britain and Japan, which exempted them from any proposed B.C. legislation.

Speaking on Mary Ellen Smith's proposed bill in the House in early December, Attorney General Manson made another outrageous comment, saying white women should not work in close proximity to Chinese men because the latter were "so often addicted to the use of narcotic drugs."

A.W. McNeill, Member of Parliament for Comox-Alberni, a leader in the campaign against Japanese immigration to B.C., took the opportunity to jump into the debate when he talked to the press during a visit to his home riding. He said a cutback of Japanese fishing on the West Coast by 15 to 25 percent a year would result in their almost total elimination over the next four years. This, said McNeill, "will restore to the white race an important industry on the coast."

An editorial about immigration in the *Province* was ironic, similar in tone to stories which appear to this day. It stated there were Canadian complaints about a new United States quota on Canadian emigration south, some 200,000 people reportedly having left the country in 1923. The Americans said the move was not so much against Canadians as it was against foreigners purporting to be Canadians who wanted admission to the U.S. through the back door. The paper ruefully noted that the new rule might have one advantage: it might keep more Canadians home.

Statements expressed in the continuing debate in the legislature were some of the most prejudiced ever heard, undoubtedly because the Asian Immigration Act had made racial discrimination an acceptable public position. William Hayward, a Tory member and mayor of Victoria, argued that legislation was needed that would stop all Oriental immigration to Canada. He stated that the 1921 census showed there were 23,532 Chinese in B.C.,15,006 Japanese, and 951 Hindus. He told the House there had been an alarming increase since then, and the willingness of these people to work for low wages threatened the employment of white British Columbians. Mayor Hayward added, "The fate of B.C. will never be realized unless we keep driving on this matter." A lot of people agreed with him.

Conservative Colonel Cy Peck spoke in favour of a proposal to help finance the move of fishermen from the Hebrides Islands off Scotland's west coast to B.C.'s coast. While he was opposed to promoting immigration, these were the "best people in the world," and the move would help rid the fishing industry of Orientals. He also recommended a policy of segregation in schools, which he termed "absolutely sane." He wanted Chinese and Japanese children to be put in their own schools with their parents made to pay the costs. Colonel Peck had strong Scottish ties and during the First World War had commanded Vancouver's 16th Canadian Scottish Regiment with some distinction. He was a war hero, a winner of the Victoria Cross and of the Distinguished Service Order and Bar.

MLA William Sloan contended that Orientals "threaten the very life of Anglo-Saxons on the west coast." He maintained 4,710 had entered the province after the 1921 census and that since then, 1,070 Chinese and 2,680 Japanese babies had been born in the province. Immigration figures from Ottawa showed that in the first eleven months of 1924 a total of 120,000 people had entered, 56,000 of them from Britain and most of the remainder from the U.S. and European countries. Sloan proudly stated that he never had any "truck or trade with the Orientals." In 38 years he had never had a piece of clothing laundered by an Oriental—one assumes he had it done elsewhere—and he had "never assisted an Oriental." During this diatribe he contended that "if people of B.C. adopted his policy there would be no Oriental problem." Sloan added that until recently eastern Canada had shown indifference to and a lack of sympathy for B.C.'s race problems.

In this atmosphere it was not surprising that four Chinese stores were torched during the night in New Westminster. Thirty people living in upstairs apartments had to scramble for safety, fortunately without loss of life or serious injury. In Victoria, while the angry debate was proceeding, some 2,000 people attended a meeting in the City Temple. They unanimously passed a resolution calling for the return of all Chinese and Japanese in B.C. to their homelands. The petition stated that the numbers of Asians were "multiplying at an alarming rate," and they were competing successfully against white merchants because of their low standard of living. The petition also stated that they were causing unemployment for everyone else and that jobs for Chinese and Japanese in industry and commerce should be restricted by legislation.

A crowd of 600 people came to the steps of the legislature to protest unemployment. The papers pointed out that more than a few in the mob had spent considerable time in city bars before moving to the building. The noisy, boisterous crowd yelled for the premier to come out and speak to them, adding that if he would not, he should be dragged out. More sober heads prevailed, however, and there was no assault on the provincial legislature despite some raging tempers and strong threats that a battle royal was about to commence. The government had ordered extra security forces to be on hand and had them in readiness, out of sight, in case there was violence.

The angry, outspoken mob viewed the number of Asians in B.C. as a major factor in the increasing rate of unemployment among whites. The same sentiment was echoed in edition after edition of the *Labour Statesman*, the weekly organ of the Vancouver, New Westminster and District Labour Council. Labour contended that it was the introduction of low-wage, non-union workers by big business (the CPR being a favourite target) that was responsible for the problem.

The labour paper seized upon the Janet Smith case with more feeling than fact. The *Statesman* maintained that she had been brought to Canada by the Salvation Army to work "practically as a serf" for $5 a month. It was wrong on both counts. She was brought by the Bakers, who paid her passage by ship and train from Paris to Vancouver, and she was paid about $20 a month plus room and board. While noting that the religious group had its good points, the *Statesman* deplored the Salvation Army for acting like a "cheap, labour-baiting agency." It blasted the "elite" for giving more consideration and money to Chinese employees than to poor working girls, claiming that they, like Janet Smith, did the drudgery and looked after the children while their socialite mothers were "out gallivanting about." The organization's deep dislike of the Chinese was also reflected in a story contending that a Chinese cook had threatened a white waitress with a knife in a restaurant argument. "We feel their presence is not only becoming obnoxious but also dangerous to the wellbeing of white men and women," added the *Statesman*.

The labour paper did not devote much attention to the Smith case as it wore on, but it did take a swipe at Attorney General Manson, not for his handling of the affair but apparently for declining to have labour properly represented on a board looking into the possibility of legalizing an eight-hour working day.

Mrs. Smith's private member's bill died on the floor of the legislature—as do most private member's bills to this day—but its extremism was easily topped by another bill proposed by the attorney general. Manson moved that industries in B.C. employ only whites. "I have no feelings against the Orientals," he told the House, "but there is an ethnological difference which cannot be overcome, the two races cannot mix and I believe our duty is to our own people." His proposal passed with only a few negative votes from labour party members. Fortunately, the law was never enacted.

On November 11, 1924, as debate in the House continued, the *Province* came up with a fanciful and totally unsubstantiated story on Lew's slaying. It claimed there were eight men involved in the killing, seven of whom received $100 each for helping the actual hit man to escape. The newspaper said the hit man received $300. The money was supposedly put up by "powerful Chinese organizations" that ordered the murder because of "the enmity Lew had gained." This story, however outlandish, bolstered the belief that the killing was gang or tong related and based on gambling, the drug trade, or prostitution. Attorney General Manson told an increasingly restless public that all leads were being followed, but there was nothing new in the Lew or Smith cases.

In a move that threw Chinatown into turmoil, the public learned that Alderman R.E. Almond, chairman of Vancouver's finance committee, had met with a representative of the Great Northern Railway with a view to moving the Chinese community away from the downtown area. Chinatown was viewed by some as valuable real estate for expansion of the city. The Chinese wondered and waited, but Chinatown stayed where it was and remains there today.

In late November there was finally a break in the Lew murder case when a man named Chong Sing was arrested in Victoria. He didn't seem to fit the role of a gun for hire, a killer who shot at close range and then fled through the streets and escaped. Chong Sing was in his 50s and slow moving. He had lived for about 30 years in Victoria, working as a cook, cleaner, and store clerk. The authorities said he was a member of the Chee Kong Tong in Victoria. The tong, outraged at the charges against one of its own, immediately started a defence fund and stated that Chong Sing was the victim of a frame-up.

White residents got priority seating at the quickly called preliminary hearing in Vancouver and were not searched for weapons. The Chinese who managed to get into the courtroom were all frisked. The Crown's case quickly fell apart because the evidence of the only white witness to the tragedy was not believable. The evidence of Mrs. M. McDonald was ludicrous, and within minutes of taking the stand it became clear she had nothing to offer. She had been in a car near the corner where Lew was murdered. The woman admitted that in a police line-up she had picked out Chong Sing only because he seemed to be the right height and build. She had not seen the killer's face. Despite this fiasco, the crown did have the evidence of Chew Fung Tao, a friend who had left the restaurant with Lew. He had been within a few feet of the gunman and had also identified Chong Sing in the police line-up. Other witnesses were less convincing, and there was controversy about their identification of the accused, who nonetheless was remanded for a trial that would not take place until the spring of 1925. In the meantime, the lack of any resolution to either the Smith murder or the Lew assassination continued to fuel racial conflict.

One calmer voice was heard in a *Sun* editorial on December 20. It stated, "If there is such a thing as yellow peril, it is not so much the invasion of Canada by Oriental immigrants, as the inability of Occidentals to keep up with the Orientals in point of industry, initiative, and resource." The editorial added that if it was desirable to keep them out, it should be based on "broad grounds of biology and economics," and not with an attempt to brand them as inferior. It was an odd argument, but in the tenor of the times, as were the comments made in naturalization court by Judge David Grant. Grant insisted that some people should not be naturalized, commenting, "once a German or Russian, always a German or Russian." The war with Germany had been over for only seven years, and the people of the western alliance were now apprehensive about the rise of communism in Russia, so neither of these two countries nor the people from them were particularly popular in B.C. The irascible Judge Grant also said that no "bootleggers, white slavers or men of loose character" would be naturalized in his court. The papers noted that in the crowded courtroom were "some well-known bootleggers and members of the underworld fraternity," all intent on becoming Canadian citizens, but there were no public complaints about Grant's views.

A Happy New Year?

The people of Vancouver largely forgot the city's murders and Chinatown's gambling and drug problems while they celebrated Christmas 1924, visiting friends, taking children to special functions, and attending church services in large numbers. Many of the Scots looked for a dark-haired man to be the first across the threshold on New Year's Day, a sign that would bring them good fortune for 1925.

As the new year began, Greater Vancouver announced population statistics marking the quarter-century. Living in Vancouver city were 135,138; in North Vancouver, 12,000; in West Vancouver, 6,000; in South Vancouver, 40,000; in Burnaby, 14,500; in New Westminster, 17,000; and in Point Grey and Shaughnessy Heights, 25,500, for a total of 250,138 in the greater Vancouver area. Half of the province's population lived within a fifteen-mile radius of the region, which meant that without the support of Vancouver, no political party striving to become the government could long survive.

The B.C. Telephone Company released statistics that showed there were 57,300 phones in use by area residents, and the B.C. Electric Company announced it annually carried 68 million passengers on street cars and the interurban rail line through Kitsilano and Kerrisdale to Marpole and the Fraser Valley.

The warm feelings of good will and progress didn't last long, however, and the hiatus in murder and mayhem ended when it came time for the hanging of Chong Sam Bow. Bow was being executed for the 1923 shooting of John C. Jones at the downtown intersection of Main and Pender, and the newspapers didn't spare the gruesome details of the event. The hanging took place only after Bow had suffered through five trials, the first held in November 1923. The first four ended in a split decision or were thrown out on appeal. He wasn't so lucky with the fifth and final hearing, and on October 21, 1924, the guilty verdict was upheld. This final trial was remarkable in its own right. Perhaps by chance or possibly by design, a woman was selected for the jury, something almost unheard of prior to this time. The *Sun* told its readers that Chong Sam Bow refused any drugs in the final hours before he stepped onto the gallows trapdoor. "He maintained the stoic state of mind generally attributed to his race during his last night on earth," the paper stated. Chong Sam Bow was a convert to Christianity, who called for "The book, the book ... " as he was led into the execution chamber. His final prayers were muffled by the black hood that was draped over his head just before the hangman pulled the lever.

The Scottish societies chose this time to announce the construction of a new $200,000 headquarters building, which would include a banquet hall and meeting and games rooms. A Burns' Night dinner held by Clan McLean drew more than 500 people. All were pleased that in the recent Point Grey elections, Scots had taken the majority of seats on the police commission on a "Janet Smith" ticket. The new commissioners promptly gave Chief Simpson a three-month leave of absence on medical grounds, but he never returned to the job. They also fired the hapless Constable Green, the man who had the temerity to suggest Smith killed herself.

Vancouver Police Chief H.W. Long began the new year by telling reporters that he would wipe out gambling in the city. The only thing louder than public laughter over this claim was the clicking of fan-tan tiles as Chinatown's gamblers continued to try their luck. Critics said gambling was the least of their worries and suggested that an increase in bootlegging could easily be halted by the opening of an all-night liquor store, something that Vancouver still had not introduced by the year 2000.

Chief Long immediately undertook the crackdown on gambling, and Vancouver police rounded up hundreds of fan-tan players in a series of raids. The Chinese, many of them elderly men, were reported to be playing a dice game called "barboodey," supposedly the latest fad.

Vancouver's feisty new mayor, Louis D. Taylor, who beat Owen in the December elections despite Owen's sweeping anti-Asian campaign, told city police to stop taking directions from Alex Manson. Chief Long immediately denied that his force was bossed from Victoria. The mayor proposed an easier approach to Chinatown, where he believed too much time was being wasted chasing minor gamblers. "The Chinese look on gambling as their pastime and as a crime it is low and the police could be more profitably engaged in checking blind pigs, dope peddlers etcetera," was Mayor Taylor's rather radical suggestion. He observed this would be preferable to "looking through peepholes" at gamblers. His two colleagues on the police commission, which he headed, were not pleased with his relaxed viewpoint, nor were church leaders and women's groups. Manson, too, was unhappy, and in deference to the public mood, the police pursuit of the gambling fraternity continued. Chinatown gambling was one of the major perceived sins of the Oriental community.

In response to Taylor's statement, Manson had one of his frequent run-ins with Vancouver's city fathers, complaining that their handling of liquor laws was lax and that bootleggers always seemed to be tipped off before raids were made on their premises. He was right, and the practice continued well into the 1960s because of archaic laws and regulations that had remained unchanged since the beginning of the century. The lucrative bootlegging business was aided by corruption in the city police department, which continued for many years and included at least one chief in the pay of the crooks.

An intriguing fracas that erupted about this time involved prominent lumberman W.R. Hanbury, whose Shaughnessy home was on Cartier Avenue. He fired a housemaid, Mrs. Lily Smith, who said she wasn't leaving until she got pay in lieu of notice. In a subsequent suit for $10,000 in damages, the domestic claimed she was injured and knocked unconscious when Hanbury grabbed her by the ankle, pulled her downstairs, and threw her out the door. The housemaid didn't have a chance. A jury took only 30 minutes to find that she was a trespasser and impertinent to boot. The proprieties of the 1920s had to be observed. She didn't get a penny; the master of the mansion reigned supreme.

Newspapers of the day carried an inordinate number of suicide announcements, possibly an indication of the social pressures under which some people lived. Women were often the victims, and their reasons were generally related to feelings of shame at being jilted by a lover, being forbidden to see a lover, becoming involved in a scandal, facing poverty alone, or worst of all, becoming pregnant prior to marriage. One of the victims of her own hand in early 1925 was Geraldine Tolmie. The niece of a former lieutenant-governor, she killed herself by jumping from a tall building in Victoria. It was not revealed which of the social taboos she had broken, or if she were mentally disturbed or had contracted an incurable disease.

The prevailing climate of racial discord was evident when the Native Sons of Canada invited 278 organizations in Greater Vancouver to discuss forming a common front that would work towards the expulsion of Asians from Canada. Most ignored the call, but representatives of 39 groups attended the meeting. The common front never was founded, but the dark spirit that called for it lived on.

On the positive side, a group of citizens was eager to erect a monument to "Black Joe" Fortes. He was a giant of a man from Trinidad who came to Vancouver and worked in a bar in the early part of the century before voluntarily taking on the job of teaching children to swim at English Bay. He eventually became a city-paid swimming teacher, and thousands of youngsters were his students. He was a loved figure, a living symbol of what the citizens saw as the city's racial tolerance, and a plaque went up in his honour after he died. It was easy to be tolerant of "Black Joe." There were only a handful of blacks in all of B.C. at the time, and not many white residents in Vancouver had ever come in contact with a black person other than Joe. He was no economic threat to the community, he had never pressed for equality, but like a good servant he had contributed to the city. (Today an upscale restaurant in the city's West End bears his name.)

Few whites felt sympathy or fondness for Wong Foon Sing, but despite the cloud hanging over him, he made no attempt to flee the city, to hide, or to go back to China, as he could easily have done. His situation was made more difficult, however, by the rantings of *The Beacon*. The first edition, ten cents or one dollar a year, was published in December 1924 by the Rev. McDougall. It contained the texts of all his inflammatory diatribes and focused on his hatred of minority groups. He lauded the Ku Klux Klan—Christian gentlemen doing their duty to their country and their God against the heathen, evil masses—and featured such articles as "How Japs Treat Their Wives" and lurid tales of the Oriental lust for white girls who were being forced into slavery. At the height of his malevolence he even suggested Wong Foon Sing could be the killer of Davie Lew. McDougall claimed he could prove Wong perjured himself at both inquests, although he never revealed his proof.

In his first edition he also asserted that in the hours following Smith's death there were many phone calls between the two Baker brothers. This statement was obviously a fabrication, as Dick did not return to the city from his European vacation until Monday. In a subsequent edition, and without apology, McDougall said the calls actually had been between Fred and his aunt, Lily Lefevre. McDougall alleged that telephone operators had told him this, but they had since been silenced on the orders of Mrs. Lefevre, a major shareholder in the phone company. Facts didn't bother the ranting minister, who twisted them all to support his own prejudices.

The city's lawyers were often a McDougall target, and he contended that members of Vancouver's Bar Association were only interested in making money. In an early edition of his paper he wrote, "Janet Smith lies under the green sod while the Chinaman like the barristers lives to enjoy his three square meals a day."

The Janet Smith affair returned to prominence during the spring because of the investigations undertaken by Malcolm Bruce Jackson, a Victoria lawyer, well-known Liberal, defeated MLA, Presbyterian, and close friend of Attorney General Manson. The attorney general had appointed Jackson as a special counsel just before Christmas. Manson described him as a man with a keen interest in crime and a talent for solving criminal cases, who had worked for the government previously. Jackson was, in fact, a recently defeated politician who needed a job. Of Scottish descent, he was born in Woodville, Ontario, in 1872 and moved to Winnipeg in 1880, where he received much of his schooling and graduated from the University of

Manitoba with a BA in 1893. Defeated when he ran for office as an MLA and then as an MP in Manitoba, he obtained a law degree in 1908, and in 1909 moved to Victoria, where he was admitted to the bar. In 1916 Jackson became an MLA, squeezing out a four-vote victory (358 to 354) to become Liberal member for the Islands. He won his seat again in 1920, but was defeated by a Tory in 1924. In his biographical notes in the *Parliamentary Guide*, Jackson inserted a line that spoke of a poignant personal grief. It referred to his son: "Lt. Hugh Arthur Jackson RAF killed in air battle France 1918." The fighter pilot was nineteen.

In the months that followed his appointment, Jackson became a central and controversial figure in the Smith-Wong story. An egotistical, publicity-seeking, garrulous man, he seemed to view himself as a mixture of Clarence Darrow, Sherlock Holmes, and Hercule Poirot. He claimed to be an expert in forensic science, but was in reality an untrained amateur. Tory critics laughed when they learned of his appointment and made the observation that in his other part-time role as chairman of the province's Game Conservation Board he was more expert at dealing with small furry animals than he was with people.

Jackson's appointment, and an announcement that there might be some action in the case in the near future, pleased the Scots, who had been pushing for a third inquest as the next best thing to a charge of murder against Wong. They tried to keep the pot boiling by stating that "startling revelations" could be expected soon. The Scots never seemed to be short of unspecified revelations, or funds, but as usual the promised new developments were slow to materialize.

Manson's special sleuth Jackson began conducting his investigation, to the chagrin of local police who said he was interfering with their efforts. Wong remained the target of the Scots, who grew steadily angrier at the inaction, but on the evening of Saturday March 20, the Janet Smith affair took another bizarre twist at 3851 Osler. This time Wong Foon Sing was the victim. His work was done for the day and he was getting dressed prior to visiting friends in Chinatown. Dick and Blanche Baker had gone out for the evening, so Wong was alone in the house when he heard loud noises coming from the usually quiet dark street. His room was in the basement and he stepped outside, into the garden, to see what was going on. He noticed two men in the street, but sensed something was wrong and hurried back indoors. Suddenly he was confronted inside the house by three men, one of whom swung a flashlight, striking him on the head. The houseboy, dazed by the blow, was knocked to the floor, his hands and feet were tied, and he was gagged and blindfolded. He heard one man say, "Give me a gun and I'll kill the bastard." The threat was intended to frighten Wong into silence and it did. He was then dragged outside and thrown into a car, which roared off into the night.

While Wong Foon Sing was being abducted, Dick and Blanche Baker were attending a dinner party not far away at the Jericho Country Club, totally unaware of what had occurred. When they returned home they found nothing out of place or unusual on the main or upper floors of the house and so retired for the night. Early next morning they awoke to find the house unusually cold. It was Wong's job to keep the furnace burning and to make preparations for breakfast, but nothing had been done.

Baker went down to the basement, calling out for Wong, but there was no answer. He noticed immediately that the door to the houseboy's room was ajar. The lock appeared damaged and the doorframe had been gouged. Going in, Baker found the room had been ransacked and Wong's clothing and personal papers were scattered everywhere. Well aware of his brother's earlier problems with the Point Grey police force, Dick Baker phoned Vancouver's main station and reported the apparent break-in and the disappearance of his houseboy. The Point Grey police never complained about Vancouver infringing on their jurisdiction and, if anything, the men from the suburbs seemed relieved to be free of any further complications that might emanate from Osler Avenue.

Vancouver Detective Joe Ricci responded to the call. He inspected the basement and the houseboy's room, and perhaps because of what had gone before and because of the aura of suspicion that hung over the case, he voiced a most unusual view of the situation. Ricci wondered out loud if the scene might have been faked to look like a kidnapping in order to cover up Wong's disappearance. Ricci suggested Wong might have fled to Chinatown or even to China, although why he thought this is unclear. The houseboy could easily have disappeared quietly during the preceding months any time he wanted to do so. There were no criminal charges against him. The Scots and others might consider him a murder suspect, but under the law he was innocent and free to go wherever he wanted. Ricci told Provincial Police Inspector Cruickshank his theory, and Cruickshank followed up on the supposed clue when he learned that the Canadian Pacific liner *Empress of Australia* had left Vancouver bound for Hong Kong earlier in the day. He stated he must find out if Wong was aboard.

Cruickshank radioed Wong's description to the liner's captain and then phoned Manson's special sleuth in Victoria to brief him on the latest developments. Jackson became agitated and developed a cops-and-robbers scenario worthy of the era's silent movies. He rushed off to a golf course where the attorney general was enjoying a round, scrambled through a hedge, and ran over the fairways to reach him. Jackson had already told Cruickshank to hire a floatplane to fly out to the liner. He repeated this to Manson and got the attorney general's permission to carry on with the hare-brained scheme. The idea of a flimsy floatplane landing on the frequently rough waters of Juan de Fuca Strait and of an investigator being hauled aboard the liner to make a search boggles the mind. The plan died before a float left the water when the *Empress of Australia*'s captain radioed to say there was no one aboard answering to the name or description of Wong Foon Sing.

Word of Wong's disappearance spread quickly through Chinatown, and the tongs met to discuss what to do. Rumours surfaced nearly as fast as they had after the death of Janet Smith. It wasn't long before there were assertions that Wong had been kidnapped by a group of vigilantes operating in cahoots with the Vancouver police and the provincial government. As time would tell, these contentions were close to the truth, but before the plot was uncovered there was a great pretense of mystery and an exhaustive, supposedly full-blown investigation.

The *Sun*'s headline on the Monday after Wong's disappearance stated bluntly, "Wong Sing Held Captive." The story quoted relatives of the young man, who were sure he had been grabbed to be grilled further on Smith's murder and likely beaten in order to make him confess or tell what else he might know. In view of his earlier abduction it was considered a distinct possibility.

The *Province* stated "White Hoods Carry China Boy Away," reporting on rumours sweeping Chinatown that described the abductors as men in long flowing robes, the ominous garb of the Ku Klux Klan. No one had actually seen the captors or their garb when they grabbed Wong, but in a later trial it was revealed white robes were the disguise they wore to hide their identity from the captive while he was imprisoned. It's interesting to speculate how the headline writers knew about the robes.

There did not seem to be much doubt in anyone's mind about what had happened to Wong Foon Sing. The paper stated matter-of-factly that the houseboy was "probably being held incommunicado outside Vancouver." There was no sense of outrage that a kidnapping had taken place, and there were no denunciations from local politicians or officials about what had happened. There is no question the *Province* had insider information as to what was happening to Wong. The paper said that a "lot of people felt Wong Foon Sing had been holding something back," and the article conjectured, "If he could be held privately and interrogated would it be possible to wring a solution to this mystery from him?"

Leading Chinese citizens met with Chinese Consul Dr. Lin Pao Heng, who was granted permission to visit the Osler Avenue house with a small group to inspect the scene. They saw damage to the door and were surprised to see an axe lying on the floor nearby. They wondered why it had not been removed to be checked for fingerprints. They were well aware of the much-handled revolver and the overlooked bullet that had lain on the floor following the Smith killing, and they could not help but wonder if this was more police bungling.

After examining the basement, the consul said he was convinced that Wong had left the house of his own free will but possibly had been lured away. It is difficult to understand how he could make such a statement. Perhaps the language barrier or diplomacy got in the way, or he may have felt, for reasons of his own, that he had to accept without question what the police told him. His statement didn't please his fellow Chinese, however, and the following day the consul, while not saying outright that he was misquoted, told reporters it was wrong to suggest that the houseboy was not kidnapped. The consul now insisted that Wong "was taken by force and he urged the police to make every effort to find out what had become of him." Dr. Lin Pao Heng offered a $500 reward for information about the missing man. The Chinese committee working on behalf of Wong felt many people, particularly the police, knew much more than they were telling about the young man's disappearance.

With events at the Osler Avenue home once again on the pages of the newspapers, Dick Baker, probably at the insistence of his father-in-law, General McRae, sent his wife Blanche and her maid on an extended visit to see relatives in the United States, where they were unavailable for further questioning about events that had taken place the night Wong disappeared.

Dr. Lin Pao Heng assured reporters it was highly unlikely that Wong had run away, gone into hiding, or left the country. He did not have much money and was still repaying the loan he received for a recent visit to see his wife in China, the consul explained. The Chinese Benevolent Society sent a letter to Manson asking for the federal justice department in Ottawa to intervene in the investigation and, if necessary, launch an official inquiry. They were obviously suspicious of local police. Manson told reporters in an evasive way, contrary to his usual positive style, that he was as "curious as the consul" to know what had happened. He carefully avoided federal intervention, which would have meant RCMP involvement. He had no intention of losing control of the case when the B.C. Provincial Police did exactly what he told them to do.

The *Sun* was not sure if Wong had been abducted, but the paper editorialized that the Chinese boy must be found and the Smith murder solved because "until it is solved, scandal will continue to lash innocent persons." A subsequent heated editorial was headed "The Menace Of Unsolved Crime." It suggested the people of Vancouver were sick of the whole Smith-Wong affair and the hundreds of theories that had been developed. Actually, apart from those who found themselves named and drawn into the case, most people were intrigued and caught up in the developing mystery. Readers were told, however, that "people are deadly tired of amateur sleuths who solve cases at the dinner table ... and of all the malicious gossip and slanderous whispers that have clustered around this case. Unsolved crime is a social menace to this community." While it took a closer look at the injustice accorded the houseboy than did other media, the *Sun* was as guilty as others in the community of happily repeating all the rumours and allegations.

Wong Foon Sing's brother, Wong Gow, a North Vancouver laundryman, said there was no suggestion that the missing man had left town. He was sure his brother was either being held prisoner or had been murdered. Given the amount of passion over the Smith death, there were those who felt that Wong could easily be at the bottom of Vancouver harbour. Wong Gow said he had been devoting so much time to his brother's disappearance that his business was ruined.

In print it was a one-sided "Holy War," as there was never a reported case of a Chinese spokesman taking a swing at the Scots, who unrelentingly hounded Wong, accusing him at every opportunity when reporters interviewed them for newspaper stories. Members of both the clans and the tongs continued to fret about the situation, but for very different reasons. They had, however, one common bond: all were convinced that the various police forces and Attorney General Manson were performing badly.

On April 4 the *Province* ran an unusual story that was another indication they had a man on the inside with access to those who were holding Wong. The information, from an unattributed source, was that the kidnappers would conduct a "secret trial" and that Wong would be punished or released depending on the information obtained from him. The story added that there had already been one "trial" and that Wong had "stuck to his story."

Dr. Lin Pao Heng announced that his three-year stint as consul was up and that he would be replaced by Ho Tsang. He would not, however, return to China immediately but would remain in Vancouver until the Wong Foon Sing disappearance was resolved.

While Chinatown continued to seethe over Wong's abduction, and the *Chinese Times* worried about his fate, it was no longer a front-page item in the mainstream press and had faded as a topic of conversation. The problems in Chinatown were brought back into sharp focus, however, when the grim details of the slaying of Davie Lew were revealed during the murder trial of the elderly ailing man from Victoria, Chong Sing. The courthouse was packed on April 14 when Chong pleaded not guilty to murder. The atmosphere was tense, and most of the Chinese were searched for weapons as they entered the courtroom. Mr. Justice W.A. Macdonald was on the bench in a trial that turned into a fiasco and provided another black eye for the administration of justice in Vancouver.

Before the trial began, the public had been well primed with stories about the lawlessness and violence that existed in the Chinese community, and they had read all the gory details of Lew's slaying in the Pekin Restaurant doorway. The *Province* said patrolling constable John Mackie found Lew bleeding badly and watched over by "a group of Chinese, impassive, looking curiously down on their dying countryman who was gasping out his life on the pavement of Pender Street, a victim of Oriental revenge and manipulation." Readers were told that Lew had been sleeping with a gun under his pillow in recent weeks and there had been an attempt to set his apartment afire. The paper maintained he had earned the enmity of some powerful tongs and gangs that felt he had betrayed them to immigration authorities over illegal entries to Canada and had also given the police information about white slavery in Canada. It noted that Lew "was one of the most vivid personalities that ever flashed across the colourful life of Chinatown," but like the inscrutable Chinese he was, the victim had told a white friend, who went unidentified, "They will get me sooner or later."

Identification of the accused was the crux of the case. The Crown didn't bring back Mrs. Mcdonald, who had told the preliminary hearing that she picked Chong Sing from the police line-up because of his size. There were now assertions that another so-called eyewitness had been told where the accused was standing in the police line-up and had simply counted off until he got to Chong Sing.

A major interest for the *Sun* reporter was Nellie Ho, the cashier at the Pekin Restaurant, who said that Lew ate there several times a week. She was described as a "stunning Chinese woman dressed in the height of Occidental fashion." The next day she was still stunning, but this time dressed in a new, different outfit right down to her shoes and "thoroughly Canadianized in manners and speech." One intriguing remark picked up in the courtroom by a reporter suggested that if Lew had married the stunning Miss Ho he wouldn't have been murdered. Lawyers must have missed the comment because questions were never asked in court about a relationship between the two.

After three days of conflicting evidence, suggestions of tong rivalries and false set-ups, and a great deal of questionable testimony, the trial turned to chaos. The sequestered all-white jury had asked court officials guarding them at a hotel if they could go for a walk. Three stayed behind, but the other nine went out, and their route took them past the murder scene, probably not by accident. When senior officials learned about this, they immediately told Mr. Justice Macdonald. He ordered the trial halted. The jury should not have been separated for any reason, he said, and members should not have gone near the scene of the murder without the accused, his lawyer, and the judge being present. The papers quickly pointed out that the cancellation of the proceedings cost taxpayers about $2,000.

When the trial was rescheduled, there were five women on the jury. This was unprecedented. There had been no more than two women on any other murder trial jury in Vancouver up to this time. Why there were so many this time was never explained.

Three new witnesses joined those who had appeared at the first trial. They testified that they were playing mah jong with Chong Sing in a room above the restaurant on the day in question. They heard the sound of several bangs, but thought they were firecrackers and not the bullets that killed Lew.

It seemed the various Greater Vancouver police organizations frequently overlooked important evidence. City Inspector John Jackson ruefully agreed with the observations of one of the jury that there could have been a much better investigation if prints had been taken from a .38 revolver left near the scene by the assassin, but none were available.

Chong Sing's lawyer, Fram Higgins, stated in his summing up, "When you consider every angle of the case, I say with confidence that you would not hang a dog on this evidence, let alone a human being." The jury agreed. In 38 minutes it returned with a verdict of not guilty.

The Dart Coon social club threw a celebratory banquet in Chinatown that night for Chong Sing. While he was 54, slow moving, and ailing, hardly the image of a hired gun, it was never satisfactorily explained why he came to Vancouver from Victoria in the first place.

Among police and reporters it was alleged that Lew had earned the enmity of a powerful group within the Chinese community in the capital city, and this gang had ordered his murder. Once again a poor investigation and an initially botched trial epitomized the criminal and legal picture in Vancouver. The killer of Davie Lew was never found, adding to a long list of Vancouver's unsolved early crimes.

The crime fighters had a little luck, however, before April ran out. Wong Foon Sing was still missing, but there was a major drug seizure from a ship. Police went to the docks and boarded the Canadian Pacific liner *Empress of Russia*. The raid uncovered 350 tins of opium hidden in the ship's coal bunkers. Each tin was worth about $50 at the time. Customs officials said it was their practice to search each ship coming into Vancouver from the Far East, but this had all the trademarks of a tip-off.

While the Lew murder held centre stage, life in the city went on. A young Chinese boy, John Wong, aged thirteen, represented Strathcona School in a city-wide spelling contest. It was a major event, with the final competition held in the Orpheum Theatre and broadcast live over radio station CFYC. John's championship hopes died when he tripped over the word "mahogany" in the final and deciding round.

In other news the same day, 88 Chinese forfeited $10 bail when they failed to show up in court after a gambling raid. The *Sun* said the future of world peace depended on understanding between the Occidental and Oriental worlds and urged the University of B.C. to set up a chair in Oriental language, literature, and commerce. The university ignored this advice, and it was a long time before UBC took an interest in Asian studies.

From the Frying Pan Into the Fire

On May 1, two major developments produced headlines on the front pages of the city's newspapers, and newsboys yelled the words that brought pedestrians scrambling for copies at downtown intersections. Suddenly Wong Foon Sing reappeared, and with him came the wildest conjecture that had yet swept the city. In keeping with the tenor of the affair since it began eight months earlier, the reappearance of the Chinese houseboy was cloaked in mystery, contradiction, and confusion. The involvement of the Point Grey police guaranteed it.

Initially reporters were told that an unidentified motorist had seen a man acting "queerly" on Marine Drive near Dunbar Street. The *Vancouver Star* eagerly parroted a police comment that the motorist had stated the man he saw "was either drunk or insane." The supposed incident was reported to a member of the Point Grey police, Sergeant Neil MacPherson, who just happened to be sitting in a parked cruiser not far from the scene. He picked up the man, whom he immediately identified as the missing Wong. As usual, confusion reigned as the Point Grey police tripped over each other with conflicting explanations. MacPherson said he phoned Sergeant Percy Kirkham at Point Grey police headquarters in Kerrisdale with the news, but Kirkham stated he had been notified by an anonymous caller, not MacPherson. Reporters were told the Chinese was confused but in good physical condition. Possibly only the Point Grey detachment could have come up with the word "confused" to describe the condition of a man who had been chained, imprisoned, and tortured for 42 days.

Wong asked to go home to Osler Avenue, but instead was driven to Point Grey police station, where he was charged with murder in the death of Janet Smith. The charge had been authorized by special sleuth Malcolm Bruce Jackson and approved by Attorney General Manson. Within hours he was remanded to Oakalla Prison.

Reporters immediately questioned the story of the arrest as related by the men in blue from Point Grey, and they soon came to their own conclusions. The *Vancouver Sun* suggested the police had been on the spot, waiting for the houseboy when he was taken to Marine Drive. The *Province* reported that Wong had been "submitted to constant questioning and the application of the third degree." Not at all troubled by the mistreatment, the *Province* blithely noted the young man now was quietly in jail after "lively days." Without any semblance of viewing the subject as innocent until proven guilty, the paper told its readers, "From fairly straight authority it is related that officials expect to be able to show a jury that Wong fired the bullet which actually killed the girl." The *Province* even knew that a private detective agency had carried out the kidnapping, saying it was handled carefully, and consequently there was little chance of the abductors being identified. The editors stopped just short of saying the kidnapping had been carried out on orders from police.

Based on the past performance of Point Grey officials, no one could be sure what the reappearance of Wong meant. In the Chinese community, anger was growing as Orientals along Pender Street learned Wong had been grossly mistreated and now was charged with murder. The Chinese consul called for a royal commission into the affair. Harry Senkler was again hired to represent the houseboy, and the Chinese Benevolent Society put up another $500 reward for new information.

The emotional Senkler became seething mad when he learned that Wong Foon Sing was being held incommunicado in Oakalla and was not allowed to have visitors. The hair-trigger-tempered lawyer threatened legal action when he was turned away. Attorney General Manson made a hurried statement declaring that Wong was being held in isolation only "until we have the opportunity to catch our breath." Manson knew he was in the wrong, and Senkler had called his bluff. Almost immediately the lawyer was permitted to see his client.

Following this initial meeting, the lawyer told reporters clustered outside the jail that he was concerned about Wong's overall health because he bore obvious injuries to his face and eyes. Senkler said the Chinese had been beaten and terrorized during his 42-day ordeal. He had been chained and threatened with death if he did not confess to the murder of Janet Smith or tell his captors what else he knew. Senkler repeated once again that Wong knew no more about the Osler Avenue slaying than had already been revealed during two inquests.

The Chinatown press reflected the anger of the community as more information came to light about the treatment of Wong, who had been shackled and blindfolded during the entire six weeks of his imprisonment. The *Chinese Times* carried a detailed story of his abduction, as told to the captive's brother, Wong Gow, and Harry Senkler when they were finally able to visit him in Oakalla Prison. Readers were told "the kidnappers often used barbarous means to force him to speak out on important evidence in the murder." Damage to his eye was "irrefutable evidence" that he had been badly treated, contended the paper.

"Wong Family Clan Cries Injustice for Wong Foon Sing" was the headline over a subsequent story, which stated that his relatives had written to the "Chinese Chamber Hall" asking for the community's support to fight the untruthful, illegal accusations and the murder charge that had been levelled against the young man.

Four days later the *Chinese Times* stated that an important public meeting had been arranged to tackle Wong's "rescue" from his predicament. The paper promised the audience would be given detailed information about the houseboy's treatment and its significance. It stressed that "the matter is related to the safety of the Chinese community. We hope our countrymen will come to the meeting enthusiastically." A large, attentive crowd was on hand to support the Wong family in its battle for justice for Wong Foon Sing. The meeting organized ten teams called "Special Donation-Soliciting Teams of the Vancouver Chinese Chamber Hall" to solicit donations for the Wong defence fund.

Meanwhile Manson all but admitted his involvement in the kidnapping plot when he issued a carefully worded statement that attempted to justify the houseboy's treatment. He said the investigation had been undertaken "quietly and persistently" by his appointee Malcolm Jackson, who had gone over "every part of the evidence that could be obtained." The attorney general claimed that the process had been difficult because of the many false rumours that caused "embarrassment and delay." He said he had received a full report from Jackson only a few days earlier, and after reading it had directed that a warrant be issued for the arrest and charge of Wong Foon Sing.

Loquacious and eager for the limelight, Jackson told reporters that the arrest was no accident and that "Point Grey [police] made it as a result of efforts with myself and the attorney general's department." His statement that this was no "accident," following closely on the words of Manson, confirmed for many their assumptions that the kidnapping and interrogation of Wong were part of a scheme that involved both the Point Grey police and the attorney general.

This form of discriminatory justice didn't bother David Paterson, president of the United Council of Scottish Societies, who stated, "I am not worrying about the kidnapping, or whether or not any statement was obtained from the Chinaman by those who are stated to have abducted him."

On May 2, the day following Wong's release, the Point Grey Police Commission confirmed Sergeant John Murdoch's appointment as police chief, replacing Hiram Simpson. Based on the information on hand at the time, the *Sun* reported that the new chief, who had joined the force in 1912 after arriving from Scotland, had been instrumental in securing Wong Foon Sing's reappearance, which of course was incorrect.

At the same meeting, Commissioner H.O. McDonald complained bitterly about the $170.50 bill he had received for costs of the second inquest, which he claimed should not be charged to Point Grey. The invoice included the coroner's and interpreter's fees, meals supplied for the jurors, and the price of the unfortunate fowl that had its head chopped off for the chicken oath demanded of Wong Foon Sing. McDonald also angrily blamed Coroner Brydone-Jack for the need for a second inquest, charging that he had botched the first one primarily because he had not seen Smith's body before it was embalmed.

The coroner shot back that everything resulted from the inadequate investigations of the municipality's own police force.

Readers of the *Province* were told that Chinatown was in ferment, with "propagandists" whipping up sentiment about a terrible miscarriage of justice. New Chinese consul Ho Tsang requested answers from Manson, and details of the affair were cabled to the Chinese foreign office in Peking.

There was much speculation about Wong's physical condition. A May 3 headline in the *Sun* sweepingly and incorrectly told readers "Wong's Condition Grave." On May 4 Senkler asked permission for doctors to examine the houseboy for head injuries. He said his client had "fully expected to be killed" by his kidnappers and remained frightened, even terrified of them. When asked why his client had tried to flee, Senkler shouted it was nonsense to suggest that Wong Foon Sing had made any attempt whatsoever to run.

Dr. P.A. McLennan reported to Senkler that Wong Foon Sing's injuries were more severe than he had expected and he wanted to bring in other doctors for additional examinations. There was now new ammunition for his case, and Senkler immediately ordered X-rays for his client. He and several other lawyers also began to question the role of Attorney General Manson. Senkler charged that Manson had ordered that Wong be charged, even though there was insufficient evidence, in order to open up the case yet again and put all the witnesses on the stand with a view to checking for discrepancies with the former evidence and "so in some manner ferret out the guilty parties." Working the accusations for all they were worth, Senkler maintained, "If this is the case the prosecution is showing a woeful weakness and a serious lack of British justice. It is a damnable thing if the Chinese boy has been thrown into the cells and charged with this crime unless there is strong evidence to his guilt. I have been kept absolutely in the dark by the crown authorities."

A *Sun* editorial echoed Senkler's views, proclaiming that the young man had been the victim of "downright banditry." The paper said if a British subject had been similarly treated in China there would have been "gunboat diplomacy," and editors maintained it was not enough for Manson to deny personal responsibility; as the province's chief law enforcer he must also identify the kidnappers. Getting flowery, the editorial stated that the affair was a disgrace to "all the British blood that has been shed to establish a British civilization."

The *Province*, which was at the time Vancouver's most conservative paper, steadfastly ignored the situation, its long editorials dealing with assorted problems in Canadian commerce, in Britain, in the Empire, and in affairs of royalty. In British-oriented 1920s Vancouver, this was expected editorially from Vancouver's "family newspaper," which supposedly studiously avoided rumour and scandal unless the story was big enough and might warrant publication of an extra edition. The *Province* outsold the *Sun* by something like 70,000 to 50,000 papers and had dominated the lucrative advertising market for many years.

Reporters rushed to get a look at Wong Foon Sing as he was taken to the Birks Building at Granville and Georgia for further medical examination and the X-rays Senkler had ordered. Their various descriptions of his ghastly appearance included his "sickly green pallor, a black eye, and a large bandage around his throat." One reporter also noted that he was "not the type of wizened Chinaman seen in the hundreds on Pender Street but was one of the modern, educated Chinese, dressed in style." There was even a description of his blue trousers, his socks, and tan shoes.

The houseboy told doctors that after being knocked down in one beating he had been kicked in the head. They found his injuries much more serious than was first believed. Doctors confirmed he had suffered a fractured skull and broken ribs. The medical team stated the fractures were old and had now healed, presumably by themselves without medical attention.

One unsympathetic response came from the *Saturday Tribune*, which made the caustic observation that it was good the houseboy would soon make a court appearance, "otherwise the daily papers would not have left him a limb intact."

Not Exactly Democracy

Wong Foon Sing's preliminary hearing on the murder charge opened May 8, a week after he was found on Marine Drive and taken to prison. It was hardly an exemplary exercise in democracy, but officials did let a handful of Chinese people into the courtroom in Point Grey Municipal Hall in Kerrisdale. During the two earlier inquests, no Chinese had been allowed to attend the hearings as spectators.

Their appetites whetted by newspaper stories, and with the memory of details revealed at the earlier inquests, Vancouverites eagerly awaited exciting new disclosures from Wong. Sensational trials had been sweeping the continent for months, providing horror tales for Vancouver's newspapers and their readers, who were now anticipating a home-grown equivalent. For weeks they had read of the Leopold-Loeb thrill killing in Chicago, where two young men killed a boy for kicks and went to jail for life. There was also the John Scopes "monkey" trial in Missouri, which questioned the teaching of the theory of evolution in school classrooms. It featured the eloquent Clarence Darrow and the great Charles Jennings Bryan and resulted in a $100 fine for Scopes.

It seemed the loquacious Malcolm Bruce Jackson saw himself as the headliner in the same kind of flamboyant case as those making news in the United States. Before the preliminary hearing began he stated to the newspapers that he didn't intend to name all the witnesses that could be called, but there would be enough of them to point the finger at Wong as the killer. He said he would weave into the testimony information about orgies, drug trafficking, infidelity, and ravishment, as well as the names of prominent people who could be involved. Jackson had obviously done some investigation after MLA Coventry's declaration in the legislature and had contacted the RCMP and Scotland Yard about Fred Baker's business dealings in Britain.

Since the Chinese houseboy's arrest, Jackson had been busy priming the press, and various stories suggested that the killing of Janet Smith was somehow drug related. Only days earlier the *Province* had finally printed a story that said, in part: "The whole story of the murder and subsequent investigations is one that has already attracted international attention and it is common knowledge that Scotland Yard detectives are working on one angle of the case, which, it is said, stretches its web right across the continent and to London. It is expected that if the full story is told it will involve a number of more or less prominent persons ... That the trail lies far afield has been admitted by Mr. Jackson who intimated that 'even England was not overlooked.' In this connection, it is stated that a former partner of one of those suspected as a 'principal' in the case when it first attracted attention was apprehended by Scotland Yard officials some two years ago and is now serving a sentence in England on drug-trafficking charges."

Fred Baker's new lawyer, G.L. "Pat" Fraser noted that he hoped Wong Foon Sing's case "would be carried out with true British justice and fair play." He urged Manson to stop Jackson from making statements, adding that "idle rumours should not get official endorsement." Until this time, Fred Baker had taken little overt action to protect himself or his family from gossip about his involvement in late-night parties, drinking, or drugs, but at this stage he decided the fanciful stories and innuendos had gone too far.

The rumours were given weight by Victor Odlum's *Vancouver Star*, which unlike the conservative *Province*, on May 4 carried a story with damaging references to Baker and his European activities in the pharmaceutical business. Special investigator Jackson was quoted again as saying that investigations had gone far afield. For the first time in print the *Star* suggested Baker was a possible suspect in Smith's killing.

Fred Baker had been represented at the second inquest by J.L.G. Abbott, a partner in the firm where he had articled before the war. The young man had undoubtedly briefed his former employer about the difficulties faced by his short-lived drug and pharmaceutical company in Britain in the hope that the experienced attorney could prevent details of the affair from surfacing, or at least defuse any suggestions that Baker himself had been in trouble in England. Abbott appeared to achieve this. Baker had moved to France when his partner Golwynne came under investigation by Scotland Yard following the arrest of an agent the firm had used on the continent. In France, Baker liquidated the firm's holdings in Europe. When this job was completed he moved on to Vancouver, where he opened a new company. Details of Baker's British company's problems had not surfaced earlier, but now they were in the public eye.

Baker's new lawyer, Fraser, apparently now decided that the best defence was an attack, and he delivered a message on behalf of his client that rattled the city's social set and had the matrons of Shaughnessy agog. He filed a slander suit against Monica Mason-Rooke, a twenty-year-old socialite who was, according to one reporter, "one of the popular girls of the younger set." Baker and his wife alleged that in conversation with acquaintances on March 20, Mason-Rooke had said, "Isn't it too bad the Bakers had the party the night before [Smith's murder]," adding "Oh yes, there was a party. I know two chaps who were there." Monica, a graduate of Crofton House School for Girls, was from "a well respected English family" and worked for her father's engineering company. The family had moved to Vancouver from the Orient about eight years previously. Fraser said the Bakers were "determined to put a stop to the flood of false and misleading gossip" that surrounded them, and their libel action broke a long silence during which they were much maligned. The new libel case did little to stem the flow of talk, however. In fact, Shaughnessy residents were soon trying to identify the two unnamed young men mentioned by Monica, and notification of the suit ignited interest in Wong's preliminary hearing.

Squeezed into the small courtroom as proceedings began were many of the same young Scottish women who had appeared at the inquests, but there were now others from

Shaughnessy, dressed in their best to attend the murder hearing. Dozens waited outside, including many Chinese, who peered through the windows although they were unable to hear what was being said. One newspaper complained that the flower beds were trampled underfoot by the throng. According to the *Vancouver Star*, the room could seat about 30 people, but close to 50 managed to elbow their way in.

Most of the crowd had never before seen Wong Foon Sing in person, and excitement ran high as his approach was heralded by the clanging of a cell door and the sound of his footsteps as he made his way to the small courtroom. Heads were craned and all eyes were on him as he quietly stepped forward. The *Star* reported that he was calm and alert under the close scrutiny of the spectators, only a slight cough and a licking of his lips betraying any nervousness. Readers were told he was neatly dressed in a brown-striped suit with a white handkerchief around his neck instead of a tie. Having already run stories casting doubt on the extent of any injuries suffered by Wong Foon Sing during his imprisonment, the *Star* noted that there was no trace of the alleged ill-treatment he had endured.

As the preliminary hearing proceeded, it became a stage for two men in particular, Malcolm Bruce Jackson and Harry Senkler. The initial technical evidence Jackson provided about the basement of the house on Osler was rather dull, and as he droned on the houseboy, as well as many in the audience, looked bored.

But then Jackson's remarks moved into the realm the audience had been anticipating. He tried to suggest that Fred Baker was involved in drug trafficking, that his house on Osler was the centre of this activity, and that Janet Smith had known about it and might even have been involved. By innuendo he reinforced a vague rumour that Smith had been engaged in a sexual relationship with Baker and was pregnant by him. Jackson's allegations were predicated on the theory that Janet Smith had not been killed in the basement. He maintained the housemaid had been knocked unconscious somewhere else in the house and had then been carried to the basement either dead or alive. He suggested that here a bullet was fired into her head in an attempt to make her death appear an accident or a suicide, conforming exactly to the verdict of the first inquest. It seemed a strange diatribe for Wong's preliminary hearing, but Jackson was, if nothing else, unpredictable. Manson had indicated the arrest of Wong was to be a "fishing expedition," and Jackson was determined to search every possible creek and darkened pool for evidence.

Manson's sleuth also played on some of the contradictory medical evidence. Could a single bullet inflict the massive skull fracture found on Janet Smith's head? he asked. Why were there no powder burns on the girl's head if the revolver was fired close to her? Why were there no fragments of brain tissue found in the basement room with her body? Why had she fallen forward instead of backward? How could the burn marks on her arm and body have been caused by a falling iron? These were pertinent points, but many were never answered by Jackson or anyone else involved.

Harry Senkler seemed to relish the battle royal as the preliminary hearing developed. He dismissed Jackson's remarks as unsubstantiated nonsense, shooting straight from the hip in his characteristic manner. He also refused any part of the ubiquitous Wong Foon Sien, who was once again being used as interpreter. He pointed out that this undesirable Chinese had been one of the perpetrators when Wong Foon Sing was snatched from the street and roughed up during earlier questioning in Robinson's office. "He was associated with the Provincial Police in the first kidnapping of the accused before the second inquest," the defence lawyer told the court. Magistrate George McQueen agreed and arranged for another interpreter before adjourning the case for the weekend until May 14.

Excitement mounted in the audience when the case resumed. There were soon interjections from the public benches—applause, boos, and hisses that grew to a volume not heard during any preliminary hearing before. Possibly because he hoped the venting of fired-up frustrations might lower the emotional tension, Magistrate McQueen and others on the bench in subsequent hearings let the furor build far beyond the level of decorum expected in a Canadian courtroom in this era. For the Scots, who made up the majority of those who had obtained seats, Jackson was a hero, the battling seeker of Smith's slayer. Senkler, the houseboy's defender, was the enemy in the pay of the Chinese. He was on the receiving end of most of their boos and hisses both inside the courtroom and whenever he entered or left the building.

Dr. Bertie Blackwood, first medical officer to arrive at the Osler Avenue home on the day of Janet Smith's death, repeated his inquest evidence. He testified that Smith's body was still warm when he arrived and estimated she had been dead for only about an hour at the most when he first saw her. He testified that the electric iron she had been using was lying between her arm and her body. Dr. Blackwood explained the plug had been pulled from its socket, probably as the iron fell from the girl's hand when she toppled to the floor.

The hapless former constable James Green, no longer a member of the Point Grey force, received derisive laughter from the spectators, described by the papers as "titters," during his explanation of what happened to his notes. Because he did not expect to be one of the main investigators, he said that when he returned to the station "I expect I threw them into the wastebasket." Jackson, who interrogated Green theatrically, picked up the alleged murder weapon and waved it about until he was asked by some members of the public to point it elsewhere. He then clicked the trigger and asked Green to identify it.

Undertaker John Edwards told the court that the order to embalm Smith's body came to him directly from the city coroner, Dr. Brydone-Jack. Edwards' assistant, Hugh Wright, gave a clinical description of the embalming process that was more detailed than many in the audience cared to hear and produced some anxious, slightly squeamish faces. Among the exhibits were Smith's broken glasses, blood-stained smock, her blue dress, woollen underwear, white stockings, and shoes.

When Dr. Archibald Hunter, who had performed the autopsy, took the stand, Jackson moved for the first time into the seldom-mentioned topic of sex, which had flowed as an undercurrent through the case from the beginning. Some women wondered privately if Janet Smith had died defending her honour against Wong. Jackson's question fell on a hushed courtroom: "Was the doctor's finding from a vaginal examination consistent with ravishment?" He didn't get the answer he would have liked. "Personally, in my opinion," said

Dr. Hunter, "I thought they [damages to the body] were due to trauma from the undertaker."

The doctor again produced the human skull he had used previously to describe Smith's fatal injuries. He repeated his evidence that the whole right side of her skull had been destroyed.

Jackson's use of previously given inquest evidence became a flashpoint for Harry Senkler. He complained that if the answers Jackson got now were not as strong as they had been earlier, Jackson was quoting the stronger words from the previous inquest transcript. Magistrate McQueen cautioned Jackson about this strategy.

The doctor offered several explanations of how Smith's body had been burned, but his most crucial statement was that he believed the burns were made by the iron after she died. The point was not pursued, but one possibility was that when Wong Foon Sing tried to lift her head as she lay on the floor, the iron had touched her body.

The question of drugs was raised again by Jackson when Fred Baker took the stand. Once more described as handsome and debonair, unruffled, with what the press reported as a cultured accent, the witness went through his story from the beginning, when he waved goodbye to his baby daughter that July morning. He said he then visited a potential rubber buyer for his export company before he received the call from Wong Foon Sing and learned about the terrible incident that had taken place in the basement of his home.

Baker and Senkler both objected when Jackson began asking questions about Baker's business dealings in England and France. The witness said neither Smith nor Wong had anything to do with his business activities, pointing out the houseboy was never in Europe and was not a part of the regular family entourage. Wong had for some time worked for Richard Baker and had been at the Osler Avenue house long before the Fred Baker family arrived.

Jackson persisted. "Was your firm engaged in the dope traffic?"

Baker answered, "We handle general chemicals."

Jackson questioned, "Heroin, cocaine and morphine?"

Baker replied, "Yes."

The answer drew gasps from the public benches and some hisses for Senkler when he objected to the line of questioning. Jackson continued with the same topic, and Baker admitted to having witnessed a $40,000 contract for drugs, which was signed with a Japanese firm. He again denied that Smith had any knowledge of his business affairs and stated that he never had drugs in his home.

As he finished, Jackson slipped in another point he wanted to make. He asked Baker if he knew of any familiarity taken with Smith by anyone, unctuously adding that he was not referring to the witness. Jackson knew, of course, that even raising the question would reinforce the suspicions of some people that Baker or Wong had been involved with Smith.

Senkler tried to defuse the drug question in his cross-examination by asking Baker if he had ever seen the houseboy take drugs. He got a negative answer and the witness again emphasized he never discussed business with Smith or the accused and they would have had no access to drugs in his home. Baker insisted he operated a lawful business and never dealt in drugs illegally. He told Senkler that he found the houseboy's story of the events at Osler Avenue to be forthright and didn't raise any suspicions.

The prosecution's case wasn't helped much by another witness, Constable F.O. Fish, who was the second policeman on the scene at the Osler house. He testified that Wong Foon Sing seemed upset but that he answered everything and didn't seem to be hiding anything.

Some of the spectators had been disturbed by the clinical description of embalming, but they were now horrified by the descriptions of some ballistic experiments carried out by the provincial police. Shots from a .45 revolver similar to the weapon found at the crime scene were fired into the severed head of a pig obtained from a local slaughterhouse. The pig's head showed extensive powder burns. Queasiness turned to revulsion when another experiment was described, this time involving a human head. Officials at Essondale Mental Hospital provided the head of a pauper who died without leaving any known relatives. The bullets fired into it were recovered misshapen, as were those pumped into the pig's head. Both heads had been placed just in front of a wall. Jackson, who saw himself as an amateur firearms expert, had come over from Victoria in order to view the experiments, but voiced no explanation or theory as to why the bullet found in the laundry room at Osler had been undamaged.

In summing up, Senkler told the court that if there had been a murder, and the evidence didn't lead to this view, his client had nothing to do with it. Wong's explanation was consistent, he didn't evade questions, and he hadn't tried to run, stressed the defence lawyer, and there was no motive for him to have killed Janet Smith. He was critical of the Crown's failure to call the two workmen who might have heard and seen Smith alive at the house on the morning of her death, even though their previous testimony had been inconclusive.

Senkler's associate, Robert Smith, said the hearing had been a persecution and not a prosecution. He criticized Jackson's attempt to link drugs to the case and said it had been built around slander and rumour and nothing else.

Jackson told Magistrate McQueen he wouldn't take long on rebuttal, but he did. He went on at great length with his scientific theories about police work, ballistics, and medical findings. His conclusion: "The ensemble and details of the entire situation prove to my mind that there was a staging of a situation intended and hoped to represent a tragedy, a case of accident or otherwise." Missing was any direct evidence to tie Wong Foon Sing to the death of Janet Smith.

In a strange and convoluted statement that added weight to the general belief that the prosecution had a weak case and didn't actually believe the Chinese boy was guilty, Jackson added, "The accused is not being asked to be tried. The Crown here is setting out the circumstances and it is only fair to the Crown and to the accused that there should be a trial of the issue as to whether or not he is responsible for this crime." The major difference for Wong Foon Sing was, of course, that he could hang. The statement may have been an effort to appease the Chinese consul, who by this time had made several complaints to the attorney general about Wong's treatment.

The magistrate had much to consider. On a sunny Saturday morning did Wong Foon Sing really decide to attack or kill Janet Smith? Was he overcome with passion while peeling potatoes for lunch? It would have been risky. The Bakers could have returned to the house at any time, and it was an era when tradesmen and suppliers made home deliveries even on Saturday morning. It was a quiet street and if builders working nearby could hear Smith singing, were they not likely to hear her if she screamed? Jackson's entire case was one of assumptions and circumstantial evidence.

After pondering the question over a weekend, Magistrate McQueen took no chances and decided the houseboy should stand trial. He was conscious of public sentiment and perceived prudence took precedence over weak prosecution. A newspaper headline on May 18 announced "Wong Sent Up." The houseboy was unmoved at the decision. He expected to go on trial at the fall assizes, but the assizes were not scheduled for months. Wong had already spent three months in captivity, half of the time with his kidnappers, the other half in provincial custody. He now faced more than four months in jail awaiting a trial based on what many legal experts saw as an extremely shaky Crown case.

A special assizes court to hear the case would cost $2,000, so Senkler suggested that Wong's trial be moved to Victoria, where there was a scheduled spring court session. His proposal was rejected. Senkler lost his temper and swore to do everything possible to get Wong out of Oakalla Prison. The day after Magistrate McQueen's decision, Senkler said he would appeal. He told reporters he was highly critical of the magistrate's citing of an 1819 British legal decision related to a sheep-stealing offence. It stated that unless a magistrate is convinced a charge is laid from malice and is also groundless, he should not discharge an accused. Senkler stressed the obvious: the British case was more than a hundred years old, from a time when the criminal law was different. He also believed that Jackson's citations should have been based on Canadian decisions, not English ones.

The *Chinese Times* gave a straightforward report of the preliminary hearing, describing the large crowd that attended and the many who were unable to enter the small hall and were forced to remain outside. The paper's language grew stronger when it reflected on the mounting temper of the Chinese. It noted that Chinatown was seething with angry comments of "unjustly treated ... western hooligans arrogantly abusing Chinese ... getting worse and worse." The paper praised the ready generosity of average working Chinese in subscribing to the defence fund. It proudly congratulated them for contributing to "the purpose of pursuing and capturing the kidnappers." Following Wong's commitment for trial, the paper pledged to support the community's drive to ensure there was enough money for his defence at the fall assizes.

The Vancouver Bar Association was neither bold nor quick to voice its condemnation of injustice, kidnapping, or the vigilante treatment of the houseboy. It waited until its regular monthly meeting in mid-May to issue this statement: "The Vancouver Bar Association in the most uncompromising manner expresses its condemnation of the illegal, unwarranted and cowardly kidnapping or abduction of Wong Foon Sing; and this Association deeply regrets the fact that in this city and country an outrage could be perpetrated upon any individual under any circumstances; that the members of this Association go on record as being firmly in favour of law enforcement and administration of justice by properly constituted officials and is unalterably opposed to the idea of lynch law, mob law, secret societies, Ku Klux Klan or third degree methods of any kind." The association also called on the attorney general to spare no cost or effort in seeking to solve the case.

Following the belated release of this statement, the Chinese press commented that this was one example of protest from the white community about the unjust treatment of Wong and the misuse of the justice system by provincial authorities.

While the *Province* continued in its normal manner with long, detailed editorials about affairs of Empire, the *Sun* ran an editorial that had the Scots seething. It stated that B.C. was poised to inflict possibly the greatest injustice ever perpetrated in Canada. "Is B.C. going to try to answer this question [the Janet Smith case] with open-minded deliberation or with mob vengeance in its heart?" the editorial asked. "Any person found guilty must be the murderer—anyone will not do ... Is Wong being tried on evidence or on prejudice? Is he being brought to trial to satisfy justice or to satisfy mob thought. Public opinion in Vancouver is highly inflamed … All this is no reason to pick a victim haphazardly."

John Sedgwick Cowper, Scottish editor of the *Saturday Tribune*, fumed that the *Sun* was anti-British and anti-royalist and that it had perpetrated an underhanded attack on B.C. courts and the administration of justice to protect Vancouver's elite in Shaughnessy. Cowper's name would soon become indelibly linked to the case.

With Wong Foon Sing languishing in Oakalla Prison, Senkler said he would proceed to file a writ of *habeus corpus* to free his client. He had been dismayed by the houseboy's state of mind when he visited him in jail. Not surprisingly, Wong was depressed and lethargic. There was nothing, however, to support Chinatown speculation that he had been beaten up by his jailers.

By this time the story of the murdered migrant Scottish lass had appeared in British newspapers. As flamboyant, sensational, reckless, and rumour-filled as today's tabloids, Britain's *The People* published one of the more outrageous stories, written by Dora Bates. It had all the melodrama of the silent-movie maiden tied to the railway tracks in the face of an oncoming train. The problem was that the provincial police couldn't find anyone with that name to question about the lurid allegations. Dora was probably a figment of *The People*'s circulation department.

From Vancouver, the *Province* interviewed Janet Smith's father in England, who said she had become embroiled in a "terrible conspiracy." He was critical of the handling of the case by law enforcement agencies in B.C.

The image of B.C.'s Chinese community was also tarnished again on May 20 when a shootout at a Port Moody shingle mill claimed three lives. It resulted from festering feuds within the Shon Yee Benevolent Society over some $40,000 that had been raised in the province to build a hospital near Canton in China.

Newspaper readers were told that Lum But, well known in Vancouver as Fred Lambert, had driven out to McNair's Shingle Mill with a carload of men. One story reported that he went out simply to get some donated money, but given the number of people involved, it appeared that the visit probably was a shake-down. Other reports said that a man named Mark Dip had been loaned

$2,000 to help his parents in China, and the visitors were checking out claims that the money never left Vancouver.

The police tried to sort out the colourful and confusing stories about what happened after Dip pulled a gun. He shot and killed Lum But, wounded another man who later died, and then put the gun in his mouth and blew off his own head. Bullets flew in the yard, but it was never clear how many men were firing. Two of Lum But's companions were hurt when their car overturned as they tried to flee. Two others were charged with murder.

Tempers soared in Chinese sectors of Vancouver, New Westminster, and Victoria resulting in thirteen arrests for fighting as feuds between tongs flared following the shingle-mill shootout. Raucous meetings were difficult to control, and one Victoria paper reported, "Sinister figures were to be seen lurking in the shadows of doorways and alley entrances as long as the palaver continued." In Vancouver, the *Sun* stated that in Chinatown "just a shove could start a riot, just a word." In a trial, months later, characterized by much confusion about the identity of individuals involved and who did what to whom, the two men who had been arrested were found not guilty.

Before the month was out the public read another detailed story of the hanging of a Japanese worker on Vancouver Island, who was found guilty of killing a mill foreman. Locally, Vancouver police asked that a drug charge against Dorothy How be dropped because she had been framed by Chinese enemies. How was the recipient of a rare and unexpected break. Newspapers were ever vigilant in their coverage of the crimes of people from Asia, seldom reporting much in their favour.

Improbable Plots, Twists, and Turns

One reporter noted that the Janet Smith affair had all the ingredients of a dime-store novel: bizarre characters, improbable plots, lies, cover-ups, violence, kidnapping, death, and more twists and turns than the Fraser River.

A leading role in this melodrama was about to be played by an unlikely figure. John Sedgwick Cowper, former Liberal MLA, was now a flamboyant, crusading newspaperman of many talents and editor of Vancouver's tabloid *Saturday Tribune*. He was an avowed Unitarian and the father of four daughters. Born in Liverpool, England, in 1867, Cowper, the son of a naval officer, attended public schools there. Married in 1898, he and his wife came to Canada in 1901. Cowper worked for the *Toronto Globe* from 1905 to 1910 and moved to Prince Rupert, B.C., in 1911, where he became editor of the *Prince Rupert Daily News*. It was while he resided in this northern coastal town that Cowper met a young lawyer named Alex Manson, with whom he formed a fast friendship. Cowper joined the Liberal party on Manson's recommendation, and it was with Manson's encouragement that he ran successfully for a seat in the provincial legislature in 1916. Unfortunately he was not prepared to toe the party line, and his maverick behaviour lost him the re-nomination in 1920. Cowper blamed Manson for his rejection by party members, and the once firm friendship turned sour.

Cowper had been the MLA for Vancouver, and as a consequence he had moved to the province's largest city in 1916. Among his many talents was his skill as a cabinetmaker and carpenter, and when he was not employed as a reporter or

MLA, he made his living as a woodworker. He was outspoken, well-educated, an iconoclast, and a resolute crusader for any cause in which he believed. He had little fear of authority, but among his weaknesses was a willingness to believe almost anything that supported his views, which were often outlandish judged by today's standards. In any of his written diatribes there was only one side to the story, and that was his own. A competent writer, his attacks on perceived enemies were often vitriolic and his words could be savage. Fortunately for his readers, his writing was also frequently tinged with humour. A complex man, John Sedgwick Cowper spoke several languages, and one of his more eccentric interests was a belief in the occult. In a social setting he was extremely articulate, often charming. He was a sought-after guest at social gatherings and often appeared at Liberal events in Vancouver.

In 1924 Cowper began working for a small weekly publication in Vancouver, the *Saturday Tribune*, in which he also had some financial investment. With him as editor it fittingly billed itself as a "journal of vitriolic opinion" and developed into a popular Vancouver tabloid. It was in a far different vein than Rev. McDougall's monthly ravings in *The Beacon,* which featured lengthy tirades without a single line of humour.

The *Tribune* was an odd publication, an amalgamation of several previous newspapers, including the *B.C. Ladies Mirror.* As a consequence, the *Tribune* featured extensive coverage of women's fashions and social events in its eight broadsheet pages, along with other stories about everything and anything that appealed to its editor. It was a reflection of Cowper's many and diverse interests. In addition to his other talents, Cowper was a stock investor and promoter, and in the pages of the *Tribune* he lavished praise on opportunities he advocated for investment in the mining industry.

Cowper liked to run big headlines. On January 3, 1925, the front page carried a banner that read: "In A Mad Orgy Of Self-Gratification The Daily Province Forces Christmas Hampers On The Public And Creates The Impression That People Here Are Starving Like Dogs." He wrote that crime in Vancouver was so bad that people from the B.C. Interior would not go to the city to "risk holdup, sandbagging or murder."

In the same edition, Cowper recounted a tale (probably apocryphal) about a group arranging a visit to Vancouver by the New Zealand All-Blacks rugby team. The team was composed of whites and Maoris and got its name from the colour of its uniforms. The sponsors were seeking funds to entertain the team during its visit to the city. They went to city hall asking for financial help with a planned social event and dance, and the *Tribune* quoted an unnamed alderman as allegedly grumbling, "You know, I don't think it is proper for our white girls to be seen dancing with niggers."

Cowper's odd sense of humour made the tabloid popular reading, and at one point he ran a continuing saga that was a take-off on a romantic series that ran at the same time in the *Vancouver Sun*. The *Tribune's* parody ran under the heading "The Slapper's Wife," with "Apologies to the Vancouver Bum." The characters included "Gloria Grogan, a beautiful, bobbed barber of Cordova Street," who had married "Dick De Slick, a struggling young bootlegger," after falling in love with his "balloon pants and varnished hair." All of the tongue-in-cheek writing pointed a finger at some of the continuing problems that plagued the young city of Vancouver.

There were no by-lines on local stories in the *Tribune*, but most of them bore the unmistakeable style of the editor. He was opposed to smallpox vaccination and railed about the "pus." He also took exception to the elite, Asian immigration, politicians, and even the Salvation Army for some of its actions. Cowper's hatred of Manson could not be contained, and in the pages of the *Saturday Tribune* he charged Manson with turning "a blind-eye to blind-pig bootleggers." He stated that justice in B.C. was "tainted at the fountain head" and also labelled Manson "Mr. Facing Both Ways," contending that he had a different outlook on everything depending on whether it involved his elitist friends or the working people of Vancouver.

Readers of the *Tribune* were treated to columns-long stories about seances, spiritualism, and clairvoyants, who were particularly popular in Vancouver at this time, and it was Cowper's involvement in this area that eventually drew him into the courtroom as a defendant.

The Janet Smith case had consumed him for many months. Cowper heard the sharp criticism that followed the first inquest into Smith's death and took up the cause. His friend-turned-foe Manson was his chief target, and he lambasted the attorney general's handling of the affair. Cowper charged there was a massive cover-up to protect members of the establishment and accused Manson and the police of a "conspiracy of silence" in Smith's murder. The far-from-modest Cowper even offered to solve the slaying "if clothed with the necessary power to conduct an inquiry."

During the winter of 1924–25, the Janet Smith murder and all the ramifications of the case had become an obsession and were featured prominently and wildly in the *Tribune.* Because of his interest in spiritualism, Cowper had read extensively about crimes being solved by assorted psychics and clairvoyants in Britain and also had heard recently of the mystic claims of a local woman concerning the Smith affair.

Barbara Orford was a plump, rumpled woman of about 35, who said she was the daughter of a former British army officer and who claimed her mystic powers came through her mother because she was the seventh daughter of a seventh daughter. She was an eccentric, outlandish woman who briefly captured the headlines following Smith's death because she was the latest star in an occult fad that had swept the moneyed ranks of the city. At night she held seances and worked herself into a trance to put the gullible in touch with their dear departed. She became well known in the city's table-tapping circles, and Richard Baker had attended at least one of her sessions. Some visited her for simple amusement, particularly young women seeking a prediction from the fortune teller about matrimonial possibilities. (Janet Smith herself had paid a visit to one of the city's many fortune tellers, though probably not Orford.)

John Cowper got in touch with Orford through a meeting of the Council of Scottish Societies. The two had several areas of common interest in addition to the occult. Orford, who had arrived in Vancouver from Australia, worked in a department store by day, a representative of the Designer Publishing Company, which sold fashion patterns. Orford's involvement in women's fashion made her a natural feature for the women's section of the *Tribune.*

Cowper had his doubts about some of the clairvoyants operating in Vancouver but was impressed with one of Orford's seances, which he attended with several other reporters. He and the woman developed a close friendship and he soon shed any doubts he may have had about her. He completely swallowed the story she told him in March 1925. Orford claimed that on three consecutive nights she had the same vision. She saw Janet Smith pouring drinks at an Osler Avenue party and watched a brawl between men in an upstairs room where the young girl was struck on the head. Then, following the sound of a gunshot, Orford saw Smith lying on the floor with a gaping head wound. Orford recognized some of the men in the room, but just who was responsible for Smith's injuries wasn't revealed in any of the dreams. Somehow, perhaps through one eccentric's appeal to another, she convinced Cowper her vision was true.

The editor of the *Tribune* was doubly prone to believe her when he learned Manson had brushed off her attempt to relate the story. If Manson didn't like it, Cowper automatically did. Orford said she had also failed to interest Jackson and various policemen in her theories. Cowper helped her write a story for the *Glasgow Sunday Mail*, a Scottish paper interested in any paper-selling revelations about one of its own, a poor murdered immigrant lassie way out in the wilds of B.C. Maybe it was rewritten by the scandal-loving *Mail* to perk up interest, but the version that appeared suggested Smith was raped. Orford's persistence finally got her an audience with Harry Senkler. He was still trying to get Wong out of jail and, accompanied by several other lawyers, attended a meeting with her. Orford gave a lengthy version of her visions, which was recorded by a stenographer, Herbert Maişie, who later declared he thought she must have been "drunk, doped or crazy."

As her audience grew, Orford's claims became wilder. Now she maintained that she knew what had happened not from revelations, but because she had attended the Osler Avenue goings-on in person. She saw it all with her own eyes, she said. Confronted by a now uncertain Cowper, Orford confessed she had made up the story about dreams and revelations rather than have anyone think she had actually been present when Smith died. It must have been his hatred of Manson and his belief in the occult, but Cowper once again bought the unbelievable. He set out to tell Orford's story in his paper. It plunged him deeply into the middle of difficult legal proceedings, but he was driven by a desire to be an undaunted, courageous reporter. He also had a genuine concern for injustice and, of course, a burning eagerness to confront Manson at every opportunity.

The Kidnappers Are Caught

Vancouverites enthusiastically followed developments in the Smith saga that ranged from the factual to the totally outrageous. Nearly all had a theory and cheerfully contributed to the boiling pot as the plot thickened. Many had become familiar with courtroom procedure after reading the lengthy accounts of two inquests and Wong's preliminary hearing on the murder charge. They eagerly awaited new disclosures.

June was a complicated month for followers of the convoluted case. Senkler worked to free the imprisoned Wong by filing a writ of *habeus corpus*, a move that many lawyers felt would be unsuccessful because of the preliminary hearing decision to commit him for trial at the fall assizes. On behalf of Chinese Consul Ho Tsang, Harry Senkler also asked Attorney General Manson on June 4 to persuade the government to offer a substantial reward for new information in the Janet Smith case. And he requested another medical examination for his client, whose health was deteriorating still further while he languished in jail.

Deputy Attorney General W.D. Carter told reporters that he would go to Vancouver personally to fight Senkler's *habeus corpus* application. He stressed that it would be "strenuously opposed," refuting the defence lawyer's argument that there simply was no evidence against Wong.

Two days later John Cowper ran a story in the *Tribune* that was basically a reprint of the Orford story already circulated by the *Glasgow Sunday Mail*. It maintained that Fred Baker had lied in the witness box during the inquest when he testified that there had not been a party at Osler Avenue. The story also hinted that Baker was involved in serious business, a reference that many readers took to mean he trafficked in drugs.

Cowper and his "journal of vitriolic opinion" always lived on the edge of libel because of his willingness to print almost anything that supported his own pet peeves. Often he was furthering his war with Manson. Why the attorney general didn't take legal action is a mystery, but he may have felt that this would only stir up a bigger wasps' nest. Fred Baker was different. Within hours of the *Tribune*'s publication he filed libel charges against Cowper. These were both criminal and civil actions, which would be heard at separate trials. The outspoken journalist was immediately arraigned and remanded. Following court appearances, Cowper's criminal libel hearing was set for June 29.

At the same time, Manson told reporters that Barbara Orford had made several statements, including one in the presence of Senkler and her own lawyer, Hamilton Reed, that was almost twenty pages long. The attorney general emphasized it was not made under oath and so had little validity. On June 9 the papers speculated as to whether Orford would appear as a witness at the Cowper libel trial, and if so, would it be as a prosecution or defence witness?

Obviously fleeing a floundering story, the *Sun* confessed without a blush that one of its favourite and most lurid rumours about Janet Smith was a "canard." The paper had alleged that Smith had been drawn into an Osler Avenue orgy, had fled into a bathroom, been killed when she fell and hit her head on the tub, and then had been taken to the basement where a bullet was fired into her head. It was a story that had resurfaced several times, obviously reinforced by the seances and visions of Barbara Orford.

On June 16, lawyers jammed Chief Justice Gordon Hunter's chambers to listen to Senkler and Carter argue the application for *habeus corpus*. The judge then adjourned briefly to allow counsel to familiarize themselves with the citations presented. Senkler argued that there was evidence his client had been beaten and subjected to third-degree methods. Carter maintained Wong's story "would not hold water" in light of all the circumstances. The deputy also challenged the chief justice's decision to review the evidence in the case, contending that his only responsibility was to look into the jurisdiction of Magistrate McQueen, who had committed Wong for trial. The judge disagreed and remanded the hearing for another week.

Orford's fanciful story wilted and died on June 17 when morning headlines screamed that Manson had denounced her tale as a hoax. The attorney general told reporters that the provincial police had gone over her statement (the one Senkler heard) very carefully and confirmed they found "no foundation" for her claims. Manson pointed out that her descriptions of the prominent men she claimed she saw at the house were totally inaccurate, and it also seemed that she had never actually laid eyes on Smith. The statement ended Orford's participation in the case, although her claims were the basis of the problems Cowper now faced in criminal and civil libel suits. There were a few red faces in official circles, where some people had given her story credence. Orford protested the statement made by Manson, maintaining that she was a true clairvoyant who knew what she saw, but she was now dismissed as a screwball.

A few hours later the list of prominent officials involved in the case expanded dramatically when senior police, leading lawyers, and court officials arrived for a meeting at the courthouse. It was obvious there was a major development arising in the case, and reporters hurried to the scene. A quickly called press conference blew the kidnapping mystery wide open, but no one had anticipated the far-reaching charges that were about to be laid in connection with the abduction of Wong Foon Sing. Officials supposedly investigating the crime were now named as conspirators, responsible for Wong's kidnapping. They were: Point Grey police commissioners H.O. McDonald and H.P. McRaney, Police Chief John Murdoch, and Detective Sergeant Percy Kirkham. Also arrested were David Paterson and Mrs. F.H. Stratton of the United Council of Scottish Societies, and A.S. Matthew, a city insurance man and long-time Scots society member. Oscar Robinson of the Canadian Detective Bureau, his son Willie, and his employee Varity Norton were arrested when Inspector Cruickshank, armed with a search warrant, headed a four-man squad in a raid on the Bureau's offices. Robinson reluctantly opened his wall safe on the inspector's orders and watched as one of the men removed a gun, two police badges, and several documents. The police had an arrest warrant for another employee, K.W. Wrightson, who was believed to be in California but was never found. Another of Robinson's employees, Mrs. Elizabeth Donnelly, was also later charged with kidnapping. Rounding out the list of accused was John Sedgwick Cowper.

It didn't take the deductive powers of Sherlock Holmes for the public to realize that Wong's disappearance had been no real mystery to a lot of people. There were many who knew exactly what was going on, or could easily have found out. Evidence later showed that Manson on more than one occasion deliberately avoided hearing information about the houseboy. He and Inspector Cruickshank admitted that shortly after Smith's death, Robinson had suggested kidnapping Wong Foon Sing to try to make him tell what he knew. It would have been easy to bring Robinson in for questioning had any of the officials wanted to do so. And a tail on Robinson or his employees after the houseboy disappeared would easily have led to the small house at 3543 West 25th Avenue, a dark brown bungalow with cream trim and roses growing round the door. In outward appearance the house was no different from other homes in the area, inside; however, it was different. There were five holes bored in a bedroom floor through which chains were fastened so the Chinese houseboy could be shackled to a bed. In addition to the holes chopped in the ten-by-twelve-foot bedroom floor, the whole house was filthy and there was damage to many of the walls and floors.

Vancouver had seen some wondrous happenings and amazing and colourful characters and politicians in its fairly short life span, but never before had a municipality had the majority of its police commissioners, its chief, and a sergeant charged with kidnapping. Their alleged crime followed the investigation of a fatality that set a new mark for police incompetence. Reporters also dug out information about suspicious happenings that snaked their way back to Victoria, Attorney General Manson, his appointee Malcom Jackson, and the provincial government. B.C.'s politics had always been fiery, but this was a naked flame in a dynamite factory.

A large group of reporters and photographers, along with some very curious neighbours, were outside the house on West

25th on June 18 when police and lawyers arrived, accompanied by Senkler and Wong, who had been brought from Oakalla. Among those at the scene was a distraught gentleman, William Walker, an injured First World War veteran living on a pension. Walker had innocently rented out the house in March for $47 a month to a man he identified as one of the accused, Varity Norton.

Senkler said there was no doubt it was the house where his client had been held, even though Wong had been blindfolded when taken in and out, and the blinds had always been drawn. The young Chinese easily identified the house, as he had learned a great deal about its dimensions during his long captivity. He had also heard children playing, and Lord Kitchener School was only a block away. He heard carpenters working on a new house, and there was a house under construction just down the street. He heard streetcars, and a line ran down Dunbar Street about 150 yards from the house. Newspapers ran pictures of the small bedroom with the holes bored in the floor where Wong had been held captive.

One unusual story that ran in the *Sun* that same day was given a by-line, which was not a common practice for a paper in this era. The reporter's name was J.A. Macdonald, and the story purported to be an interview with Wong Foon Sing, although it didn't exactly say so. More likely it was an account given to the writer by somebody else, possibly Harry Senkler. The by-line could have been used to try to add to the article's authenticity and disguise the fact it came from the lawyer.

Macdonald wrote dramatically, "Wong Foon Sing's own story of his abduction, detention and torture can now be told. It is a story of inhumane cruelty and bodily harm from which he still suffers and which makes it difficult for him to stand even the strain of telling about." The story quoted the houseboy as relating that on the day he was kidnapped he had first heard a dog bark, he looked outside to see if the dog was in the yard, then he returned to the basement where he was confronted by three men. "I pulled back and I yell 'Murder, help,' and scream hard as I can but nobody came," wrote the reporter, but they were words that were never uttered by Wong in evidence. Macdonald also quoted Wong as stating that he was struck on the head and now "my head buzz buzz all the time." The story added that while making the statement, Wong held his head, leaving readers to believe that Macdonald was there and had talked one-on-one with the young man.

Senkler later told reporters that he hoped the charges against the twelve accused kidnappers would quickly clear up the Janet Smith case. Robinson and Norton were in jail, unable to raise bail; Willie had been turned over to juvenile authorities; and court officials were on the move throughout town, handing out summonses.

Recently elected Point Grey Reeve James A. Paton publicly admitted that Robinson had been hired by the municipality to do detective work on the Smith case for a fee of $1,250, which was paid to him secretly. The reeve declared, however, that the kidnapping had been done without his knowledge or authority. In Victoria, Manson said he was considering suspending McDonald and McRaney as police commissioners. When McDonald was told of this, he stated defiantly, "Let him go to it." Paton, head of the commission as well as reeve, said he saw no reason why they should not stay on. After meeting with police and the prosecution, Manson told reporters that the documents taken from Robinson's safe indicated that Wong had said nothing new or incriminating during his six weeks in captivity.

The fiasco was all fodder for the *Sun*'s campaign for a consolidated police department. The paper said police work was important and couldn't be treated the same as public works. The law was delicate, it needed careful and skilled handling, it was more "than construction of a sewer," stated the paper's editorial.

On June 22 the *Sun* dug up a letter sent to Malcolm Bruce Jackson by Varity Norton, one of the kidnappers, demanding money he felt he was owed for his part in the affair, a letter that finally resulted in the decision to free Wong. The next day Mr. Justice Hunter ruled against a writ of *habeus corpus*, but said he would allow bail for Wong. This was highly unusual in such circumstances, but this was no ordinary situation. The judge stated after reviewing the evidence, "There is some evidence. True it is scanty and due to the powerful examination to which it has been subjected by Mr. Senkler I don't see how any court could convict on it." He agreed that Wong was in the house, that there was blood on his clothes, and other evidence was offered to refute suggestions of Smith's suicide or accidental death; under the law, however, the magistrate could rule as he saw fit. This was a major win for Senkler, who immediately demanded bail be set. Carter, the deputy attorney general, was left with little choice and agreed, "Candidly I think it is a case for bail." Discussions on the amount of bail required began, and Senkler immediately asked Chinese community leaders to put up the money.

Public criticism about Jackson's role in the affair was now becoming louder. The press asked if he had hampered the police investigation and wanted to know how much he was paid. They lambasted his appointment as nothing more than political patronage. Manson came to Jackson's defence, but dodged the question of pay. He said criticism based on partial knowledge was "harmful and unjust" and declared his appointee had done his utmost to secure Wong Foon Sing's release from the kidnappers, although evidence that emerged later showed the government's hand had been forced. Wong had been kidnapped, terrified, and tortured, but now Manson piously called for fair play for Jackson. "Let us be British," he intoned, "and have conscience that justice is administered fearlessly and fairly in British Columbia."

Jackson also hit out in his own defence. "This story is a perversion of facts. It is a smokescreen for the purposes of protecting someone. The whole thing is maliciously wicked and perverse propaganda," he contended. Always keen to add to the confusion, he declined to tell reporters who the "someone" was. He stoutly maintained he never knew where Wong Foon Sing was during his disappearance, but said Cowper did know and that he had tried to work through the newspaperman to free the houseboy.

After being held captive since March, first by the kidnappers and then by the law, Wong finally was freed on June 24. Senkler said the $10,000 bail had been quickly raised by Chinatown merchants. Undeterred by all he had been through, the houseboy quietly went back to work at Osler Avenue and to his room in the basement.

Kidnappers in Court

June 25, the date set for the kidnappers' preliminary hearing, was a lovely sunny day, albeit with a certain poignancy. The Scots made sure to draw public attention to the fact that this would have been Janet Smith's 23rd birthday. Once again, Scots matrons were in the van of the hundreds who flocked to the small courthouse in Kerrisdale for the accused kidnappers' court appearance. Conscious of the mob scenes at previous hearings, the police were out in force this time to handle anything that might develop. There were hot tempers outside as the crowd vied to get in, but there was no violence. Inside, however, observers said the audience created some of the rowdiest incidents ever seen in the public benches. As proceedings wore on there was applause, hissing, boos, shouts of "Liar," and one man even charged to the front of the courtroom demanding to be heard. Onlookers pushed and shoved as they moved about the room in conversation. As at earlier hearings, Magistrate McQueen allowed more leeway than was customary, intervening only when disturbances became particularly boisterous.

The twelve accused (Norton was dealt with separately) and their lawyers crowded into the front benches, spilling over from the tiny prisoner's dock to seats at a nearby table. All the lawyers with an interest in the case scrambled for seating. It was warm and stuffy in the airless room as an early heat wave hit the city. The second day produced the highest temperature recorded up to that time in Vancouver: 92.4 degrees, topped by Victoria's 95.

Wong had been released from Oakalla jail the day before and was driven by friends to the Kerrisdale courtroom. He had become a recognizable figure in Vancouver after a photographer's studio portrait appeared in all the newspapers, but since then he had been locked up in a house or behind bars in jail. Many were anxious to see what he looked like now. In the picture the handsome young man sat at a table, elegantly dressed, poised, and confident. In the courtroom he looked the same, his feelings under control. He seemed unfazed by the dozens of eyes that searched his face and watched his every move.

He was the first witness called before Magistrate McQueen, and he took the stand in the same box he had occupied earlier when facing accusers who claimed he had murdered Janet Smith. McQueen was the same magistrate who had committed him to trial for murder. Wong was temporarily out of jail, but his life still hung in the balance.

Alex Henderson, the lawyer for the Scots, made the same demand he had made at the second inquest, insisting that Wong take the chicken rather than the fire oath. Magistrate McQueen turned him down. Lawyer John Oliver, representing Robinson and his son Willie, drew immediate applause from the Scots with the biased statement, "I don't take the word of any Chinaman." The lawyer was the son of Liberal premier John Oliver, ironically defending two of the accused from prosecution by his father's attorney general.

Wong Foon Sing told his story in a calm, straightforward way, and the courtroom was generally quiet as the interpreter translated his words. The *Sun* told its readers, "It was a story of brutalities such as one would associate with the dark ages of civilization and seemed incredible his describing incidents which occurred in the present year in the peaceful district of Point Grey." The paper added that his abductors had put the Chinese youth "through tortures of a most un-British character that savoured of the Spanish Inquisition."

The houseboy told of being snatched from Osler Avenue, beaten, handcuffed, and blindfolded. Careful of what they perceived, probably correctly in most cases, as the tender sensibilities of their readers, the papers said Wong Foon Sing testified that one of the kidnapping trio said if he had a gun he would "kill the blankety-blank."

After they had transported him to the house on West 25th and removed his blindfold, the witness said he saw his kidnappers for the first time. "The men had white hoods over them with holes for the eyes and nose," said Wong, who recognized the gowns as the style favoured by the racist Ku Klux Klan. He indicated to the court with his hands that the hoods had high crowns and that the white robes came down to their feet. (Among the items entered as exhibits at the preliminary hearing were receipts taken from Robinson's wall safe including one for lengths of chain—$1.96—and another for white cotton and electric tape.) The captors he saw for the 42 days of his imprisonment were always dressed like this except for a fourth man who sometimes appeared wearing a red handkerchief mask. Wong Foon Sing testified that when he was taken from the bedroom to the bathroom, he always was accompanied by two men, one carrying a revolver.

Some women laughed in an embarrassed way when the witness described the most terrifying moments of his weeks in captivity. The kidnappers had urged him to tell what he knew, he said, and then had produced a length of rope and staged what he feared was to be his own lynching.

"They hanged me up once," he testified. "They showed me my wife's photo [taken from his Osler Avenue room] and said I would not see my wife any more. Then they locked my hands behind my back, gagged and blindfolded me and said they were going to hang me." They took him into the bathroom. "There is a skylight there with a beam across it. They put a stool at my feet and stood me on the stool, then they put a rope around my neck and hanged me up. I was faint and everything went black and I was unconscious. They put me on the bed and spilled water on me. Then blood came from my mouth." As Wong testified, the now hushed room was transfixed. He told of several beatings and pointed to bruises on his face. The houseboy also testified he was examined by a robed man he believed was a doctor. He told the hearing that three times he was taken into the front room of the house and had his picture taken. For one shot they placed a picture of Janet Smith in the background.

When the hearing adjourned for the day, some of the spectators and three of the accused—David Paterson, Mrs. Stratton, and Alex Matthew—went to Mountain View Cemetery for a ceremony to mark what would have been Janet Smith's

23rd birthday. The wreath they placed on the grave was bought with a one-pound note that her mother had sent from Britain. Some 500 people attended a service that was part religious ceremony and part rally of support and encouragement for the three accused. Paterson repeated his claim that they were victims of "trumped-up charges." The rabid Rev. Duncan McDougall, who first listened to the accusations of Cissie Jones and then preached that Wong Foon Sing was a murderer, led the crowd in prayer for justice in a time of "Holy War."

When the preliminary hearing resumed, the court had to arrange for an evening sitting because one of the accused, the busy John Sedgwick Cowper, was appearing in another courtroom for the start of the preliminary trial on his criminal libel charge.

A provincial policeman told of interviewing Cowper in mid-April after a picture, apparently of Wong Foon Sing in captivity, was run in the *Tribune*. Cowper told him that the shot had been delivered to his office by a messenger, whom he was unable to identify. He did not know who might have sent it, he said.

Henry Floyd, Point Grey municipal clerk, told of money payments made to Chief Murdoch for secret transfer to Robinson for his detective work. An unusual witness was Hyman Jay, 18, who said he could not spell his last name because he never used it and who testified that he delivered groceries to the 25th Avenue home rented by Robinson's agency.

Confessed kidnapper Varity Norton had the court wrapped in silence as he contended that the provincial government and the Point Grey police and politicians had planned the abduction, paid for it, and assured him and the other kidnappers that they had immunity and would not face any criminal charges.

It was Norton's complaint about not being paid, and his pitch for more money, that actually forced the government's hand in the kidnapping and resulted in the release of Wong. On April 16, Jackson had received correspondence from Norton stating he was one of the kidnappers and Robinson owed him $200 for his work. Norton obviously believed that Jackson, whom he claimed was one of those behind the plot, could solve his problem. But Norton added a touch of blackmail. In a covering letter dated April 14 he said he had addressed copies of the documents to the Chinese consul, the editor of the *Province*, and two other men, political opponents of Manson, and these would be released if he wasn't paid. The witness said he had given the copies to a friend with instructions that if he hadn't heard from Norton in a week, he was to mail the letters. By threatening to send them to the newspaper and political foes, Norton thought he would get his money. Unusual as it was, his story leant some credibility to his claim that he had been promised immunity. If he didn't believe this, his letter to Jackson, the money demand aside, was an admission of being a party to the kidnapping.

Jackson, in the face of potential whistle-blowing, had little choice but to set in motion the meetings with the Point Grey Police Commission that led to the freeing of Wong Foon Sing from the house on 25th Avenue. To Norton's dismay, he found out quickly there was no immunity. He was arrested and charged with kidnapping. Norton testified he was unemployed when Robinson hired him in the spring of 1925 and gave him a role in the kidnapping. He was to be paid $7.50 a day, but Robinson later told him he hadn't got all the money needed to pay him, despite the $1,250 from Point Grey, and this had triggered Norton's letter to Jackson.

The newspapers said Norton's evidence established definite links between the provincial government and the kidnapping. Norton also identified Paterson and Mrs. Stratton as having been outside the Osler Avenue home when Wong was snatched. He admitted his role in the crime, but denied that he used any violence against the captive. Norton claimed that the mock hanging was not as bad as Wong claimed and it hadn't drawn blood from the houseboy.

He told the court that during Wong's captivity the house was visited by Point Grey Chief John Murdoch, Commissioner H.O. McDonald, and John Cowper. He said that Sergeant Kirkham had supplied the revolvers and handcuffs. Norton added that McDonald told him, when Wong was freed from the house, that arrangements had been made for him to be held in jail for several months until the fall assizes, although this pre-arranged scheme collapsed because of the efforts of Harry Senkler. The witness said that prior to Wong's release he rode in the back of the car with the houseboy, while Kirkham drove. For some time they followed a circuitous route, telling the captive that he was being returned to Canada from the U.S. He was let out on Marine Drive and immediately picked up as part of the plot and charged with murder. Asked if he was involved just for the money, Norton replied, "I wanted to help to solve the mystery." He meant Janet Smith's death. The kidnapping, of course, had been no mystery to him.

Norton stated that after Wong was released on Marine Drive, he went back to the house to try to patch up some of the damage that had been caused during the preceding six weeks. There was, however, nothing that could be done about the holes bored through the bedroom floor, and they provided stark evidence of Wong's captivity and the chains that shackled him.

Mrs. Donnelly, the former detective agency employee, identified Jackson in the courtroom as someone who had visited Robinson's office while Wong was being held. She said the special prosecutor came twice and that on one occasion she heard him say, "Fifteen to two thousand dollars." The woman said Robinson replied, "It's not a matter of a bribe, it's justice and the reward I'm after." The distraught witness raised the excitement in the packed, stuffy room when she fainted and collapsed in the witness box.

Point Grey reeve James Paton readily testified that the municipality had agreed to pay Robinson $1,250 to try to solve the Smith case. He didn't spell it out, but observers assumed that the Point Grey Council felt this was necessary because it had little faith left in the competency of its own police. Paton stressed that kidnapping was not the intention and that he had cautioned Robinson to keep within the law.

On July 3, Norton, as part of the Crown strategy, appeared before Magistrate McQueen on the kidnapping charge and waived his right to a preliminary hearing. He was remanded until the fall assizes.

When the preliminary hearing of the others resumed, the Crown asked that the charges be dropped against Alex Matthew, whose only connection to the case was that his name appeared on a list of "supporters" in one of the documents taken from Robinson's safe in the police raid. The enthusiastic Scots-born insurance man and former Council of Scottish Societies executive member apparently was prepared to help bankroll Wong's kidnapping, but proceedings against him were not pursued. In lengthy arguments on July 9 the counsel for the accused moved to have all charges dropped, but the magistrate disagreed. He ruled that they be stayed against Paterson, Mrs. Stratton, and Point Grey police commissioner H.P. McRaney. He committed all the others—Robinson and son Willie, Cowper, Point Grey Police Chief Murdoch, Sergeant Kirkham, and Commissioner McDonald—for trial at the fall assizes.

A Pair of Irrepressibles

It was predictable that the flamboyant John Sedgwick Cowper would have an equally colourful, aggressive lawyer representing him when the preliminary hearing on his criminal libel charge opened on June 29. That lawyer was Gordon Wismer, young, brash, publicity conscious, at this time making a name for himself in legal circles, and happy to be involved in a high-profile controversy that would garner attention. As well as being Cowper's legal counsel on this occasion, he was also associated with him in business, as Wismer was solicitor for Empire Mines, a project in which the newspaperman held a major interest. Fiercely Liberal, Wismer was later elected to the legislature and became attorney general in the government of Byron (Boss) Johnson. Like Manson before him, Wismer was to become a controversial attorney general, although the reasons for his notoriety were quite different. Wismer took to being driven around Vancouver in police cars to visit late-night clubs and mingle with the crooks and gang leaders of the era. He was closely tied to a major scandal in the 1950s when a royal commission found the Vancouver police department was graft ridden and its chief, Walter Mulligan, a close friend of Wismer's, was in the pay of gamblers. For four decades Gordon Wismer was the Liberals' Mr. Fixit both in and out of office, at the provincial and federal level, a man with connections to all segments of society from Shaughnessy to skidroad.

Cowper's defence was one of Wismer's early cases, and it was simple. The newspaperman had believed the stories of Barbara Orford, even when she said that instead of receiving revelations about an orgy at Osler Avenue in a dream, she had actually been there. Cowper felt it was his duty as a newspaperman to disclose her allegations, particularly when the investigation seemed stalled and she had been given the cold shoulder by the police, Manson, and special sleuth Jackson.

Fred Baker was first up in the witness box before Magistrate J.A. Findlay and another standing-room-only crowd that watched with fascination as Gordon Wismer met his match. In all the hundreds of thousands of words printed in the stories that filled the papers for more than a year, Fred Baker received consistently favourable coverage, and he did not bow when Wismer decided Cowper's best defence was an attack on him. Wismer played on every slice of speculation, every rumour, even the slightest suggestion that Baker might have been involved in supplying illicit drugs or having sex with Smith.

Throughout the wide-ranging assault, Baker was poised and unflustered, exhibiting a steely determination to combat the slurs and accusations made against him and his family. His charges of libel against Monica Mason-Rooke, and the more serious one of criminal libel against Cowper, were evidence he would no longer take anything lying down. He might ignore minor rumours, but once they began to damage his business or his family, Fred Baker stood his ground. He was now a businessman of stature in post-war Vancouver with a reputation to protect. The questions raised about drug deals cast an unwanted shadow on his name and character, as well as on other members of his family. There is no doubt that his brother Dick and sister-in-law Blanche, as well as General McRae and the wealthy Mrs. Lefevre, were advising him and were as anxious as he to shed the suspicions they had begun to hear in the drawing rooms and club lounges of Shaughnessy.

As Wismer began his interrogation, Fred Baker confidently and vehemently denied all Barbara Orford's allegations. The lawyer knew the story of the orgy had already been discounted by Manson and the police, but that was not enough for Wismer, who carefully raised and deliberately asked all the lingering questions about Baker's commercial involvement with drugs both in England and France before he returned to Vancouver. Baker insisted his importing business was perfectly legal, including a publicized transaction involving the $40,000 sale of narcotics to a Japanese customer. Baker denied a suggestion by Wismer that one of his former partners had been jailed in Europe for dealing in opium. (It was not a partner, but an agent for the company who was jailed.) Baker even kept his temper when Wismer demanded to know if there had been any drugs concealed in furniture that he brought back from France. "Absolutely none," Baker responded without raising an eyebrow. When Wismer tried another titillating topic, bringing up Orford's claim that Smith had told her she was pregnant with her employer's child, Baker bristled and said in steely tones, "Absolutely ridiculous, a malicious lie."

Wismer went a little too far in bending the facts when he alleged that during the second inquest Archibald Hunter had testified that the embalming of Smith's body had wiped out any evidence of the pregnancy. Baker's lawyer, Pat Fraser, immediately interrupted and shot back, "Dr. Hunter made no such statement."

By this time Magistrate Findlay had had enough of the unabashed Wismer and told the lawyer that his statements besmirched not only Baker's name but also Janet Smith's, and she wasn't there to defend herself. The preliminary hearing wound up quickly, with the magistrate committing Cowper for trial at the fall assizes. These were now developing into an almost all-Smith event, to be presented case by case, chapter by chapter, in a saga of epic proportions.

Outside the courtroom, Fred Baker did his best to step out of the limelight and stated that he had let gossipy socialite Monica Mason-Rooke off the hook, dropping his libel charge against her. Baker explained that the young woman had admitted she knew nothing of a party at his house the night before Smith died. She had merely exaggerated some previously heard gossip and had not intended to speak disparagingly of him or Mrs. Baker when she had talked about the case. Baker said that the flood of stories and gossip about a party were "utterly without foundation" and were by now untraceable. He explained that at first he thought the rumours would subside and fade away, but they did not. Then a friend alerted him to the tale told by Mason-Rooke to her friends. It was the first authentic report he had received about the source of the persistent rumours, and it had led to his charge against her. All was now forgiven, he said, as the young woman had admitted there was no truth to her statements. His Shaughnessy friends were pleased with his decision, and Baker said everyone would soon see there was no truth to the story because of the evidence that would emerge from Cowper's upcoming appearance in court.

The irrepressible Cowper still carried an advertisement in his paper that touted the clairvoyant powers of Orford, trying to capitalize on her brief fling at fame, or perhaps infamy. She gave a lecture in the Empress Theatre billed as "The Girl Who Knew." Admission was 80 cents, 55 cents, and 30 cents for different levels of seating, and she was introduced by one of the city's other leading clairvoyants. However, she attracted only a sparse crowd to what proved to be her only stage appearance. The debunking of her claims in the Smith affair had ended her brief career as a newsmaker.

Before June ran out, the *Sun* opened up another can of worms by writing about meetings held in mid-April when houseboy Wong Foon Sing was in the kidnappers' hands. The paper reported the talks had been initiated by Jackson during a meeting with the Chinese consul and Wong Gow, Wong Foon Sing's brother, who insisted that Harry Senkler must be consulted before any further discussions were held. Jackson then approached Wong's lawyer, asking if he would agree to be taken to see Wong Foon Sing in captivity if it could be arranged. Jackson also asked Senkler to help the Chinese consul compose a letter urging the houseboy to tell the whole truth and all that he knew about Janet Smith's death. Senkler refused to go along with the outrageous proposition. There's little doubt that the wily lawyer leaked news of the meeting to the press, enjoying Jackson's discomfort when the story hit the streets. The special investigator had his own version of events, but had to agree with the basic facts in the newspapers while maintaining he had not known who had seized Wong or where he was being held. Jackson insisted that he had hoped to work through Cowper, who knew where the houseboy was being held.

The Kidnappers' Plot Uncovered

With the filing of a dozen new charges against the accused kidnappers, the Janet Smith case became so involved that only true devotees of the long saga of events could sort out the mounting lists of characters, charges, and the plots that had developed around each one. There had been a break in developments early in 1925, but the fast-moving episodes beginning in March, with the kidnapping of Wong, and leading to the sensational events of June had made Janet Smith's death into a criminal epic. Since July 1924 the Scottish girl's demise had dominated news in all Vancouver daily newspapers and weekly journals. Included by this time were these facts:

- There had been two inquests in 1924, the jury in the first ruling accidental death and the second jury finding she had been murdered.
- Wong Foon Sing had been kidnapped in March, released by the kidnappers in May, and immediately arrested by police, charged with murder, thrown into jail, and committed for trial. He then was released on $10,000 bail.
- Fred Baker and his wife Doreen had rattled the establishment in the spring of 1925 with their libel suit against one of their own, gossipy socialite Monica Mason-Rooke. After discussions between the two families and an apology from Monica, the suit was dropped.
- Following the June 6 edition of Cowper's *Saturday Tribune*, the Bakers had laid criminal and civil libel charges against him and he was now committed for trial at the fall assizes.

- The city was amazed in mid-June to learn the details of the kidnapping plot and the names of the accused, which included three members of the Point Grey Police Commission, the municipality's police chief, and a sergeant.
- The charge against a thirteenth kidnapper, Mrs. Elizabeth Donnelly, was dropped as part of the involved strategy developed by prosecutors, with Manson the master manipulator pulling the strings in the background. The woman had agreed to testify against the others, as had Robinson and Varity Norton. It hadn't taken long for the gang to start looking for ways to try to save their individual skins. Their actions were not surprising, since the penalty for kidnapping carried a maximum sentence of 25 years in prison.
- The final decision on the fate of the kidnappers was to be determined at three separate trials. There would be one trial for Robinson and his son, another one for John Cowper, and yet another for the Point Grey police commissioners and policemen, assuming they were all committed for trial after preliminary hearings. Norton had pleaded guilty. All sentences were to be imposed at the end of the fall assizes. Charges against David Paterson, Mrs. Jessie Stratton, and Alex Matthew had been dropped.
- Norton was a key witness and would be dealt with first. Cynics said his ultimate sentence recommendation would depend on what he revealed at the trial, or, perhaps more likely, what he didn't reveal.
- There was little doubt that the crown would do whatever it could to keep Jackson out of the limelight, though Harry Senkler was one of many who wanted to get the investigator in the witness box to testify under oath. Senkler hoped Norton would reveal incriminating evidence against Jackson and establish a direct link between Manson and the kidnappers.

The Smith-Wong affair was now broadening its scope beyond Shaughnessy and Chinatown, beyond the petty manoeuvring between Vancouver and Point Grey police departments, and moving rapidly into the stormy realm of provincial politics. The attorney general was subject to mounting criticism in the legislature, in newspapers, and in public discussion about his own and Jackson's involvement in the kidnapping.

In addition, Manson faced an attack on his integrity from another direction. He was under investigation by the B.C. Law Society for an unrelated matter. Ironically, Senkler was also leading this charge against his long-time foe, which threatened to push the attorney general from the frying pan into the fire. Manson was accused of withholding medical evidence in a murder trial that showed the accused, a Japanese workman, was mentally incompetent to stand trial. The Oriental millworker was convicted and sentenced to die on the gallows, but the medical officer who had examined the man complained his report had been suppressed. Premier John Oliver bypassed his attorney general and made a successful bid to Ottawa to have the death sentence commuted. Not only was Manson in the premier's bad books, but the Law Society then decided to investigate his handling of the case in the fall. If the society did proceed with its inquiry, it came to nothing and today there is no record of it.

Summer Hiatus

Aficionados, those who religiously read every newspaper story and the hundreds of thousands of words written about the Janet Smith affair, were happiest when concocting their own theories about what happened. They had to wait through the long hot summer, however, before the drama resumed in the fall of 1925 with the opening of the assizes.

In the meantime Cowper continued to write articles in the *Saturday Tribune*, and they were still sprinkled with assorted asides and sardonic comments. Already charged with criminal libel, he ventured close to the legal limits with his articles that summer, most of them fuelled by his hostility towards his one-time friend Alex Manson.

In Vancouver, the whack of tennis balls could be heard at private clubs and public courts all over town. White was the colour on the courts and at the cricket pitches where cricketers bowled their overs and broke for tea and scones at Brockton Oval. Olde England was still very much alive on the coast that summer, especially in Stanley Park, which had been a mecca from the time it was designated a park in 1886. Now outdoor lovers were happy when the federal government gave a second $8,000 grant for work on the seawall, although it would be about another half century before it was finished. Later in the summer, 6,000 Tories attended a political rally in the park.

With 327 hours of sunshine, July 1925 was the warmest since 1906 and provided the perfect setting for an idyllic summer. Even those who faced the fall assizes with apprehension were able to enjoy Vancouver at its best. One unfortunate affair, however—an outdoor dance on the Georgia

Viaduct—turned into a disaster despite the best intentions of the city fathers. They had arranged to have music, played by a nine-piece band, piped to the viaduct over a loudspeaker system. Unfortunately the shuffling feet of the dancers drowned out the music, and the crowd of young people became incensed, demanding a refund of their 25-cent admission.

Residents of English Bay might have appreciated a little rain to dampen the spirits of young revellers that summer. Instead, they complained about the noise coming from the swimming pool run by Pleasure Piers Ltd. The owners suggested the complainers should remember that the bay was a resort area and they should not be killjoys.

One responsible fourteen-year-old, Agnes Rabbit, was commended for her bravery in rescuing two young swimmers who got into difficulty at Kitsilano beach. At the same time there were complaints about other fourteen-year-olds who were shocking women on the street by repeating "filthy rhymes" while making "flirtatious advances that in sophistication would shame a roue."

Attorney General Manson received considerable support, as well as some opposition from the clergy, when he announced that any electoral district that came up with the signatures of 40 percent of its residents could hold a plebiscite on serving beer by the glass and, providing the populace approved, introduce beer parlours. The *Sun* warned that such establishments could become "places of assignation for prostitutes" and advocated the simple solution would be to keep all women out. Until the 1960s, Vancouver had beer parlours for men only, with other sections for ladies and escorts.

In the summer of 1925 the Woodward family opened its new department store on Hastings at Abbott, the city's largest. It flourished as a major retailer for close to 70 years. In 2000 the building lay scruffy and empty, its future still undecided.

Arthur Battersby won the 25-yard men's potato race at the sixth annual picnic held by Vancouver's Spencers Department Store, now also defunct. The 1,700 employees and their families travelled to Bowen Island for the occasion, using two Union Steamships steamers, *Lady Alexandra* and *Lady Cecilia*. The nimble-footed Arthur won several events.

Moviegoers flocked to see Gloria Swanson in *The Coast of Folly*, which sounded like it could have been about Vancouver and Janet Smith but wasn't.

Ah Soo, described as a pretty Chinese waitress, got a break from Magistrate J.S. Jamieson, who dismissed charges against her for selling liquor in a Pender Street cafe. He labelled the Chinese operatives of the B.C. Provincial Police, who ordered the drinks, "lowdown plants."

The 1924 salmon pack was reported at 1.7 million cases, the biggest ever, in a fishing industry that employed 8,136 fishermen and 6,123 packing house workers.

Houses in Point Grey similar to the one where Wong Foon Sing had been held captive were selling for $3,500, and a two-acre orchard with house at Lonsdale and Queens in North Vancouver was listed for $1,800. For years it was known as the Stoker Farm and was home to a prominent North Vancouver family.

Many were horrified to read that one in twelve marriages was ending in divorce. Vancouver already had many widows and single women who had been the fiancées of men who marched off to war in 1914–18 and didn't return.

Some feared the onslaught of a more permissive society, heralded by everything from the fourteen-year-old cutups at English Bay to the unfortunate Evelyn Campbell, who died at age nineteen from an "illegal operation" in which four men were charged. Her grieving family told a reporter that "her troubles were in part due to public dances." Some wondered if the dances that Janet Smith loved and wrote about in her diary played any part in her death on the basement floor.

It was an era of reasonable prosperity and plentiful jobs although as always the most plentiful were at the low end of the scale. There was a mounting feeling of class consciousness and growing gaps in society, heightened by the much publicized death of Janet Smith and highlighted by events and outrageous rumours of the goings-on in Shaughnessy.

And as a reminder of the court cases looming in the fall, Point Grey solicitor A.G. Harvey announced that all those in the municipality charged with kidnapping would be paying their own legal costs.

Clan Wars

Battling the English was one of the main preoccupations of the clans in old Scotland. If there were no English to take on, the fractious clansmen accepted second best and warred among themselves. That was the case at the end of the summer when David Paterson resigned as president of the Scottish Council. In a bitter attack, he publicly charged the executive with diverting funds raised to investigate Smith's death to defray the costs of the Point Grey police charged with kidnapping. Paterson said a "political clique" within the organization had blocked the investigation in order to protect its friends, but he wouldn't name the clique members. The ex-president said the investigation committee, which included himself and Mrs. Stratton, had been "persecuted at every step."

Acting president Mrs. James Robertson struck back quickly, contending that Paterson had been forced out over differences in dealing with the Smith affair. She said no politics were involved, no funds had been diverted, and she emphasized that the Council investigation would continue. Divisions had developed between those who were firmly convinced that Wong was the killer and those who felt there was no evidence against him and were embarrassed by the revelations of his treatment at the hands of police and provincial and local officials. They disagreed especially with Rev. McDougall's declaration of a "Holy War" at Smith's graveside. Cowper's *Tribune* summed up Paterson's resignation with a succinct headline: "Chairman Of The Scots Society Gets His."

But the Scots were united when some 4,000 people gathered again at Mountain View Cemetery on Sunday afternoon,

On two occasions at the site of Janet Smith's grave, Rev. Duncan McDougall preached to the assembled crowd that it was a time of "Holy War."

September 27. Over the course of the year the Council had raised the money for a permanent headstone for Janet Smith, and now it was to be unveiled. The crowd spilled from the gravesite south of 41st Avenue onto Prince Edward Avenue to hear the service of dedication. Point Grey reeve Paton pulled away the tartan cloth covering the soaring eight-foot pillar of the monument to reveal a tombstone built in the old Scottish style. Following tradition, the top of the column had been chipped roughly away to signify that the deceased had come to an early end. The inscription on the base read: "Erected by the Council of Scottish Societies for British Columbia. In loving memory of Janet K. Smith who met her death while in the bloom of youth at Shaughnessy Heights on July 26, 1924, aged 22 years 1 month and 1 day. 'On earth one gentle soul the less, in heaven one angel more.'"

The Rev. J.S. Henderson, who had officiated at her funeral, asked the crowd to sing two verses of Smith's favourite hymn, "Nearer My God to Thee." The Rev. Richmond Craig stated that the mysteries of life and death could not be solved by the human mind but "that all was in the knowledge of God."

Cowper Takes the Stand

John Sedgwick Cowper's criminal libel trial opened the fall assizes on October 1, the first of the cases arising from Janet Smith's death. The flamboyant, eccentric Cowper faced two libel charges as well as the kidnapping trial. He was still represented by the aggressive, cocky Wismer, while the venerable E.P. Davis, probably the city's most respected lawyer, was the prosecutor. Mr. Justice D.A. McDonald presided.

Although no one could have anticipated it, the more the public learned of Cowper, the more they liked him. To the Scots he was their champion in the cause of justice for Janet Smith. They had all but given up on Manson, much to the delight of non-Liberal politicians and even to some in his own party. Cowper was now the implacable foe of the attorney general and a crusader for the Scots. To the few not emotionally involved in the politics of the day he was an amusing figure, a slightly dotty crusader riding a swayback horse, a regular Don Quixote.

The Bakers told their now well-known account of events, rejecting once more all of Orford's claims that there had been a party at Osler Avenue. Baker said he felt that the press had inflamed public opinion between the first and second inquests, resulting in the second decision that pronounced the death a murder. Wismer brought up the drug question, and Baker again answered "Never" when he was asked if he had ever been involved in trafficking. Asked if he thought Wong was the killer, Baker defended the houseboy, stating that the evidence wasn't there.

In the witness box, Cowper played on his claim to 25 years of fearless newspaper reporting, donning the cloak of a martyr. "I find the murder of Smith is more important than putting me in the box," he told the court. Prosecutor Davis dryly commented, "Oh, yes, we know your duty is the outstanding point of your character." Completely unabashed, Cowper contended, "If ever in my life I realized my duty as a journalist, I felt it then."

Cowper told of meeting Orford, hearing her story, and believing it, although she had deceived him by claiming psychic revelations of an orgy and then maintaining she had actually been present at the party. One of her claims was that Smith had been attacked in an upstairs room and had then fallen and smashed her head on a radiator. Orford told Cowper that if the carpet in the room was lifted, a blood stain would be found. He now revealed that a private detective had been hired who managed to get into the house and take a sliver of wood from the floor, which did appear to be stained. The detective was not named, and Cowper admitted that a scientific test could not identify the substance that had made the stain.

During his two hours of testimony, Cowper said he had been told, presumably by Wismer, not to be tricked by the prosecution into calling Orford as a defence witness. He didn't explain how the "trick" was supposed to work, but the prosecution claimed it had not sought her as a witness. Cowper said he last saw the woman about two weeks before the trial, when she informed him that someone had invited her to take a holiday in Hawaii. Some observers may have wondered who paid her fare, but this question was never asked.

The defendant said Orford had maintained there were seven prominent people at the Baker house party. Pressed by Davis, Cowper identified two of those Orford had named as B.C. Lieutenant-Governor W.C. Nichol and his son Jack. This assertion brought an immediate denial from Government House in Victoria, the words almost spluttering out of the angry statement. In fine vice-regal fashion, the king's representative in B.C. described Cowper's claim as not only a "gratuitous impertinence, but an unqualified falsehood." His Excellency exclaimed that not only had he never been in the Baker house, he didn't even know where it was.

Davis, a member of the provincial establishment, was eager to remove any slurs against his prominent friends and tried to introduce Jack Nichol as a witness in the case. The younger

Nichol, a well-known playboy, had a broken leg and shuffled to the front of the courtroom on crutches, intending to testify that he was nowhere near Osler Avenue on the date in question. The bid to introduce his testimony was, however, rejected by Judge McDonald, who said it had no place in the trial. Nichol had been a First World War flier like the Baker boys, and he was a family friend of the judge.

In summing up, Wismer said the Crown could not dispute the fact that Smith had been murdered. Davis interjected, "I absolutely do." He was supported by Judge McDonald, who said he agreed with Davis, adding, "The only evidence was the finding of a coroner's jury and another coroner's jury found absolutely to the contrary."

Wrapping up his case, Wismer asked the jury to acquit his client, maintaining in stock flowery fashion, "If this friendless, homeless, Scottish girl who lies murdered in her grave could rise from her ashes this afternoon she would ask you to acquit this innocent man." Judge McDonald, in his charge to the jury, said the newspaper played an important part in Vancouver life and was something that many people turned to morning and evening for information. "It is protected by law, the paper is not muzzled. It may report anything said in the court of justice," he stated, but added, "There are limitations." He expressed sympathy for the Bakers, contending "the name of Baker has been bandied throughout the city in a way that you and I would give ten years of our lives to avoid."

The jury considered Cowper's plight for four hours and twelve minutes before finding him guilty. The decision didn't seem to upset the indefatigable reporter, who still had to stand trial on the Wong kidnapping charge and the civil libel case. Baker's lawyer told the judge that his client didn't seek retribution, only to clear his name. Judge McDonald remanded Cowper for sentence until the end of the assizes, with continuation of his $500 bail.

Murder Charge Thrown Out

After all the waiting, it was almost anti-climactic. On October 9 the headlines in big black type screamed, "Wong Sing Goes Free." It took a grand jury less than two days to find that there was no evidence against the Chinese man to warrant sending him to trial for murder. The shadow of the gallows had finally been lifted from Wong's future, fourteen months after Janet Smith died.

The lawyer's presentations began before Mr. Justice D.A. McDonald and a jury that included two women. They heard the now familiar stories from witnesses ranging from the ham-fisted Point Grey police to the doctors at the autopsies, and they reviewed the evidence from the preliminary hearing. The next morning the jury requested some technical detail and returned at 12:45 p.m. to tell McDonald there was no evidence and the houseboy was free. The jury also stated there was nothing to prove that Smith was murdered by anyone, effectively taking the affair back to the beginning, to the first inquest where her death was ruled accidental.

Wong received the decision calmly, and the Chinese community was pleased and surprised that their countryman had finally received justice, although it had taken much too long to be delivered. The papers reported that the news of the decision spread with "astonishing rapidity" through the courthouse and out into the streets. The papers rolled off special editions that were eagerly snatched from newsboys. One reporter noted, "It was a surprising turn in the case following a series of sensational events." Many residents of Vancouver, not just those of Scots ancestry, believed Wong had killed the girl.

The Scots were stunned by the verdict, and they greeted the jury's pronouncement with a deafening silence. In Victoria, Manson and Jackson were outraged by the decision, claiming that the grand jury had overstepped its duties, although it had done exactly what it was set up to do.

There were mutterings in the capital about the possibility of another charge being laid against Wong, but nothing came of it. Fred Baker was pleased, having contended from the start that Smith wasn't murdered.

The *Sun* summed up the situation: "Flat as a punctured tire lies the Smith murder trial." It added, "Thus ends, or nearly ends, one of the most sensational 'cause celebre' that ever agitated the people of two nations."

The Scots-Chinese "Holy War" ended with Wong a winner. As he did after the preliminary hearing, the houseboy quietly went back to work at Osler Avenue. If anyone ever had cause to protest mightily about the injustice inflicted upon him, it was Wong Foon Sing, but he didn't. In today's litigious world the list of people he could have sued ranged from Manson and Jackson to the Point Grey politicians and their police force, not forgetting the newspapers, John Sedgwick Cowper, Oscar Robinson, and company.

Thankful that justice had finally prevailed for one of their own, the *Chinese Times* carried a simple, non-recriminatory story following the grand jury's decision. It stated that Wong's release had been achieved "through the concerted efforts and cooperation of the Chinese community." The paper praised Vancouver's Chinese people for "their warm support and generous donations."

While Wong had been found not guilty, the kidnappers' trials were yet to come and the ramifications of Janet Smith's death were far from over. In the meantime, English-language newspapers continued to publish lengthy stories about the crime and violence that coloured Chinatown. The *Sun* told its readers that "the Greedy God of Jealousy fanned the flames of hatred in the heart of a disappointed Oriental lover disappointed in his suit for the hand of a demure little Chinese singing girl which is thought to have led to the assault and serious injury of Woo Shun in the dark resources of a Chinatown alley." The paper quoted police as stating that the area was torn with more strife since singing girls had been imported to act as waitresses and entertainers in Chinese restaurants.

Even the Chinese would have been hard pressed to make a sympathetic case for Chang Hai, the subject of another story, as a worthy resident. He was in possession of burglar tools when shot in the leg by a private security man while fleeing from a Seymour Street break-in. At the time he had just got out of jail. The court was told that since Chang Hai arrived in Victoria in 1899, he had spent almost all of his time, eighteen and a half years, in jail for various crimes. For the latest one he got two more.

On Sunday, October 4, a Chinatown tribute harkened back to an earlier crime when an estimated 4,000 people jammed Pender Street to observe the funeral of Lum But and Ng Hor, killed in the shingle-mill shootout at Port Moody in the spring. The papers didn't say why the funeral occurred so long after the incident, but again the police were on standby in case of violence. The community remained sharply divided over the money raised by the Shon Yee Benevolent Society, ostensibly to build a hospital in China. Two vehicles preceded the two hearses. They stopped on Pender outside the Society headquarters for a ceremony, which the *Sun* reported was entirely in Chinese. Mourners then fell in behind the cortege and followed it on foot to Main and Prior, where 60 taxis were needed to transport those wishing to attend the burial at Mountain View Cemetery. Despite the state of emotions in Chinatown, there were no incidents that required police action.

It is ironic that it took a paid advertisement to tell some of the other side of the story of the Chinese presence in Vancouver and B.C. On October 25 a full-page notice ran in the *Vancouver Sun* under the heading "Yip Sang Pioneer Extends Greetings To British Columbia." It was printed in celebration of the 80th birthday of a remarkable man and his equally remarkable family.

In 1880 Yip Sang arrived in San Francisco on a sailing ship from Canton after a two-month trip across the Pacific. He went to Victoria and then New Westminster, intending to start a business, but instead became the superintendent for the Kwong On Company, labour contractors for the Canadian Pacific Railway. He worked on the stretch from Kamloops to Port

Moody, the Onderdonk Contract as it was known to old-timers. Immigration records in Ottawa state that from then until completion of Canada's first trans-continental railway in 1886, the CPR brought in about 15,000 Chinese. It was tough, dangerous work that involved tunnelling through mountains and building bridges over roaring rivers. Some 600 Chinese were killed doing jobs that others had turned down. The dynamite used to blast through the rocks was particularly volatile and responsible for many of the deaths.

On completion of the line, Yip Sang opened his first trading company, Wing Song Chu at 51 Pender Street in Vancouver. He also continued to work as an agent for the CPR, handling the company's Chinese business.

The achievements of his family were outstanding. By 1925 one of his sons had graduated from McGill University in Montreal; a daughter had graduated from Columbia University in New York and was teaching at Canton University; a son was in fifth-year medicine at Queens University in Kingston; and his youngest son attended the University of B.C.

Yip Sang's business had expanded and prospered since its beginnings in Chinatown and he was now engaged in international trade. The newspaper message stated he was instrumental in introducing B.C. salt fish to the Chinese market. Yip Sang was still active in community events. His main achievement was founding, at the turn of the century, the Chinese Benevolent Association. He was its first president, and in 1925 his son, Yip Mow, headed the organization. From 60 members it had grown to more than 6,000. It occupied a four-storey building in Chinatown, one of the floors dedicated to the teaching of English. Among its many activities it provided aid to people in need, and at that time Wong Foon Sing was one of the recipients. The Association actively supported his case both morally and financially, providing a portion of the funds for his defence. There were many stories about the Chinese population in the papers, but it took a paid advertisement to record the 80th birthday and the achievements of this important B.C. pioneer and his family.

Detectives on Trial

Wong Foon Sing had been legally cleared of murder, but many Scots and others who supported their efforts still believed he was a killer who had escaped the noose. They sought ways to have him punished, to have him charged with something, almost anything. If there *was* anything to pin on him, it might be uncovered at the kidnapping trials, which promised to be one of the highlights of the fall season.

There was rising speculation about Alex Manson's involvement, and excitement grew when it was discovered that the Scots' former friend turned foe was about to take the stand. Perhaps some of their questions would be answered. Would Manson's involvement in the kidnapping be revealed? Had the abduction and interrogation been directed by the attorney general from Victoria while Malcolm Jackson played the management role with the plotters in Vancouver? Was there any indiscretion in writing that tied either of them to the house on 25th and the events that had taken place there? Manson was a shrewd, wily, experienced lawyer and politician, but could he have made a false step somewhere, even a small one? Could the impulsive, brash Jackson have left a trail that led back to Manson's office?

The Robinsons, father and son, were slated to go on trial November 5, but first there was an exciting new development. Special counsel Malcolm Jackson's name was added to the list of the accused, and he was charged with complicity in Wong's kidnapping. In an out-of-the-blue turn of events, Oscar Robinson named Jackson as a participant in the whole ugly undertaking. Vancouver justice of the peace Earl Robinson, no relative of

Oscar, filed the charges on the basis of information supplied by the private detective. Four others also were charged: David Paterson, Jessie Stratton, Commissioner H.P. McRaney, and Point Grey reeve James Paton, chairman of the police commission. It was never known whether the justice of the peace believed Oscar Robinson's claim that all five of them had been involved, or if he was just another person picking on Jackson because of a grudge against him, the attorney general, or the Liberals. Whatever the case, there were smiles on the faces of many Scots, despite the fact that members of the Council of Scottish Societies were once again being charged. The sight of special investigator Jackson in the box, being grilled about new aspects of the Smith affair, was a spectacle no one wanted to miss. The spectacle would have to wait, however, until the trials already scheduled were concluded.

Jackson immediately denounced Robinson's charge as a malicious act against innocent people. He claimed it was a smokescreen, meant only to add confusion prior to the beginning of Robinson's own trial. There seemed some reason to suspect this might be the case, but the charge, bogus or not, added more fuel to the fire and it was soon evident that a new chapter was underway in the dime-store-novel saga of Janet Smith.

If the attorney general was feeling pressure when he took a seat in the courtroom for the Robinsons' trial, he didn't show it. Manson, who seldom smiled at any time, was appropriately serious for the event. As with all the trials held in connection with the Smith-Wong case, the room was packed, every seat was occupied, and an unhappy overflow crowd waited impatiently outside. Mr. Justice D.A. McDonald was on the bench and the Crown prosecutor was again the veteran Charles Craig. The judge, in his first decision regarding the trial, rejected a plea by the Robinsons' lawyer, J.E. Bird, to have all those accused of kidnapping Wong tried at the same time. The Robinsons were to face the music alone.

During these assizes, Wong Foon Sing was once again at centre stage, a major player in the unfolding drama. In the witness box he said that he had been in Canada about eleven years and had worked in "white men's houses" and laundries. Then he repeated his story about being seized in the basement by two men after he heard strange noises and went to investigate. Prosecutor Craig unwrapped a parcel containing three white, hooded gowns and three masks, which Wong identified as those worn by his captors. He also indicated that two guns and a pair of handcuffs produced by the prosecutor looked like the ones he had seen in the house on 25th. During his testimony he said that his captors had read excerpts to him from transcripts of evidence given during the two Janet Smith inquests. He explained that they based many of their questions on this material and demanded that he give them answers.

Any lingering suggestions that Wong's disappearance was a mystery to the accused were dispelled when B.C. Provincial Police inspector Forbes Cruickshank testified. He said he had hired Robinson's agency to help with his investigation following the first inquest. This involved snatching the houseboy off the street in Chinatown shortly after Smith's death and grilling him for several hours. This was before the district of Point Grey employed the same agency to go after Wong again. Asked by defence lawyer Bird if he ever suggested to Robinson that Wong should be kidnapped, the policeman said no, then quickly added, "Only once when I said to him that the police would have nothing to do with it." He added that the plan had called for Wong to be held until he confessed or incriminated others in a signed statement.

Robinson's wife, Mary, mother of co-accused Willie, had the rapt attention of the courtroom when she told of a visit to her home by Malcolm Bruce Jackson two or three days after Wong's second disappearance. Her husband had told her to stay hidden outside the living room but within earshot while he met with the special investigator and got Jackson to repeat his promise of immunity for all those involved in the kidnapping.

She testified that she heard her husband say he had talked to Manson and he wanted confirmation of immunity. Mrs. Robinson said Jackson replied, "You have nothing to fear; the province will protect you." She insisted that Jackson said Manson knew everything but that his hand could not be revealed. Jackson also assured her husband that he would not be "disturbed" by the provincial police, who were on side, said Mrs. Robinson. Bringing the whole plot into the open, she named other visitors to the house at various times. They included Inspector Cruickshank and other policemen, lawyer Alex Henderson, and Point Grey police commissioner H.O. McDonald.

When Mrs. Robinson stepped down, she was followed by John Sedgwick Cowper, who testified, in his colourful fashion, that he was in Robinson's office when the detective talked to Jackson by phone. He said he heard the detective say he was tired of holding Wong without getting any money and that Jackson should bring him some. During the time of Wong's incarceration in the suburbs, Cowper had started a drive in his *Saturday Tribune* to raise funds for additional sustenance for the houseboy while he was in captivity. The drive was an odd approach and obviously one of the factors that put Cowper in the witness box. At the very least it indicated he had to know how to contact those responsible for the abduction. The public had subscribed some $50, and Cowper had given the money to Robinson with the stipulation it be used to purchase food for the captive.

Cowper also admitted that during this period he had visited the house on 25th Avenue and said he donned a disguise when he spoke to Wong, who mistook him for a doctor. The disguise was likely one of the KKK robes. Cowper stated, "I held his pulse and I asked him questions. Every time I led him away from the beaten track of his story, his pulse would jump. This is one of the methods used in ascertaining if a man is lying."

The courtroom burst into roars of laughter when Mr. Justice McDonald grinned, leaned forward, and remarked to Cowper, "We haven't got that opportunity here." When the howls died down the judge smilingly stated, "I must apologize but I couldn't pass up this opportunity."

Cowper said he had gone to the house to take a picture of Wong because he was concerned about the man's health. He had asked Wong to remove some of his clothing so any mistreatment might be confirmed, but Cowper said he saw no signs of cuts or bruises, adding that Wong also looked well fed. During this performance on the stand, Cowper did his best to tie Attorney General Manson and Jackson to the kidnapping plot.

Manson sat gravely shaking his head when his old antagonist Harry Senkler took the stand at the request of Crown prosecutor Craig. Wong's lawyer said Manson had paid him a visit in order to recount the gist of a conversation the attorney general had had with Point Grey police commissioner McDonald. Under questioning Senkler revealed that, according to the attorney general, McDonald had started to tell him about the kidnapping, but Manson had stopped the commissioner, saying, "I don't want to know anything about it." Senkler said he told Manson he found this refusal peculiar.

Robinson was next up, followed by his son Willie. The Robinsons' defence was simple. They believed they had immunity from prosecution and they pleaded not guilty on this basis, admitting to the kidnapping and to the six-week imprisonment of Wong at the 25th Avenue house in Dunbar Heights.

Robinson explained that he had met Manson in Victoria in September 1924 and the attorney general had asked him what he thought of the first abduction of Wong from the street in downtown Vancouver. Glaring at Manson, who was sitting beside the prosecutor, Robinson stated, "I can look him fairly in the eye and tell him. He asked me if I thought it would clear the matter up if Wong were to be held for a longer time than on the first abduction. I answered 'Yes,' and then Manson said, 'Why don't you go ahead and do it, then?'"

The court was shown a copy of a letter Robinson later wrote to Manson referring to their meeting. It asked that Jackson be given Robinson's name in the event the investigator needed help. He said the attorney general didn't reply, but Jackson did write back saying he could not use his "valuable services." The accused maintained this was a cover-up letter written on Manson's orders and that Jackson did get in touch with him in person at a later date. Glaring this time at Jackson, Robinson said the two of them met about twenty times before the kidnapping took place. Jackson told Robinson he had been recommended by Paterson, at that time the chairman of the Council of Scottish Societies, as the best man for the job. The two met again in mid-January when the final decision was made to seize the houseboy. Robinson blamed Manson's hand-picked man for all the grief that followed.

Robinson said Point Grey police visited him unannounced, but clearly on orders from Jackson, to discuss the plans for Wong's interrogation. Shortly after this meeting he received an advance of $200, the first payment in the approximately $1,250 he was to receive from Point Grey through secret juggling of the municipality's books. He said a special signal code was worked out with the police in case he might at any time need their help.

Grilled by prosecutor Charles Craig, Robinson insisted he had been assured immunity and that the assurance came from Manson. The accused said he believed it was "an honest-to-God" transaction backed by the government. He said he had been confident that Manson could legally empower him to commit a crime.

Judge McDonald asked Robinson if he had laid information against several others, referring to Jackson and the four he had just accused of complicity. Robinson said yes. McDonald asked, "Do you intend to do all you can to see that the prosecutions are carried out?" Robinson answered firmly, "Yes, I do." His determination was clear and Jackson and Manson knew it.

Willie Robinson then testified that he stood watch at Osler Avenue when his father and Varity Norton grabbed Wong in the basement. Willie said that David Paterson and Mrs. Stratton, executives of the Scottish Council, were outside on the sidewalk when the man was kidnapped. Young Robinson was one of the robe-wearing guards who had been on duty throughout Wong's captivity. Willie testified that his father paid him $5 a day for his participation. He identified Cruickshank as one of the policemen who visited their home and Alex Henderson, the lawyer for the Scots, as another person who knew about the Wong abduction.

The crowded courtroom now eagerly awaited Manson's performance. He was duly sworn in and then described a second meeting with Robinson following their earlier Victoria discussion. Manson said that when Robinson started to discuss a plan to kidnap Wong, he interrupted, telling him this was Canada and such a thing could not be done. The attorney general's evidence seemed to show that he knew who had kidnapped Wong, yet this point was not developed further. Craig was in an extremely difficult position, essentially interrogating his boss.

The attorney general made it clear that he favoured a "fishing expedition" murder charge against Wong. This was the transgression of basic justice that Senkler and several others had protested when Wong was imprisoned at Oakalla. Manson said he and Jackson discussed in January the lack of progress in the case. They felt the houseboy should be put on trial so that whatever evidence had been gathered could be presented and further developed in a court of law. If Wong was acquitted, the public at least would know what evidence the police had. Manson said they decided to lay a charge because they felt there was a possibility of further developments. Before any charge was laid, however, the kidnapping took place.

The attorney general was questioned several times about the existence of written minutes covering various meetings that were held or of any written notes or instructions. He was asked if there were copies of instructions he had given to Jackson. Manson maintained it was all done by word of mouth and there were no records.

Although he had shaken his head when Senkler recounted his conversation with Point Grey commissioner McDonald, Manson did not deny telling Senkler that he refused to listen to McDonald. When questioned further by defence counsel Bird about the meeting, Manson proudly pointed out that he was a lawyer of vast experience who had started his legal career in June 1908.

For the first time in his two hours of testimony there was now pointed questioning about specific events, and electricity filled the air. Manson agreed that McDonald had come to see him of his own volition in April. Bird then asked, "And he came in and was prepared to open up to you in all regards in this matter of this abduction that you say your department was anxious to obtain information concerning?"

Manson answered, "With regard to that, I can't say, Mr. Bird. All I can say is that I judged from his first few words that he was going to discuss the matter and I considered it fair to warn him that he could not talk to me in confidence."

Bird followed up, "And that was exactly the impression you gave to Mr. Senkler in talking to him, that he was opening up on the whole thing and you said in horror 'No, don't talk to me about that!'"

Manson replied, "There was no horror about it; there was a plain fair statement, telling him that in substance he could not talk to the attorney general on that subject in confidence."

Bird then asked, "Did he ask for this matter to be kept in confidence?"

Manson shook his head. "I don't think he did."

"Then don't you think it was your duty, as the chief of the justice department of this province, to apprehend him [McDonald] if he was a party to Wong's abduction, and call a policeman?"

Evading a direct answer, Manson said, "Had that information come to me, well and good."

Bird followed up, demanding, "But you stopped the flow of information to you?"

Manson indignantly responded, "I did, and did it quite deliberately, and have no apology to make for having done it. I considered it the fair thing to do. A man might come to me—and I believe he did come to me—thinking that he could talk to me in confidence, and I certainly disabused his mind at once."

Bird turned from this verbal fencing to quiz Manson about several other aspects of the case and drew the statement that the attorney general had the utmost confidence in Provincial Police inspector Cruickshank. Manson said he had received police reports by "the bushel basket full," but he hadn't read them all. When Bird said he would like to see them, Manson airily commented he could give him a general impression of what they said.

Doing his best to catch Manson out, Bird then suggested there had been a bid to get a confession from Wong, that Manson was an accessory, and that somebody else was guilty of the major crime in Smith's death. The attorney general calmly responded, "My position in that is this: all the evidence we had was entirely circumstantial. It attached itself to Wong in this respect, that he on his own admission was alone in the house with the girl at the time of her death. The crime did not look to me to be one that was committed by the Chinaman. I had no right to arrive at a positive judgment in that respect. I did not know whether the Chinaman was guilty or whether he was not. I knew only the evidence we had for what it was worth and I made up my mind it was worth submitting to a jury composed in the public interest and let them try the matter so that they would know there was no attempt to protect anyone."

Manson did not spell out who needed protection, although it was clear that Wong, who had needed all the protection he could get under the legal system, had not received much from the chief law enforcer. Manson's statement conveyed the impression that he felt Wong could be sacrificed to appease public opinion and, in political terms, shore up voter confidence. Bird jumped on the point. He demanded, "Do you think it was right or do you say that it was reasonable under these conditions where a man was being held illegally by you to suggest the getting of any kind of a statement from him whatever under these circumstances?"

Manson bristled and shot back, "I do not know, Mr. Bird, if you mean the phrase illegally by me."

The defence lawyer replied, "You knew that he had been kidnapped by somebody."

Wrapping himself in the dignity of his office, Manson stated, "If you make any suggestion of that kind then I frankly say I have not the respect for you that one would expect to have towards another member of the bar. You know perfectly well I had no knowledge of that Chinaman being kidnapped and knew nothing."

Bird had every reason to think that Manson lied, but he pulled back, having made his point. "I withdraw that statement," he said, and Manson, in a tone of more sorrow than anger, commented, "It was a rather contemptible one, you know."

The defence lawyer pressed on, but Manson stated he was confident of the course he followed. When he left the witness stand, the attorney general had used all the fencing experience he could muster during the sharp exchanges with Bird. He hadn't given an inch, maintaining that he was far above any of the questionable tactics suggested by the defence lawyer, who had given him a fairly rough ride after the velvet-glove treatment from Craig. Manson's evidence was carefully couched in legal language, and he gave an unconvincing account of his role in the affair. He left the impression there was more to it all than had been divulged.

Manson had made it clear that apart from his late April meeting with McDonald in Victoria, the proposition of a kidnapping had been put to him months earlier by Robinson, who had discussed the same plan with Inspector Cruickshank, who in turn was answerable to Manson. According to the attorney general there had been "bushels" of police reports, most of which he had never read, but strangely enough there were no written records either in notes from Manson to his men or from them to him.

In contrast to the icy calmness of the attorney general's testimony, Jackson was like a snake-oil salesman on the stand, fast-talking, with arms waving, hard to follow and difficult to believe. He too used legal jargon to confuse, and like his boss he denied having any prior knowledge about the kidnapping.

The papers commented on the obvious: Jackson's rapid-fire delivery and his charged-up presentation. The jury tried to sort out his all-embracing claim that "Never, in any way, shape, or form did anyone connected with this department [attorney general's] or anyone connected with this matter, neither know of, or anticipate, suspect, expect or desire the abduction of Wong Foon Sing, and nothing was more surprising to me or the department than the events that took place at that time, on the twentieth of March, and furthermore, it was contrary to our expectations of being able to successfully, if not to bring conviction, get the truth of this tragedy developed." It was amazing that this statement, with all its conditional clause links, could be delivered without having to be read. Jackson was adamant that when Robinson suggested kidnapping Wong, he rejected the proposition.

Jackson said his meetings with Robinson were much fewer than suggested, claiming that there were only about three. Trying to impress the court that he was on dangerous work, Jackson said that when he met Robinson he ensured that he had a bodyguard standing nearby. Jackson didn't elaborate as to why he thought this necessary. He maintained the detective had told him he knew who was holding Wong captive, but Jackson insisted that he was unaware who the captors were. The special investigator maintained he asked Robinson for proof of the kidnapping and in return got a roll of undeveloped film. He had it processed and the pictures were some of those taken of Wong at the house on 25th Avenue.

Jackson also contended that he felt Wong was being held somewhere in the Gulf Islands, but exactly where, or why he thought this was the location was never explained. Jackson said that he believed Cowper knew who was holding Wong, and the reporter offered to act as a mailman and ensure that any communication Jackson prepared would be delivered to the kidnappers. Harry Senkler, however, had scuppered the investigator's proposal for a letter to Wong from the Chinese consul.

In light of Robinson's earlier suggestion that Wong be kidnapped, Jackson knew who the obvious suspect was when the houseboy disappeared. The same proposition had been heard by Manson, Inspector Cruickshank, and the Point Grey officials. It was much less than a closely kept secret. More a charade than a mystery.

After two days of testimony, the prosecution, defence counsel, and Mr. Justice McDonald delivered their charges to the jury. Prosecutor Craig said the father-and-son accused had gone into the witness box and admitted the crime. He said the judge would tell them that even if the attorney general had authorized them to carry out a kidnapping, it was no excuse for the crime. Craig said he doubted the jury would even have to retire to give a verdict.

He stated that if he had objected to much of the irrelevant evidence they heard they would not have learned all the details of the kidnapping. "The effect would be that the attorney general was not willing to face the music; that he was not willing that any suggestion of his wrongdoing might be told and heard in open court. The reputation of the attorney general was in a way committed to my care and I could not leave open a suggestion that he might have been willing to condone any crime. As between the attorney general and Robinson you do not have to decide. The public will do that." It was a statement that seemed more concerned with Manson's reputation than the facts of the crime.

Bird, in a bitter address, suggested the whole thing was a whitewash put on to protect the attorney general. He said it was a highly unusual case and the honour of the government of B.C. was at stake because either the government or the prisoners were guilty. "One or other of these," said Bird, referring to the prosecution and defence witnesses," is an awful liar; Robinson and his wife or the attorney general and Jackson. It is for you to determine."

He said the jury verdict would have a major effect on the administration of justice in B.C., and he attacked the government and the police for not investigating Robinson from the outset. Dealing with the sweeping power of the chief enforcement office, Bird said Manson even had the power to halt any prosecution in B.C. Judge McDonald cut in, stating, "Not while I'm here he can't."

The prosecutor gave a reason for Robinson not getting the immunity he had been promised. "There was such a blast of public clamouring as to blow Mr. Manson clear from his chair and the emoluments of his office if the immunity promised had been carried out," Craig maintained. He then stated that the only recourse was to have Manson impeached on the floor of the legislature. Mr. Justice McDonald quipped, "I hope you are not going to do it here."

The judge's charge was surprisingly short in light of all the evidence presented. He said he had permitted a great deal of evidence that did not bear directly on the charge because he felt the jurors would be able to differentiate the testimony. His main point was: "Both the accused admitted under oath in the witness stand that they had committed the crime with which they were charged. I tell you, this defence has nothing to offer that constitutes a defence."

Mr. Justice McDonald asked the jury to render its verdict without retiring, but the members declined his suggestion. They withdrew shortly after noon and returned within a half-hour with guilty verdicts against Robinson and his son. An addendum brought a wide smile to Robinson's face. The jurors strongly recommended that leniency be extended to the accused, intending that their urging would save the pair from long sentences. It was a brutal kidnapping, but after all, this was a second-rate detective confronting the police and the attorney general. The Robinsons found comfort in Mr. Justice McDonald's words to the jurors. "I will take your recommendations into serious consideration," he stated. "I was anxious that we retain our dignity and do what the public wants. I appreciate the confidence you have expressed in my charge."

Some wondered if it was not the court's duty to deal with the matter under the law rather than concur with the swell of pubic opinion, which ranged from the bigoted views of the Rev. McDougall and his believers to the moderates who wanted justice dispensed according to the statutes. Some assessed the jurors' verdict and recommendation for leniency as meaning that while they could not find the pair "not guilty," they had considerable doubts about the evidence of Manson and Jackson. Robinson was returned to jail, and son Willie was sent back to his mother pending sentence at the end of the assizes. The three directly involved in the kidnapping, the Robinsons and Norton, had been dealt with. Now the public eagerly awaited the trial of those said to be behind the crime: the Point Grey group, Jackson, and the four others from Point Grey charged by Robinson with complicity.

Cowper in Court Again

Before the trial of the big three from Point Grey began, the second trial of John Sedgwick Cowper took place. Throughout his first trial and conviction for criminal libel, Cowper had maintained an appealing, optimistic outlook that had intrigued his audience. The new trial on kidnapping charges opened on November 10 with a twist that would have been difficult for some but not for Cowper. He acted as his own counsel because his new lawyer, W.E. Haskins, was appearing on his behalf in another court, presenting a motion that Barbara Orford be added as a defendant in the upcoming civil suit for libel laid by Fred Baker. This motion was turned down, but for the time being it left Cowper representing himself in court.

It was vintage Cowper to take the part of a man seeming to play tennis by himself. He didn't exactly rush back and forth between the lawyers' table and the witness box to ask himself questions and then reply to them, but at times it seemed he did. The crowded courtroom watched the performance with fascination.

Cowper pleaded not guilty and convinced Mr. Justice D.A. McDonald, who by this time knew the facts inside out, to order the charge of kidnapping against him be dropped. The remaining three charges involved assault and forcible confinement, aiding and abetting in the abduction, and aiding and abetting in the imprisonment of Wong.

Prosecuting again was C.W. Craig, who told the jurors that anyone implicated in a crime was just as guilty as those who committed it. He said Cowper was a man who didn't have the courage to be a kidnapper but would let someone else do it and then go along with it as far as he thought the law permitted.

Wong was among the now well-known list of witnesses who testified. Cowper questioned them all about the many meetings and conversations he had been party to during the houseboy's imprisonment. He admitted giving Robinson $50 that he had raised through the paper as a sustenance fund for the houseboy. He also admitted taking pictures of Wong at the house and asking him to open his clothing to check his physical condition, but denied stripping him.

Cowper insisted that his interest in the affair was simply as a newspaperman who was endeavouring to help solve a mystery and get a scoop for his weekly sheet. Prosecutor Craig asked him, "And you did this all simply as a newspaperman? You were willing to risk a penitentiary term for this?" Loving the role of ace reporter and martyr to the cause of press freedom, Cowper answered, "Yes! Newspapermen often risk their lives, and as a matter of fact I believe I risked my life in this case."

The trial was over quickly. Mr. Justice McDonald gave a brief charge to the jury before lunch time. He told them that Cowper had no defence and that his admissions made that clear. The judge said there was only one possible verdict: "Guilty."

The jurors retired, went for lunch, and then came back to amaze the court with an unexpected and surprising verdict. Despite the evidence and the instructions given them by the judge, they found Cowper "not guilty." His luck, his quixotic personality, his perseverance, and his version of events had won them over. Maybe they felt he was already in enough trouble with the libel charges and the new charges of complicity. It was, nonetheless, an amazing decision, which infuriated Mr. Justice McDonald. The judge cited two instances alone that convicted Cowper: giving Robinson money to help sustain Wong during his captivity, even though it had been donated by readers in an appeal through the *Saturday Tribune*; and the removal of the captive's clothes, which constituted assault. McDonald spoke to the twelve in no uncertain terms. "I must tell this jury that they have failed in their oath. There was only one charge to return and I charged you on that. You have deliberately refused to accept my charge to you and you are discharged."

Prosecutor Craig urged the judge not to accept the verdict, but the very angry McDonald rejected the suggestion, possibly because he'd had enough of Cowper and most definitely of the jurors. The jury's decision and its lenient approach, however, gave added confidence to the next men on the stand, the trio of officials from Point Grey.

Point Grey Trio's Trial

Less than a day after they were severely censured by Mr. Justice McDonald for finding Cowper not guilty, five of the jury members found themselves back, weighing the evidence in the new case that opened on November 11. They were selected from the jury panel to hear the trial of the Point Grey contingent and were presumably picked in part by the defence counsel in the hope that they would be as sympathetic toward these three men as they had been to Cowper. They had defied one judge, why not another? In the dock were police commissioner H.O. McDonald, police chief John Murdoch, and Sergeant Percy Kirkham. Mr. Justice Aulay Morrison presided.

The accused, all of Scots descent, had the support of the crowd that jammed the public benches. Some onlookers arrived as early as 7 a.m. to line up for a seat. Officials wanted to avoid the mob scenes that had occurred earlier, so, as one newspaperman noted, "the usual quota of constables was augmented to prevent displeasures and interruptions." Extra brown-uniformed provincial policemen were on duty to maintain order throughout the assizes. When the doors opened at 9 a.m. the crowd surged forward and quickly filled the available seating. As usual, hundreds of disappointed would-be spectators were left outside.

C.W. Craig was prosecuting and told jurors that this was perhaps the most important case to be heard during the long fall assizes because of the positions of trust held by the three accused. Craig stated that the motives of the Point Grey police were to find the killer of Janet Smith. He sounded more like a defence counsel than prosecutor when he stated that "they tried to do what every honest man wanted to do, to solve the riddle that was confounding a whole community."

Craig added, however, that good motives were no excuse for committing a crime. He told the jurors that at Robinson's trial he had occasion to say he did not believe the accused's story. Now it was up to the twelve to decide if they believed him. The court was hushed as he exclaimed, "Personally, I wouldn't convict a dog on Robinson's evidence unless it was corroborated."

For the umpteenth time, Wong entered the witness box to tell his familiar story, but at 11 a.m. his evidence was halted as everyone in the room rose to observe two minutes silence on this November 11, Remembrance Day, in tribute to those who fell in the First World War. Vancouver had sent many men and nursing sisters to the front, more on a per capita basis than any other Canadian city, and many of these young men and women had paid a cruel price during the four-year conflict.

As the trial resumed, Wong Foon Sing identified Chief Murdoch as one of the men who visited the house and was present when he was finally removed from the house on 25th Avenue. Varity Norton repeated his story and also identified the chief as a visitor to the house.

The public expected something new when Robinson took the witness stand, and they got some interesting details. He told of meeting with Chief Murdoch and Commissioner McDonald several times when the kidnapping was in the planning stages. Robinson said these discussions covered the crux of what he was hired to do. He commented that the police commission and the men of its force didn't want to be directly involved in the kidnapping, but they believed it was necessary in order to find out all that Wong knew. Robinson also verified that both Murdoch and McDonald were at the meeting, along with Commissioner McRaney, in late April when he asked them what they wanted to do with Wong after he had been chained and held captive for about six weeks. The three men had agreed that McDonald should go to Victoria to get advice. This was shortly after Varity Norton's barely disguised blackmail attempt and his letter to Jackson in pursuit of money he felt was due him. They knew the jig was up and they had scrambled to get out of a tricky situation.

McDonald took the stand, and his testimony covered his meeting with Manson in Victoria. There is no doubt it was extremely damaging to the attorney general. The witness said Manson had stated, "Perhaps if you don't tell me anything it would be better. I am in a very peculiar position. Don't say anything to me but go back to Vancouver to Mr. Jackson and take your instructions from him." McDonald told a quiet, attentive audience that Manson said at the end of the interview, "I'll give you a message to take back to Vancouver. We will pay Robinson a reward—I'll leave it to you and Jackson as to what it shall be—keep it as low as possible. Now get back to Vancouver and forget you ever saw me." McDonald said that when he met with Jackson, the investigator initially disagreed with the reward proposition, saying he had not discussed it previously with Manson. The witness said Jackson maintained that all he had been told to pay was "that," and he held up five fingers.

McDonald testified that Jackson told him "to go get the Chinaman [out of captivity], if you have to pay go ahead, but don't get the government mixed up in it. I don't want that." He met with his Point Grey colleagues and cooked up the story about Wong being found wandering on Marine Drive. McDonald maintained he didn't know that Robinson had kidnapped the houseboy until the meeting at McRaney's house, when the detective asked what they wanted to do next with Wong.

At the mention of the house on 25th Avenue there was a disturbance in the court. Ex-soldier William Walker, who owned the bungalow in question, got emotional and demanded to be heard. He was stopped by court officials as he headed towards the front of the room, shouting that he was being persecuted. He already had yelled out "Liar" during testimony, angered at having been rebuffed by officials in his claim for compensation for damages to his house in Point Grey. It was just one more unexpected outburst in proceedings that were studded with them.

Manson's testimony was summed up in a newspaper headline that stated "Manson Memory Is Hazy." The attorney general was being watched closely by his political enemies. They gloated over every detail, hoping that something would emerge to incriminate him beyond any doubt. His political future was still very much in the balance. His abrasive arrogance combined with his legal combative approach had earned him his fair share of critics and enemies, so he was accustomed to being on the firing line. In the witness box he was cool and unruffled, showing no signs of confusion, even though his answers were carefully worded and he constantly weaved and ducked. His steely style spoke of someone in charge. Even his most vocal critics acknowledged that he was very tough and unlikely to crack. Manson and his deputy, W.D. Carter, were both fuzzy on some points but adamant about disputing McDonald's version of the Victoria meeting. Carter's support meant nothing, however, when he admitted under cross-examination that he might have left the office before Manson and McDonald finished their conversation. The evidence was similar to what had been presented at the Robinson trial. One reporter noted that McDonald sat smiling through all of Manson's repudiation of the evidence presented. The court was spared another performance by Jackson, who surprisingly hadn't been called as a witness.

Outright denial of the evidence presented by other witnesses was the basis for the defence of the three accused. Chief Murdoch, an eleven-year police veteran, said he did not know that Robinson had kidnapped Wong and declared he had never visited the house on 25th Avenue until the night the houseboy was released from captivity. It was never clear if he was responsible for the original report that Wong had been spotted wandering on Marine Drive by a passerby. That report had quickly been labelled a complete fabrication and pronounced "unbelievable."

Point Grey policeman Percy Kirkham's story was the often-heard refrain that he was only carrying out orders when he supplied Robinson with weapons and handcuffs. The sergeant stuck to the claim voiced by the others: he "didn't know the private detective had kidnapped Wong." He also disputed much of Norton's version of the freeing of the captive, denying he rode in the car with Norton and Wong to the drop-off point.

Defence counsel Stuart Henderson told the jury, in summing up, that Manson's selection of Jackson as his special investigator was an "unfortunate choice." Henderson said he did not believe that the attorney general or his deputy, Carter, had purposely told lies, but he also did not believe they could not remember details about the crucial meetings with McDonald in Victoria. This complicated pronouncement didn't dissuade many from the belief that the lawyer meant they were liars. He said the evidence of Wong, along with other testimony, was more than sufficient to establish the guilt of the accused.

In his charge to the jurors, Mr. Justice Morrison said an inference could be drawn from the fact that Jackson, the man who was supposed to have known all about the Chinese being held captive, had not been called as a witness. The judge noted that Manson was fully empowered to secure legal assistance and to ensure that each assistant was competent and above reproach, stressing that failure to do so was a dereliction of duty. Justice Morrison didn't name any names when he stated that the attorney general must not surround himself with "foul-mouthed, blasphemous blackguards or plantigrade [flatfooted] fools." Jackson filled at least part of this description, as much of his performance was foolish. Robinson and his squad obviously were the "foul-mouthed, blasphemous blackguards."

Mr. Justice Morrison warned the jurors they must not convict if they thought the accused were possibly guilty, but only if they thought them really and truly guilty beyond any shadow of a doubt. He stressed that any doubts they had must go in favour of the three men in the prisoners' box.

Two days after the trial began, with testimony from eighteen witnesses completed, the case went to the jury on the afternoon of November 13. There were four charges: kidnapping, assaulting by force of arms, confining beyond reach of the law, and illegally imprisoning. As in the other trials, the kidnapping charge was the one that mattered.

Three hours after they retired, the jury came back with not guilty verdicts on the key charge of kidnapping and on the count of assaulting by force of arms. They disagreed on the other two. The judge urged them to try to reach a conclusion and gave further explanations of the charges of confining beyond reach of the law and illegally imprisoning. It took the jurors only five minutes to decide the trio was not guilty of these crimes either. They came back with the verdicts that freed all three men of any role in the kidnapping of Wong Foon Sing.

Spectators cheered and applauded the decisions, crowding around the men to pat them on the back and offer congratulations as they left the courtroom. For the Scots it was a major win in their crusade, but the big one still eluded them. Wong was free, even though they were uncompromisingly confident that he was the man who took Janet Smith's life. They still hoped that somehow he would be punished for the crime.

The clearing of the officials from Point Grey closed another chapter in the saga. Norton had pleaded guilty to the charge of kidnapping; Oscar Robinson and Willie had been found guilty; Cowper was guilty of criminal libel, but he and the Point Grey trio had been found not guilty on all kidnapping counts. All that remained was Cowper's civil trial and the late and unexpected count of complicity against Jackson and the four others based on Robinson's charges. If they came to trial, the chances of conviction were slim due to the jury's finding in the most recent case, which in effect repudiated Robinson's evidence of the kidnapping. Political opponents, however, still hoped Jackson might be caught out if he was forced to testify, and there was always the outside chance of bringing Manson down with him.

Manson Battles Political Foes

While in public he still appeared to have the full support of Premier John Oliver, Manson was becoming a questionable asset in the ranks of the minority Liberal government, whose chances in the next election looked bleak, even without the fallout from the Smith affair. Critics charged that the attorney general merely *talked* about "British justice," but didn't practise it. He had also lost considerable support among his staunch Scottish followers. After all that had transpired in the long legal process, the question still remained, "Who killed Janet Smith?" Some even doubted there was a "who" involved. Despite all the evidence that had been presented, particularly that of the medical men, there were those who believed Smith's death was accidental or perhaps a suicide, as the first inquest had ruled.

The opposition finally had Manson on a spit in the legislature in Victoria. Their attacks were hot, heavy, and often vicious. For too long the attorney general had lorded it over his opponents in the House; now it was their turn. They attacked his appointee Jackson as a ham-fisted, egotistical, incompetent, amateur dabbler in crime who should never have been appointed to his job and who had disrupted an already floundering investigation. It was perfect fodder for the papers, which happily added their own condemnation, damning him for third-degree brutality and lynch-mob treatment of the Chinese suspect. Even the *Province*, which earlier touted Wong's guilt, now joined in the criticism of Manson.

Manson knew his foes were biding their time in the legislature, but he didn't show any concern on his return to Victoria when he rose in the House to respond to their attacks.

His supporters had expected fireworks and a barnburner response from the usually combative Manson, but he disappointed them with a relatively unimpressive defence. He followed the well-worn path of slamming the media and blaming the papers for almost all his troubles, focusing particularly on the machinations of Cowper and the *Saturday Tribune*.

He attacked Cowper as a diabolical man who had discredited B.C. in the eyes of the world by printing the grossest of slanders in his "slimy sheet." He went on in the same vein before abruptly sitting down after a much shorter speech than had been expected from the usually long-winded veteran. Then suddenly Manson resumed and became quite emotional. He boomed out, "Let the honourable members attack if they will any other part of my administration, but I beg them to leave justice alone unless, indeed, it be true they are assured that I am unworthy to administer it. If it has come to that, then the sooner I am removed the better. I leave myself to the judgment of you, Mr. Speaker, and of my fellow members. There are big things in the province to engage our attention, great problems, let not lust for power divert us from things that are worthwhile."

His statement surprised the opposition because it raised the question of his removal from office, a decision that lay with Premier Oliver alone. Manson had been one of the strongmen in a lacklustre cabinet, and the possibility that he might be dumped from the portfolio hadn't been considered, despite all the evidence of his interference in the Smith affair. Opponents began to wonder and hope there was a major development on the horizon, unknown to them, one that was about to break, discrediting Manson, and a forerunner to his possible downfall. They waited for Jackson's court appearance with great expectations.

The next day, November 17, the Robinsons and Norton appeared for sentencing at the assizes. Hopeful that the jury's recommendation for leniency would be observed, Robinson heaved a sigh of relief when he was given a year in jail, with the four months he had already spent there to count as time served. He was lucky, as were all the others. The court treated son Willie like an errant child, sending him home to his mother with an admonition to stay out of trouble. Norton got nine months. In the criminal libel case, Cowper was fined $200 or six months in jail. He still faced the civil action.

While awaiting his next trek to court, the irrepressible Cowper delighted in badgering Manson in the pages of the *Saturday Tribune*, narrowly skirting the minefield of libel, trying to avoid any further trouble with the law, but still getting in as many digs as possible at the attorney general.

The civil action against Cowper opened November 30, with Mr. Justice Francis Gregory presiding. The Bakers told their story one more time, Mrs. Baker referring with some amusement to the nasty, anonymous letters the couple had received, including one that advised her to take her troubles to a priest. The Bakers repeated they had nothing to do with drug dealing. In the last of his many appearances, Baker once more denied any dealing in illegal drugs but rather in substances "like Epsom salts."

It was over quickly. Mr. Justice Gregory was obviously keen to get rid of what he termed "unfounded charges" that had dogged some people for months. Charging the jury, Gregory stated, "I do hope this is the last time we will hear of these unfounded charges. People have been dragged in who clearly were not there [at Osler Avenue], but their names have been on the public tongue for months to their detriment." He was perhaps thinking particularly of his friends Lieutenant-Governor Nichol and his son Jack. The jury took his advice this time, and after only 44 minutes found Cowper guilty. The financial damages and award were to be worked out at a later date.

All that remained in the marathon was the case of Jackson and the four co-conspirators, but it hung over Manson like a black cloud. If the preliminary hearing went to trial, the case would not be heard until the spring of 1926, and the attorney general knew the media would worry the affair for all the intervening months. This could seriously affect the shaky government's future. In an election, the Smith affair would be used to attack the government on every husting. Because it was unresolved, Manson also worried that some unrevealed detail might emerge, bringing with it devastating damage. If this happened, would Jackson accept the role of sacrificial lamb? It didn't seem his style.

The Curtain Comes Down

The curtain came down abruptly on the last act of Janet Smith's sad story after nearly sixteen months of inquests and trials that had filled the pages of the papers and entranced the public. The preliminary hearing of the charges against Jackson, David Paterson, Mrs. Stratton, Point Grey police commissioner H.P. McRaney and reeve James Paton opened in a Vancouver city courtroom on December 1.

City prosecutor Major W. McKay rose to his feet, and the courtroom was suddenly silent as he told Magistrate H.C. Shaw that he had received a message from Victoria staying the charges against all five accused. There would be no prosecution. The unexpected, audacious move startled attendees and reporters alike. There were many who had wanted to see Jackson get his comeuppance. Instead of hearing new testimony, they listened as Shaw read a message from Deputy Attorney General Carter in which Carter maintained that the legal move was entirely his own decision. He didn't bother to appear in person, and there were not many who believed him, feeling without doubt that it was a direct order from Manson. Jackson was Manson's man, and while there seemed little new to be unveiled in further testimony, a new trial always provided a possibility of more scandal.

Carter maintained that the order could have been made earlier, but he had decided to wait until all the significant evidence was in, particularly the case against the Point Grey trio who had been found not guilty on all counts. He stated that these decisions constituted a repudiation of Robinson's evidence and his allegations against Jackson and the others. The deputy cited the assizes court jury's finding of guilt as proof that Robinson's story was beyond belief. "No public good can come from further proceedings," stated Carter, knowing it was a very hard sell with a skeptical audience, but insisting that Manson had left the decision entirely in his hands.

Carter contended that Robinson had not laid his charges in good faith and that the attorney general's department "should not lend itself to such a method." He added it would be an insult to ask the court now to consider such evidence and "it ought not, in common fairness, be permitted." Carter maintained it would be a "useless waste of public money and should be stayed." His hypocritical statement spoke of a justice that certainly had not been accorded Wong Foon Sing, and expenditure of public funds had not been a consideration in hounding of the houseboy. Nevertheless, the charges were dropped and the five were free.

Manson faced another round of sharp attacks from politicians and the public because of this latest move. It was reasonable to assume that the strategy had the backing, however reluctant, of Manson's colleagues and the premier, who had deemed that it was preferable to face attack over the move than risk possible disaster with Jackson on the stand again. One member, C.F. Davie, said Manson had abused his prerogatives with the stay of proceedings and that it swept away all confidence in him as the province's chief law enforcement officer. "It was the most shocking blunder and misuse of justice this province has ever known," he declared. Davie insisted that Manson, as the man in charge, should not have left something of this importance to his deputy.

The assault went on, with R.R. Pooley telling the legislature that Manson knew if Jackson was found guilty, the attorney general was equally guilty of criminal actions. Manson argued back that it would have been in his interests to have the case go ahead, but it would have been an abuse of the courts. The opposition moved a motion to slash Manson's $7,500 salary to $10, but his colleagues hung tough and defeated it in a vote.

With his party standing publicly behind him in the House (although in private some members voiced differing views), and in the face of Manson's stonewalling, the opposition attack and the furor finally died. The politicians had other issues to deal with and an election was looming. They also perceived that apart from objections made by the die-hard Scots, the trials were over and the decisions made, interest was waning, and even the media seemed prepared to live with the mystery of Janet Smith's unusual death.

It wasn't all over, however, for the unfortunate Cowper, the man who faced the largest number of charges and made the most court appearances. So far he had one win and two losses, being acquitted of kidnapping but convicted of the criminal and civil libel charges.

On December 7 the judge told Cowper the civil case was going to cost him a large sum of money. He was to pay the Bakers $2,000 plus the costs of the action. Baker's legal bill was expected to be about $1,500. In 1925 this added up to much more than a year's wages for most people. Two days later a writ was issued to set aside the transfer of Cowper's home at 1032 Pacific to his wife's name. Cowper turned over a $2,000 cheque to Baker and negotiated a lower damage bill. He was poorer, but he was neither cowed nor penitent. He still flailed away in his paper in support of his causes and against his arch-foe Manson.

Cowper wrote in the *Tribune* that if anyone thought the heavy financial penalties imposed on him would mean the end of the paper, they were very much mistaken. Despite attempts to take away his house, his "weekly paper of virile comment and opinion circulating throughout B.C." could not be silenced.

He was relentless, even when his fate and the amounts to be paid in the civil action were still before the courts. In November he had cockily announced a contest, the winner to be the person who made the closest guess as to the number of ballots cast in a "Should Manson Resign" poll. The winner would get transportation for two to Victoria and an introduction to the attorney general, something which Manson naturally knew nothing about.

In mid-December the *Tribune* announced the results, which came as little surprise. Ballots favouring Manson's resignation totalled 1,238, compared to a meagre five opposed and four spoiled. Cowper said the closest guess to the 1,247 votes cast was submitted by Mrs. E. Todd, who lived on West 20th

Avenue. The *Tribune* said her steamer tickets to the capital were on the way, but didn't mention the introduction to Manson. It's highly unlikely that Mrs. Todd and the attorney general ever met face to face.

The Cowper contest was one example of the reasons his *Saturday Tribune* was for a time a popular best seller, but its appeal didn't last and it faded away like so many papers and magazines that flourished briefly in Vancouver's early days. Undaunted, Cowper went on to other challenges.

The Unsolved Mystery

The court cases were finally over, there were no appeals, but still the question remained, as it will forever: exactly what happened to Janet Smith? Into the late 1920s the unresolved mystery still concerned some of the ardent Scots, but they were never able to revive the case, despite strenuous efforts. The only certainty is that the 22-year-old woman died at the Bakers' Osler Avenue home from a bullet fired into her brain. It cannot even be stated with certainty that she was murdered, although there seems little doubt that she was. Officially one inquest jury said her death was accidental, the second said she was murdered, and the case against the only man ever charged with her death, Wong Foon Sing, was thrown out quickly by the grand jury because there was no solid evidence linking him to it.

All that remains are some conclusions and assumptions, along with various theories that may or may not be true. One theory suggested that she committed suicide, but this seems unlikely. In her short life, Janet Smith had been born in Scotland and raised in England in a working-class home where money was scarce. She was bright, but circumstances forced her to seek work rather than pursue a better education. Her life had become more colourful and exciting than the average domestic's, however, after she answered the Bakers' advertisement for a nursemaid. She had enjoyed the sights and delights of Paris before agreeing to go on to Vancouver. Her diaries told of her life in the city, her church attendance on Sunday, her flirtations and romantic dreams, going to the dances she enjoyed so much, but they also told of the demands and restrictions of life at Osler Avenue. She had received at least two proposals of marriage, but had decided not to marry either of the young men. She even went to a political meeting and found it extremely boring.

Janet Smith had the Bakers' guarantee that they would pay her way back to England if she wished after finishing her initial one-year term of employment in Vancouver. She was not trapped, alone and destitute in a strange city. She was definitely not despondent. There was absolutely nothing to suggest she wanted to kill herself.

The medical evidence at times was contradictory and frequently incomplete, but it also seems to refute a verdict of suicide. Provincial police ballistics tests indicated there should be powder burns on Smith's forehead if the gun had been fired from no more than ten inches away. The medical team manipulated the woman's arms as she lay in the morgue and estimated she could have held the .45 a maximum distance of about ten inches from her body, although if she had pointed it at herself, the muzzle would have been only six inches from her head. This meant there should have been powder burns on her face if she committed suicide. There were none. Even if she was only examining the gun, as Baker suggested, and it had gone off in her face accidentally, there would have been powder burns. It also seems highly unlikely, despite Baker's contentions, that she would have taken the gun to the basement and stopped in the middle of her ironing to inspect it. There were those who thought she might have taken the gun in order to protect herself against Wong, or in fear of another intruder, but both of these suggestions seem far-fetched. If suicide and accidental death are discounted, murder is all that remains.

Forensic medicine was in its infancy in 1924, and methods in Vancouver were far behind what was then state of the art. Some facts did, however, emerge from the various inquests and trials. There were documented cases of a gun being fired at close range and leaving no burns on human skin. Many factors could be involved, including the calibre of the weapon and its condition, the type of ammunition and its age, even the humidity at the time it was fired.

There were questions about why no brain tissue was found on the basement floor or walls, evidence that could be expected following the impact of a heavy bullet. Possibly it was there initially, but was missed by the original investigators who also apparently failed to see a bullet lying in full view on the floor. By the time the police got around to taking a second look, the room had been cleaned.

Medical experts disagreed as to the cause of the burns found on Smith's body. Some contended the hot iron could have burned her skin without leaving scorch marks on her clothing. Others disagreed. The iron could have brushed Smith as Wong tried to raise her head, but it would probably have touched clothing rather than skin. The issue was never resolved. There was testimony by Dr. Blackwood that the iron was still warm when he arrived at the scene and examined the body. He estimated she had been dead slightly more than an hour, but would the unplugged iron have retained its heat for an hour?

Nearly all those investigating the case were of the opinion that Janet Smith should have crumpled forward when hit by the bullet through her right temple, but she was found lying flat on her back. Malcolm Jackson hammered away on this point but was unable to come up with any corroborating evidence for his argument that her body had been placed in the position in which it was found after she was killed elsewhere. It is undoubtedly possible that the impact of a large bullet from a heavy weapon at close range caught her off balance and threw her backwards. There also was one medical opinion that she could have suffered instantaneous muscle spasms that drove her backwards as she died.

One of the major blunders of the case was the failure of the Point Grey police—or anyone else—to establish that the bullet found on the basement floor several days later was the one that killed Smith. According to testimony, the bullets fired through the head of a pig and through a human skull in police tests were damaged, but the one found on the basement floor was not. Was it actually the bullet that killed her? Was it possible the bullet wasn't there when Constable Green made his first investigation? Did somebody put it there later? If so, who and why? Could the discovery of the bullet have been part of an elaborate attempt to hide the fact that Janet Smith had been killed elsewhere and her body carried to the basement?

How many people knew Fred Baker had brought the gun to his brother's house when he, his wife, baby Rosemary, and Janet Smith moved there temporarily in May? On that July day it is likely only four people knew where the .45 was after the houseboy moved it upstairs: Fred Baker, Doreen Baker, Janet Smith, and Wong Foon Sing.

As soon as he arrived at the scene, ham-fisted Constable Green wiped out what could have been valuable evidence when he picked up the weapon by the butt. Other investigators also examined it, totally destroying any chance of identifying fingerprints of Janet Smith or her murderer. Both Baker and Wong reported that the gun was jammed when it hung in the front hall and they couldn't release it. When the gun was found at the scene, Green asked Baker to hold it as he tried unsuccessfully to free the magazine. If it was still jammed after Janet Smith was found dead, was it actually the weapon that killed her?

The girl was found in a small basement room, but none of those first on the scene reported noticing any trace of an odour of gunpowder, and Constable Green didn't smell the barrel to try to determine if the gun had recently been fired.

Leaving aside the confusing physical evidence, who might have had the means and the motive to kill the nursemaid? If Fred Baker had reason to kill Janet Smith, he couldn't have done it that morning. He was too far away to commit the crime. Wong telephoned him within a few minutes of hearing a shot and finding the body. Baker could not have killed Smith and then driven from Osler Avenue to his downtown office in time to take that call. Could he have hired a hit man if he was worried that Smith suspected him of being involved in illegal drug deals? In the great welter of rumours tossed about by the public, this was one of the implausible possibilities.

Doreen Baker was running a number of errands downtown that morning by herself. Was it possible she wanted to kill Smith after hearing rumours of an affair between her husband and the housemaid? Her lawyer produced witnesses to testify to some of her activities—banking and shopping—but did the police check cab companies to try to determine if she returned home that morning? There was no mention that they did. Under any circumstances, however, it would be stretching the imagination to the absolute limit to consider her a suspect.

Arthur Dawson, the soon-to-be-dumped fiancé according to Smith's diaries, was clearly established to be working upcoast near Roberts Creek on the Sechelt Peninsula the day she died.

How much did the police question John Lake, a spurned suitor according to the woman's diary entries? It was never revealed in court, and the newspapers never presented him as more than a concerned friend. How bitter was his disappointment when Janet turned him down? If he wanted to kill her, would he have chosen to strike at Osler Avenue on a Saturday morning when he knew that Wong was in the house? Had Smith mentioned that the gun was in the house or told him where it could be found? It seems unlikely that he would have chanced prowling the house long enough to find the gun, even if he knew one was there. The fact remains he was in Vancouver that day and his precise whereabouts during the morning of July 24 were never thoroughly investigated.

Could any of the other men mentioned in the diaries have been a disappointed swain? Could one of them, or even a stalker, have known where to find the gun that lay beside her body on the basement floor? She wrote that her flirting made some women jealous, but it would be wild supposition to suggest that any rival in love came into the house and killed her.

Medical evidence stated that the very slight damage to Smith's vaginal area was in all probability caused by the embalming process, carried out on the controversial instructions of Point Grey police and Coroner Brydone-Jack before a full medical inspection had been performed. The hasty embalming prevented verification of a perplexing question. The doctors believed Smith had not been raped, and there were findings from the second autopsy to suggest that she died a virgin, but this could never be completely verified.

There was no evidence of an assault before she was shot, and her clothes weren't ripped or torn. Wong never mentioned hearing screams or any unusual noise coming from the basement before the shot rang out through the quiet house. The men working next door heard someone singing earlier that day but heard no screams and saw no unusual activity. Janet Smith either knew who fired the gun or was killed so quickly she had no time to cry out, speechless with surprise or fright.

Some elaborate theories circulated about Jack Nichol's role in the affair. Nichol was the son of the province's lieutenant-governor, the man who had hobbled on crutches into court during Cowper's criminal libel trial to say officially that he had nothing to do with Smith's death. He was prevented from testifying by the judge's ruling that his desired refutation had nothing to do with the case. Nichol, well connected and well heeled, was known as a fun-loving playboy and a prime candidate for gossip within high-society circles. He had an alibi for the day of the killing—he was out of town. But for many years he remained in some minds the likely suspect in Janet Smith's death. He was the man people envisioned as her killer at the infamous Osler Avenue orgy, despite the fact that there was no evidence any such party ever took place. If the workmen at the house next door were accurate that they heard Janet Smith singing Saturday morning, she could not have been killed Friday night. Dr. Blackwood's estimate of the time of death also made this clear. Elaborate, implausible theories, however, contended that Jack Nichol sneaked back into town for the alleged orgy, tried to rape Smith, and then killed her, despite all the evidence to the contrary. The break-up of his marriage about this time added to the speculation.

Barbara Orford's colourful claims about an orgy were nonsense. The imaginative shop assistant-cum-psychic lied originally by stating it all came to her in revelations, then claimed she had actually been there herself. She had made her reputation by dreaming up stories, and a new one about scandal among the hoi polloi was all she needed to make headlines, possibly attract new influential clients, and increase her fees for a seance or a look into the future. She guaranteed her own notoriety by naming prominent men in the community, like Lieutenant-Governor Nichol and his son. Among the points made by police to refute her story was the fact that an all-night orgy at Osler Avenue would have brought more traffic than usual to the quiet street, but there were no reports from neighbours of activity in the early morning hours of July 24. The total debunking of her story was never challenged. Orford had been persistent in getting publicity, refusing to be brushed off by police or politicians. She convinced Cowper of her fantasy and had her brief moment of notoriety before disappearing from sight, a confused woman with a vivid imagination. Long after she was gone, however, her fantasies lingered on in the minds of many who still believed a wild party had brought death to Janet Smith.

The young woman's diaries were used extensively by defence lawyer Harry Senkler. He challenged the assertion that she had been afraid of living in the same house as Wong by asking why she had not written of her fears? There were only scant references in the diaries to the houseboy, and if anything the comments described how well the two got on together. She helped him preserve fruit and he gave her some gifts, which she accepted. It seems likely, despite the racial divisions of the time, that the handsome Wong had developed a crush on Smith, who was an admitted flirt and probably encouraged his attentions, but there's nothing to suggest their feelings for each other went any further than that. Like many Vancouver Chinese of the time, Wong was a long way from home, separated from his wife and child, and no doubt lonely on occasion. Smith had taken pictures of him happily holding the Baker baby, Rosemary. Doreen Baker testified that Wong and Smith got along well and she was sure the nursemaid would have told her if she felt at all threatened by her co-worker. She never heard a word.

One conflicting factor was the unanimous testimony from Smith's friends that she told them she was frightened of Wong. Were they lying? Had they all been influenced by vengeful, persuasive Cissie Jones? Or is it possible that Smith, whose diaries told of romantic interludes with herself in the starring role, created stories she thought would excite her friends? Did she paint herself as a dauntless young woman—akin to the heroines of the silent movies—carrying on bravely despite the constant threat of an amorous approach from Wong? She frequented the movie theatres, but she was also well travelled, had lived in Paris, and had some experience of life. She seemed self-possessed and level headed in most things. Was what she told her friends real or an imaginative tale to pass the time at afternoon tea? Did she overtly encourage the excitement of an affair with Wong or did she live in fear of him? Was her annoyance at the restrictions placed on her by Mrs. Baker enough to prevent her from telling her employer of her concerns?

And if for some reason Wong wanted to kill Janet Smith, would he have picked that Saturday morning? The two were alone in the house, but he was bound to fall under suspicion if for no other reason than because of the racially charged feelings in the community. Was it likely he was overcome by passion or hatred while he was peeling potatoes and she was doing the ironing, with the Bakers due back for lunch? He was victimized in the press and hounded by the Scots. He was the target of the police and politicians. He was charged with murder on shaky circumstantial evidence because he was in the house when Smith died and public opinion maintained he had to be the murderer or, at the very least, was somehow involved in the killing. This was the thinking of Attorney General Alex Manson and his special sleuth, Malcolm Jackson. Wong didn't hide or run away to China as he could have done, despite months of accusations and intense pressure. In a land far from his home and family he lived in an atmosphere of hatred and contempt, enduring the shadow of execution. He was kidnapped, beaten, and held captive in chains for six weeks. He told of the horrors of having a noose placed around his neck. After he was committed at the preliminary hearing and let out on bail, with the noose still a possibility, escape would have been simple. His life was on the line and he had experienced the worst of B.C. injustice, but still he remained. His story never wavered or changed from the first interrogation to his testimony at the inquests, his appearances at the preliminary hearing on the murder charge, and finally in his evidence at the trials of the kidnappers. Yet for years and years there were those who contended he had to be the killer, one who covered his tracks so well that he couldn't be caught and so got away with murder.

How could the death of a young nursemaid have occupied centre stage for so long, raising doubts and suspicions about so many people, affecting their reputations, liberty, and even life in the case of Wong? The fact that some of the leading lights in Vancouver and Victoria were named as participants in the case, coupled with the determination of the implacable Scots, who got their dander up and wouldn't let go, were two principal reasons the affair went on and on. In this race-conscious era, Wong was an easy target.

Some people, including Manson's special investigator, Jackson, were aware that Fred Baker's activities in the drug business had been investigated by authorities in Britain, France, and Hong Kong. Neither he nor his partners were ever charged, although an associate was charged with trafficking, found guilty, and jailed. This fact lay behind the questions on drugs that produced theories suggesting Smith knew something and was killed to keep her quiet. Jackson pushed the issue but didn't get very far with it. Baker responded that Smith and Wong didn't have any knowledge of his business activities.

Was Smith's death the act of one person—rejected lover, drug-ring assassin, prowler, robber, rapist, or resident at 3851 Osler Avenue—or were others involved? Was there an incident, innocent or otherwise, that led to Janet Smith's killing and made it the impetus for a twisted, vindictive, racist plot that spun out of control and eventually involved provincial and municipal politicians, several police forces, administrators of justice, private eyes, leading citizens, an enthusiastic if misguided newspaperman, and a nutty clairvoyant?

Why did Manson become so drawn into the affair? He didn't like Asians and he was very proud of his connections with the Scots, who represented a great many votes for a troubled government heading for an election, but he was also an experienced politician who knew the dangers and pitfalls of becoming involved in such a high-profile case. Was political ambition the reason he took such a risk? If his early moves were meant to appease, they quickly unravelled, because the Scots complained bitterly of incompetent police work and a failure by Manson to push harder for prosecution. Did he become trapped and sink more deeply into the affair than he planned? The Smith case badly damaged Manson's reputation, putting an end to his hopes of becoming premier of the province.

The bungled investigation and the Wong kidnapping led to only one definite conclusion. The Point Grey police department was totally incompetent and inadequate to handle the needs of a community that was larger than the City of Vancouver in area and was growing at a faster rate. It was abundantly clear that policing throughout the region needed change. This was no help to those directly involved in the case, but the amalgamation of the three police forces, which took place finally in 1929, was a move in the right direction.

Wong Foon Sing, after a two-year struggle, received justice of a sort, probably all that was open to him under the laws of the day, especially considering that he was not a citizen of the country. No one knows how Janet Smith died, so justice for her is unattainable, but her death left an irremovable stain on the justice system of the day.

Wong Forsakes the Golden Mountain

For Wong Foon Sing, Vancouver had been far from a "Golden Mountain" that he would climb in search of prosperity. When he left China, he could never have dreamed, even in a nightmare, of what awaited him over the next dozen years in the strange new land. He expected to work hard, and he did, but he never anticipated becoming a key figure in a tragedy that tore at the very heart of Vancouver's ethnic and social structure. Wong had been beaten and persecuted, shackled and held captive, but he nonetheless remained determined and steadfast in his proclamation of innocence. It wasn't ethnic typecasting to call him stoic in the face of prejudiced authority.

In 1926 he was still employed at the house on Osler Street, and he refused to run, even when rumours again swept the city, pushed eagerly and desperately by the Scots, that another charge might be laid against him. His Scottish foes always feared he would slip away from B.C.'s legal jurisdiction, but he hadn't tried to do so to this point. Legally, there was nothing to hold him.

In March 1926, however, Wong had made up his mind, and one evening in early spring he stood at the rail of a gleaming white Canadian Pacific Empress liner as it pulled out of Vancouver harbour bound for the far east. A few friends and his uncle were there to say goodbye. His departure was no secret; Senkler ensured that the authorities knew.

Wong must have had mixed feelings as he watched Vancouver fade into the distance: joy that he was free from persecution, but disappointment that his dreams and ambitions had been dashed. A dozen years earlier he had arrived with high hopes; now they were all gone. He was returning to Fujian province, to a life from which he had previously fled. There would be few opportunities for him in a land where poverty and overpopulation were the normal conditions. The fact that Canadian law did not allow him to bring his wife and child to Canada may have been the deciding factor in his return to China. At the very least he deserved compensation for what he had suffered, but this was unlikely to happen in the 1920s. It is doubtful that any lawsuit filed in the city on his behalf would have succeeded. At the least it would have been blocked for years in expensive legal entanglements. Harry Senkler apparently didn't advise him to launch any action, and the lawyer had been a tireless battler for his client's rights.

Manson no doubt was thrilled to see Wong, the thorn in his side, sail for the far east. There was nothing new and nothing to warrant further charges, no matter how the Scots felt. While Wong remained in Vancouver he was an embarrassment to the attorney general and a political threat to the Liberals because of suspicions about the kidnapping. The media had abandoned the Smith case for the time being, but even a whiff of a new, exciting rumour would put the story back on the front page. Wong went quietly home, probably with not much more in his pocket than when he arrived. Vancouver never heard of him again.

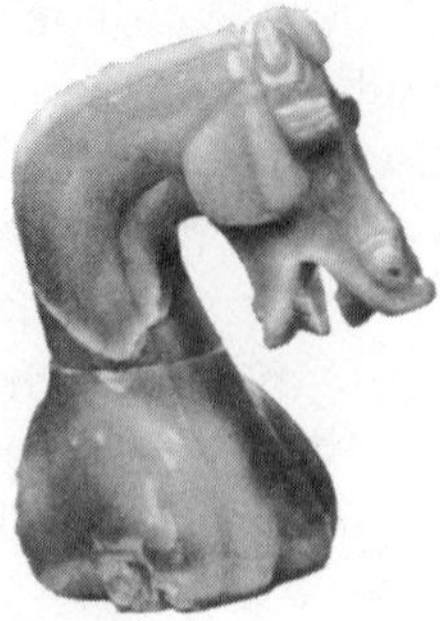

The Judgments of Mr. Justice Alexander Malcolm Manson

If Wong Foon Sing went unrewarded, this was certainly not the case for Alex Manson, whose later career was outrageous and even frightening for those with respect for the judicial system. The man who directed the investigation and prosecution of Wong, and whose key role in the kidnapping plot was all but proven, was an avowed racist who became a judge.

Manson had entered politics in 1916 and was elected for his local riding as the member for Omeneca. He was appointed deputy speaker of the House in 1918, and shortly thereafter became speaker, holding that position until he was appointed attorney general and minister of labour in 1922. Manson survived the 1926 election despite criticism of his role in the Janet Smith-Wong Foon Sing affair, even though the Liberal government went down to defeat. The controversial case had put many new dents in the government's battered armour, and Manson became merely a member of the opposition.

A Liberal government returned to power in British Columbia with an election win in 1933, but Manson's political career was over. He had been an MLA for several years and held the key post of attorney general, but now he found himself a backbencher. The new premier, Duff Pattullo, didn't want any part of Manson and his controversies, and the former senior minister was not appointed to cabinet. Manson was outraged and looked for somewhere else to go. In a move that was politics' gain but justice's loss, he was appointed two years later to the B.C. Supreme Court—a surprise to many, particularly in the legal field. There were other men who could have been chosen for the post and it was difficult to understand why the Liberal government in Ottawa selected him in view of his record, but he did have friends in high places. Some believed that the federal ministers bowed to the entreaties of their fellow provincial Liberals to get Manson out of B.C. politics.

To make an erratic politician a judge was a dubious call. Those who questioned his fitness to hold such power had their misgivings borne out many times in his 26 years on the bench. His conduct made him one of B.C.'s most controversial and notorious justices. Manson was soon dubbed "a hanging judge," and his rulings were changed and altered on appeal more often than those of any other man who ever sat on the bench. He seemed to stalk controversy. His actions and comments both in and out of court, on a daunting range of topics, frequently caused consternation in his audience and guaranteed him headlines.

During the Second World War the Canadian Labour Congress called for his dismissal from the War Services Board, stating he was "unfit to hold the position." The B.C. Pulp and Sulphite Union was among those over the years who demanded his removal from the bench, contending that his outspoken anti-labour views made him unfit for his position. Manson knew well the controversy he stirred up in a province where the union movement was well-embedded and powerful. He ignored all the demands of his critics and stayed on the bench at a time when judges were on a taller pedestal than they are today.

Alex Manson's colourful, turbulent career came to an end in September 1961, much against his wishes and with more controversy. He was forced out under a new federal law that set the retirement age for judges at 75. He was 77. Manson was highly critical, claiming that judges were appointed for life, but this time his loud objections changed nothing.

Scrappy criminal lawyer Angelo Branca was twice ordered out of Manson's court under escort when they clashed during trials. While he disagreed with many of Manson's views on life in general and matters of law, Branca developed a love-hate relationship with the former attorney general. He recognized Manson's many failings in the political field, but Branca knew that the man's tireless energy and determination to have things done his way were more suited for the hustings and the legislature than the dispensation of justice. Branca's biography, *Angelo Branca: Gladiator of the Courts*, was entrusted by him to writer Vincent Moore, who also worked for many years as a court reporter. Moore probably was voicing the view of Branca when he wrote in the book, "After years spent around courts, seeing dozens of judges at work, I rate Mr. Justice Manson the worst judge I ever knew."

Possibly it was because they were both combative and unafraid to take on challenges that Branca admired some of the quixotic aspects of Manson's mind. Branca was a champion of the underdog and he was intrigued by Manson's personal concern for the future of some of the people he jailed after they got out, while he unmercifully crucified others who appeared before him.

It is significant that Manson called on Branca to represent him in his unsuccessful bid to avoid forced retirement from the bench at the age of 77.

Manson always was good fodder for journalists because of his actions and eccentricities, and in a farewell interview he told a writer what many had known and his record showed: "As a judge I broke all the rules." During his quarter century on the bench he delivered some 460 judgments, including the imposition of a dozen death penalties. Manson said he was not a hanging judge "but a fearless judge." He claimed that personally he was opposed to the death penalty but was required by law to impose it, although critics always felt he showed an unhealthy interest in the execution process.

On his retirement, Manson said, "Some think it is the sole duty of the court to protect the accused. But it is also its duty to see that society is protected. I don't fear death and I have never lost a night's sleep over a capital case." He considered drug traffickers "worse than murderers," and they got some of the stiff fifteen-year to life penalties he handed out. Manson was adamant that modern society was going to the devil with loose morals, a lack of responsibility, and a lust for money. He noted sadly, "The rock pile has gone and the preachers have done away with hell."

His retirement comments included a swing at the Vancouver police department, whose detectives, he said, were "blundering and inefficient." He said the force needed an overhaul in its training methods, and for once most people agreed with him. Even with municipal and police department amalgamation in 1929, including the absorption of Point Grey's "Keystone Cops," the force was still graft ridden and incompetent.

In retirement Manson still managed to hit the headlines with his caustic observations and opinions. When free-enterprise premier W.A.C. Bennett surprised the province with an about-face and nationalized the B.C. Electric Company, Manson labelled it a conspiracy between the company and the provincial government.

When he died in September 1964, aged 81, there were no great tributes by fellow judges or the legal profession recognizing Manson's career on the bench or his years as a lawyer or even his service as a politician. Walter Owen, the treasurer of the B.C. Law Society at the time, gave a brief, carefully worded comment, saying no more than was necessary or conventional. He paid tribute to Manson's great personal courage and his independence. Owen's most telling observation was that "any mistakes he made were of the heart." The minister at Manson's funeral in West Point Grey Presbyterian Church said he was "a good citizen, a happy warrior, and in the Scottish idiom, a bonnie fechter [fighter]."

An editorial in the *Vancouver Sun* was less kind and more trenchant. Under a heading "Death of a Rule Breaker," the paper stated that in his long years as a judge, Manson "often made up his own law as he went along." In a sweeping understatement it noted this was his "weakness." Those he sentenced could expect the severest treatment based on Manson's view "that the end justifies the means," the editorial said. It added that he reserved this privileged philosophy for "a God-fearing, family-loving, Presbyterian moralist such as himself," and it noted that this attitude meant Manson's sentences "were frequently and critically altered by appeal courts." Few provincial judges, stressed the editorial, had been "as roundly and consistently excoriated by a wide section of the B.C. public," his problem being that he took it upon himself to correct single-handedly the cardinal sins. These were the aspects of Manson's life that many recalled on his death.

As late as 1996, Manson's conduct as a judge was under fire after the discovery of letters from 1948, when fears of the "red menace" and the spread of communism were sweeping the United States and having an effect in Canada. An article in the *Victoria Times Colonist* stated that Victoria lawyer John Saxton had found damning letters in the archives about a man he had defended in a 1948 criminal libel case. The letters between Mr. Justice Manson and Prosecutor Alex Cunliffe discussed the need for, and the best way to get, a conviction and the maximum sentence. University of Victoria's David Williams said in the *Times Colonist* article, "Manson was a very bloody-minded judge. He didn't have a great deal of respect for the legal profession."

This was the man who directed the course of justice and the prosecution of Wong Foon Sing. The 1925 *Canadian Annual Review*, published shortly after the close of the Janet Smith case, carried an unusual quote from Attorney General Alex Manson in which he stated, in retrospect, "I have tried to maintain the administration of justice untarnished in this province. I would with all my heart that these pages in our history had not been written." It was Alex Manson who had dictated much of the Janet Smith story that he now regretted. This was an unusual comment from a man who seldom admitted he could have been in the wrong.

There was no Charter of Human Rights in the 1920s, and rights depended largely on race, colour, money, power, politics, and one's rung on the social ladder. It wasn't only in later years as a judge that Alex Manson "broke all the rules." As a politician and the province's chief law enforcement officer he always marched to the beat of his own drum. Wong Foon Sing was only one of many who could have testified to that.

Other Major Players

Harry Senkler, the lawyer who battled tirelessly on his client's behalf, died suddenly following surgery at the age of 58 in March 1926, about the time Wong Foon Sing left Vancouver to return to China. His tenacious, often theatrical performances were a hallmark of the many appearances he made in the houseboy's defence. He was the senior partner in the prestigious firm of Senkler, Buell and Van Horne, and for three consecutive terms he was elected a bencher of the Law Society of B.C. At his death he held the key position of Society treasurer.

He was hailed as one of the best-known lawyers in B.C., a forceful character "who commanded the respect of an unusually large circle." The *Province* added that people liked "his many qualities, his courage and the spirit of fair play which he displayed at all times, even to those who disagreed with him the most. Impetuous by nature, he was also generous in victory and cheerful in defeat. He had few enemies and few men were held in such high regard by all sections of the community." In his younger days he had been known in amateur sporting circles as a cricketer, lacrosse player, rugby enthusiast, and rower.

A lifelong Liberal, Senkler was defeated twice in electoral tries for the legislature and the federal House. He bucked the party line when he disagreed with policy or particular people. His old foe Manson fell into the latter category, and political affiliation never detracted from Senkler's criticisms of the attorney general in or out of court. It was very noticeable that Senkler's eulogies paid tribute to his accomplishments as a lawyer, something missing almost entirely from the statements made on Manson's death.

The Baker boys went on with their lives in Vancouver. A few years after the Smith trials, Richard was the director and manager of the bond department for Gillespie Hunt and Company. Fred was the manager of the Stevens Baker Company, "importers and exporters of grain, small foodstuffs, shipping and commission merchants." Before the Second World War, Richard invested in and became the president of Vancouver Properties and manager of the city's medical-dental building across the street from the courthouse. Fred became assistant manager of the same building and retired shortly after the war.

A war hero and a man whose name became almost a household word in Vancouver in the mid-1920s, Fred Baker's death went almost unnoticed, ignored by the major dailies but accorded a small front-page story in the morning *Vancouver Herald* in the spring of 1956. He plunged 40 feet to his death from the fire escape of a downtown Vancouver hotel. He died in St. Paul's Hospital on April 30 from injuries suffered in the fall from the second floor of the St. Regis Hotel on Dunsmuir Street. Baker, 63, was at this time living in Qualicum Beach on Vancouver Island. Why he was on the fire escape wasn't known, but the story said he had undergone a medical examination in Vancouver. He left widow Doreen, three children, and five grandchildren. The newspaper story made no reference to his role in the infamous Smith-Wong tragedy more than 30 years earlier, and the death notice in the classified columns of the *Sun* and *Province* did not mention that he was a distinguished veteran of the First World War.

Although the principal was jailed for kidnapping, Oscar Robinson's detective bureau remained in business and was still going strong in 1927. Surprisingly, his business licence wasn't lifted—or perhaps it was and he ignored this technicality. Ex-cons are hardly the stuff of private investigators, but Robinson carried on, even landing in trouble for a minor misdemeanour shortly after he got out of jail. In 1928 his operation was no longer listed in the city directory.

Manitoba-born special sleuth Malcolm Bruce Jackson peaked as an MLA with a brief stint as deputy speaker. He was a long-time member of the Law Society of B.C., which he joined after moving to Victoria. Jackson lived and worked in the capital city for the rest of his life, but never again made the headlines or gained the prominence that he achieved during the Janet Smith affair. He was active in the community, a keen sailor, and an officer in the capital city's yacht club. He died in Victoria in 1947.

John Sedgwick Cowper carried on in his own inimitable style and became a feisty columnist for the *Province* after the *Saturday Tribune* folded. He died in 1946, an iconoclast to the end, but, like most of the others, he was never as dominant a figure in Vancouver as when death stalked Osler Avenue.

The Rev. Duncan McDougall's publication, *The Beacon*, lasted two years and seemed to pick up an increasing amount of advertising, particularly from the city's chiropractors, but it folded after its ravings became more than the majority could stand and when interest in the Smith case waned. McDougall went on ministering in his own particular way.

Former Point Grey policeman James Green went into the hotel business. Some Scots, who never forgave him for his role in the Smith investigation, wondered if he had used hush-hush payments, received for not telling all he knew, to buy the hotel, but these suspicions were never verified.

General McRae became a Conservative senator in Ottawa, and Gordon Wismer made it to the legislature, becoming controversial attorney general in the coalition government of Byron Johnson. Former Point Grey reeve James Paton, the man who hired Robinson for $1,250 to investigate the Smith affair for the municipality, also moved upwards in politics and became a coalition MLA. Alex Matthew, the former Council of Scottish Societies executive whose name was found on Robinson's list of those prepared to bankroll Wong's kidnapping but who was not prosecuted, became a Social Credit member of the legislature in the 1950s.

There was some solace for lumber-mill worker Arthur Dawson, who was engaged to Janet Smith when she died. He eventually married Jean Haddowe, one of Janet's many friends who had testified that she lived in fear of Wong Foon Sing.

All the other principals in the Smith-Wong story are likely long dead. Even teen-aged kidnapper Willie Robinson, if still alive, would be in his 90s.

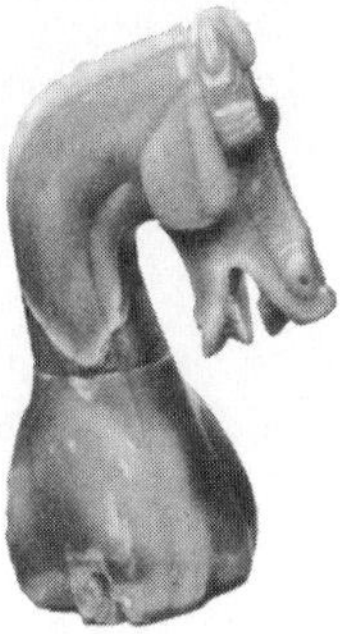

Janet's Resting Place

Mountain View is a sprawling cemetery in southeast Vancouver, with graves dating back more than a hundred years, and where burials still take place today. It is the largest cemetery in the city, covering 106 acres and stretching over twelve city blocks from north to south. There have been 160,000 people buried there since the first body was interred in 1887, one year after the city of Vancouver was founded. Then the cemetery was located in a lonely area far from the tiny community rebuilding along Vancouver harbour after the disastrous fire of 1886. Today Mountain View is entirely surrounded by urban housing, heavy traffic, and the commerce of busy East Vancouver.

The unveiling of Janet Smith's tombstone brought one of the largest crowds ever seen at Mountain View to a ceremony more than a year after her death, when the humble nursemaid was still more prominent in death than she was in life. It was estimated that over 4,000 people attended the service, the huge crowd spilling out onto 41st Avenue and Prince Edward Street. Today her gravesite is easily found in a small section of the cemetery immediately south of 41st Avenue, near John Oliver High School. It is to the right of the entrance off 41st. While many of the graves have only flat markers lying flush with the ground, Janet Smith's monument remains standing, its single pillar, with the top broken in the old Scottish style to identify an early death, dominating the area. It has weathered well the passage of some 75 years, although there are signs of a slight tilt. The inscription remains clear and legible.

Not surprisingly, there are none who go there today to mourn or to remember. Janet Smith had no relatives in

Vancouver, and the Scots who felt so passionately about her fate are long since gone. Some of those who have learned more recently of her tragic fate visit the site out of curiosity. There are many graves at Mountain View, but the cemetery's office staff, who have obviously responded to more than a few queries, quickly locate Janet Smith's resting place for visitors without having to check the ground plans for details. The unfortunate Janet is gone but not quite forgotten.

Davie Lew, Lew Hun-Chang, gunned down in a Chinatown murder a few weeks after Janet Smith was shot, also is buried in Mountain View, but today there is no visible sign of his grave. The site is on the cemetery's records, but recently even an employee was unable to locate any marker recording the life of one of Chinatown's very colourful characters of the 1920s, who, like Janet Smith, died young.

Epilogue

Laws have been made and strengthened in Canada in the 75 years since the abuse of Woon Foon Sing, and it is highly unlikely that there could ever be a repetition of such persecution, although the connivance of government and the powerful can never be discounted. The Bill of Rights gives Canadians added protection, so much so that there are those who believe it goes too far. In keeping with changing public attitudes, today's media question, probe, and challenge official government policies and processes more than they did in the 1920s, which is not to say they always get it right. In addition, today there are many more avenues for scrutinizing the unfair dictates of governments and special interest groups. On its own, the Internet provides individuals with a voice they have never known before.

While laws have changed since the victimization of Wong Foon Sing, it would be naive to suggest they are now perfect or evenly applied, but more basic protection is there. Laws, however, do not change public attitudes towards racism and prejudice based on colour, race, or religion. The federal government's uneven approach to immigration and refugees is an area that helps to harden public opinion at the beginning of the new millennium. This is particularly true in the case of illegal immigrants who are permitted to remain in the country, at taxpayers' expense, until their cases are decided, while others, who applied legally to move to Canada, are refused entry for obscure or ill-defined reasons. Immigration policies can only succeed if they are seen to be as fair as possible in the interests of this country, rejecting both the cries of extremists demanding the slamming of the door of fortress Canada and the demands of other groups that the door be torn down and entry thrown wide open.

The responsibility for eliminating racism does not lie only with the existing population, which over the years has developed an acceptance and tolerance that our ancestors did not possess. New Canadians are not asked to assimilate but to integrate, to accept Canada as it is with all its faults and difficulties, while working to improve the multicultural society we have become. Integration allows new Canadians to keep the aspects of their own culture that are important to them, but it also asks them to be a part of Canadian society, to learn the languages spoken, to attend public schools and institutions, and to become part of the fabric of the nation. Multiculturalism as sweeping as in today's Canada is an experiment of which we are all a part.

Canadians of the 21st century will gladly accept people of different cultures who want to be a part of Canada, but not those who want to establish foreign ghettos and who bring with them all their old prejudices, ancient hostilities, hatreds, and religious wars. Canadians will always be skeptical of those whose interest is where they came from rather than where they are.

The country is not one big happy multiracial society, despite well-meaning claims that it is. On the other hand, it is recognized throughout the world as having made significant attempts and indeed great strides toward accommodating different peoples. It is understandable that newcomers, especially those who must first learn the language, will depend on former countrymen for support and aid, but there is less need today for the same protective, suspicious attitudes and fears that once led to cloistering and ghettos. The argument that this is how we used to do it in some far-off place has little currency in 21st-century Canada.

There are no better witnesses to this evolution than some British Columbians of Chinese ancestry, who knew of the head tax, lived with the persecution, and needed the protection of Chinatown in 1920s Vancouver. There were no citizenship opportunities then, and blatant discrimination existed in the province until 1947. While progress was stalled in those early years, it has advanced mightily since then.

Andrew Joe (inset) was the first Chinese-Canadian lawyer in Vancouver—called to the bar in 1953.

In Vancouver today are Chinese Canadians like Andy Joe, who is proud to explain that he was the first Chinese Canadian called to the B.C. bar in 1953. Andy Joe's mother was an indentured servant with a well-to-do family that brought her to the province from China when she was nine. When his father met and wanted to marry her, he had to purchase her from the family.

In 1953 Chuck Lew was the fifth Chinese man to graduate in law from the University of B.C., and both of these B.C.-born men still practise in Vancouver. Chuck, born in 1930, smiles at the birth certificate provided by the provincial government that classifies him as Chinese. His mother, a B.C. pioneer, was born in Cumberland on Vancouver Island in 1900. Her birth certificate also stipulated she was Chinese. She lived in B.C. for

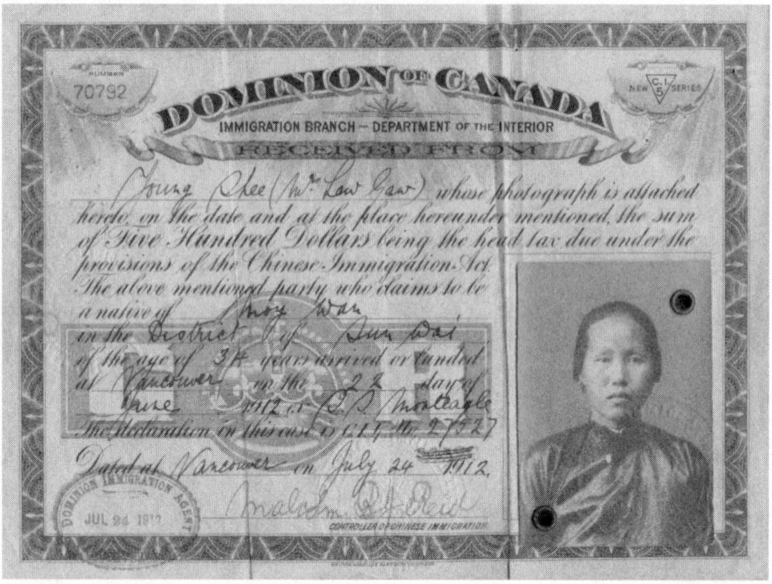

NUMBER 70792

DOMINION OF CANADA

NEW C.I. 5 SERIES

IMMIGRATION BRANCH – DEPARTMENT OF THE INTERIOR

RECEIVED FROM

Young Shee (Mrs Lew Gaw) whose photograph is attached hereto, on the date and at the place hereunder mentioned, the sum of Five Hundred Dollars being the head tax due under the provisions of the Chinese Immigration Act. The above mentioned party who claims to be a native of Moy Wan in the District of Sun Wai of the age of 34 years arrived or landed at Vancouver on the 22 day of June 1912 ex S.S. Monteagle The declaration in this case is C.I. 5 No. 27527

Dated at Vancouver on July 24 1912.

DOMINION IMMIGRATION AGENT JUL 24 1912

Malcolm R.J. Reid

CONTROLLER OF CHINESE IMMIGRATION

When Vancouver lawyer Chuck Lew's paternal grandmother, Young Shee, arrived in British Columbia in June 1912 she was required to pay a head tax of $500. Fresh off a small steam ship from China, the young 34-year-old woman carried the Canadian immigration document, with her, stamped with the date when she passed through Customs and Immigration, July 24, 1912. The document, along with Chuck's father's chop, a Chinese family identity symbol, is one of the historic items now treasured by the extensive Lew family.

98 years, for more than 60 years in the family home on Prior Street, the outer fringe of Vancouver's tightly knit Chinatown, and died in 1998. In the year 2000 the house was vacant but still standing.

Both Lew and Joe admit that by the time they attended school in the 1930s, attitudes were changing. Chuck Lew comments, "There were over 50 different nationalities at Strathcona School even in those days, so we didn't face any racial discrimination."

Lew fondly recalls his classmates at high school. Long before the creation of the ubiquitous hamburger chain, Chuck was dubbed McLew by his Scottish buddies on the football team. They even taught him the Scottish songs of Harry Lauder.

Both men belong to large families whose members have studied hard, graduated from some of the best schools on the continent, and prospered. These and many, many others are proud of their Canadian heritage and are active within the community. Their allegiance is to their province and to their country.

In Vancouver today, nearly half the inhabitants are of Asian descent, whether Chinese, Japanese, East Indian, Vietnamese, Laotian, Korean, or some less visible nationality. How long will it be before their numbers outstrip the descendants of the Scots, English, Irish, and other Europeans who arrived with the earliest settlers? A ready acceptance of a common future would remove lingering doubts and fears within both groups.

Possibly better than any laws or fretting about statistics is the growing evidence clearly visible every day on the streets of B.C. communities that things are changing. Inter-marriage is further breaking down racial barriers. The resulting toddlers are the multiracial citizens of tomorrow, those who will proudly and confidently shape and lead B.C. into the future, assured of their place in a society that is becoming an example to the world. They will have all the opportunities forbidden to Wong Foon Sing.

Appendix 1
The Chinese

On June 28, 1858, the steamer *Caribbean* pulled into small, lonely Fort Victoria at the south end of Vancouver Island. The ship had stopped at San Francisco en route to the rugged north coast after its trans-Pacific voyage from China. Aboard were 300 Chinese, the first major movement of migrants from the Orient to what was to become the province of British Columbia. The discovery of gold in California some twenty years earlier had attracted the first Chinese; now reports of strikes along the Fraser River and in the Cariboo drew them north.

The first Chinese, many from the area around Canton, landed in Victoria. Some stayed on Vancouver Island to work in the resource industries—mining, logging, and fishing. They soon established their own areas within the communities of Victoria, Cumberland, Duncan, Nanaimo, and a few other Island centres. By about 1880 there were approximately 3,000 Chinese in B.C. There were early cries from the white population that cheap "coolie labour" was taking their jobs, and the *British Colonist* newspaper in Victoria echoed the sentiment: "The Chinese ulcer is eating into the prosperity of the country and must be cut out."

It was the building of the Canadian Pacific Railway, the country-spanning line that induced B.C. to join Confederation and opened the west, that encouraged many more Chinese to enter Canada. The ambitious railway project, which many predicted was doomed to failure, had a myriad of problems, including finding enough men to tackle the backbreaking tasks involved in the mammoth construction project that would cross a wilderness of forests and muskeg, raging rivers, and mighty mountains. Prime Minister Sir

John A. Macdonald in 1882 put the Chinese labour argument succinctly: "It is simply a question of alternatives; either you must have this labour or you can't have the railway." The decision was made and the Chinese were in.

One of the most difficult sections of the CPR to build was the stretch from Kamloops to tidewater undertaken by contractor Andrew Onderdonk. It required blasting a route through the rugged Fraser Canyon and was destined to be the final resting place of many who toiled there. Onderdonk enlisted the aid of as many of B.C.'s approximately 35,000 white population as he could persuade to take jobs, along with Native people and as many workers as could be attracted from the U.S., where other railway projects were under construction and competing for available labour.

The contractor needed a work force of 10,000, and he soon looked to the Chinese, who were his only alternative and who would work for $1 a day compared to the top rate of $1.75 for white labourers. In the winter of 1881–82, Onderdonk chartered two sailing ships that brought 2,000 more coolies to B.C. He was to bring in another 6,000. Between 1881 and 1884 some 10,000 Chinese came across the Pacific to Canada and another 4,000 moved up from the U.S., although not all of them worked for the railway.

The Canadian government estimates that 600 Chinese died from accidents and sickness while working on the railway. Many were killed in premature explosions because of the sensitive nature of the dynamite used to blast through rock to build right of ways, tunnels, and bridges along the canyon walls. But it was not only the Chinese who died and suffered in the great project; illness and accident took many lives with no regard for age, race, or ability. Living conditions for anyone working on the railway were primitive, nourishment was inadequate, and health services all but nonexistent. The CPR was built on the endurance, courage, and tenacity of a great army of men of many races and nationalities, including those who died and those who were maimed or suffered ill health for the rest of their lives. There were labourers who saved some money, and there were others who blew their hard-earned wages on gambling and drink. All those who toiled along the Onderdonk section deserve the gratitude of today's beneficiaries. It is a large part of the early Chinese contribution to the development of the province.

Appendix 2
The Notables

Alexander Duncan McRae

Alexander Duncan McRae was one of Vancouver's earliest multimillionaires, an entrepreneur, politician, and leading socialite in the first half of the twentieth century. He always knew what he wanted and went after it ferociously, from a range of business enterprises to his own short-lived political party. McRae was a self-made man who slipped easily into a life of power, prestige, and wealth. It was written of him that he "wasn't too big on education but he could read a financial statement faster than any other man alive and could say 'No' so swiftly it would make your head spin." Often seen as imperious and demanding, he frowned on social assistance programs and was a believer in rugged individualism. McRae was convinced that people were better standing on their own feet than leaning on government. It was said that privately he was "friendly, hospitable and philanthropic."

Typical of McRae's style was his desire to move a California sequoia tree to the five-acre grounds of his magnificent mansion Hycroft, which stood on the slope of a hill with a sweeping view of the city, the harbour, and the North Shore mountains. The rare tree had been planted and was growing in New Westminster some fifteen miles away. McRae saw it and wanted it. Told by arborists that it couldn't be moved, McRae said it could. He bought it, had a special wagon made, and trundled the tree through the streets to his estate. Today, nearly a century later, the giant sequoia proves McRae was right.

His story was the epitome of the boy from a farming family who made good. Born near Glencoe in southwestern Ontario in 1874, he went to Duluth, Minnesota, where he developed an insurance company that he sold in 1903, making a handsome profit. He married Blaunche Latimer Howe, a wealthy American, and returned to Canada with $50,000 to invest. And invest he did, putting together parcels of land that amounted to some 500,000 acres around Qu'Appelle, Saskatchewan. Purchased for $1 per acre, they were sold six years later for $9 million.

McRae moved to B.C. in 1907 with a small fortune, "raring to go" in the quickly developing natural resource industries. With his entrepreneurial spirit he forged a role as a major player in business, adding greatly to his own wealth. He invested in Fraser Mills, Canadian North Pacific Fisheries, Wallace Fisheries, Canadian Collieries, a lumber company at Golden in the Interior, and in other enterprises. He had three daughters. The oldest, Blanche, became the wife of Dick Baker of 3851 Osler Avenue.

In 1909 he started to build Hycroft. He spent $100,000 on the 15,000-square-foot mansion with its 30 rooms on three floors, a basement ballroom with adjacent lounge, and a mirrored, brass-railed stand-up bar. The wine cellar held 2,000 bottles. There were stables, a play area for the children with a swimming pool, greenhouses, and a fountain in the oval garden at the front of the house. Some local architects sniffed at what they saw as Hycroft's pretentious, pillared-portico style, but McRae liked it. The family moved in and by 1913 the mansion became a glittering jewel, resplendent with flowers year round, but particularly with tulips in spring. New Year's Eve balls at Hycroft were one of the highlights of the winter social season, and invitations were much sought after. McRae enjoyed donning a costume for the annual fancy dress affair that brought Vancouver's top 100 rushing delightedly to the house on the hill.

McRae went overseas in the First World War and his organizational ability and drive shot him up the military ladder to the rank of major-general. His wartime role, however, brought lasting post-war criticism from his foes in the political and business world, where he was pictured as a backroom soldier who never spent a minute in the trenches or heard a shot fired in anger. The criticism was tinged with envy and dislike and was unfair. The other criticisms levelled at McRae concerned how he made so much money so fast and whether his fortune was based on his wife's money or his own. There were also questions about dubious land deals in the Fraser Valley in the 1920s. But McRae ignored his critics, always marching to the beat of his own rapid drum.

A lifelong Conservative, McRae became disenchanted with all of the province's political parties, particularly the Liberal government and the way it spent money. He announced he had a better financial plan for B.C. Sidestepping the established Conservative party, on October 29, 1923, he organized the founding meeting of what was to be known as the Provincial Party. He attracted many of the city's business leaders to the first gathering in the Dominion Hall on West Pender. Many abandoned old party affiliations and loyalties because they were unhappy with the existing government and the alternatives. Alex Manson led the Liberal attack on the new group, infuriating McRae by questioning where the multimillionaire had made his money and what his current aims were. An angry McRae challenged Manson to a debate in which he promised to account for every bit of his wealth. Manson did not pick up the gauntlet and was savaged by McRae at the meeting for failing to show up and for his role in the government's poor performance. McRae also kept his promise, outlining in broad terms how he amassed his fortune.

At the same meeting he unveiled his financial policy as leader of the Provincial Party: "We must keep expenditures within prospective income and there must be no resorting to increased taxation but rather an effort made to reduce and more evenly distribute them." McRae pledged to "end extravagance, incompetence and dishonesty" in government. Those attending the inaugural meeting also adopted a proposal to look into the gradual replacement of Asians in the labour force by white workers. Among those on the party's advisory committee were Fred Baker and Harry Senkler, the lawyer who was to defend Wong Foon Sing.

In the election of 1924, McRae discovered that while money helps in politics, it carries no guarantees at the ballot box. He missed winning his seat by less than 100 votes in his personal bid to be elected in Vancouver. He was not alone in losing, as most of the other candidates for the Provincial Party were also demolished. It elected only a handful of members. As quickly as it rose, the party disappeared from the scene. McRae kissed and made up with the Conservatives and was a winner in the 1926 federal election as the Tory MP for Vancouver North, only to lose four years later. He never again tried for elected office. His promotional and organizational skills were credited with doing much to sweep R.B. Bennett to the prime minister's role in Ottawa in 1930, and McRae was rewarded with a Senate appointment a year later.

He was embarrassed when his family was drawn into the Janet Smith affair, with the fatal shooting taking place in July 1924 in his daughter Blanche's home. She and husband Dick were on vacation in Europe, so were obviously not directly involved, but in McRae's view the situation was too close for comfort. Over the years he had built up enough enemies—newspaperman Victor Odlum noticeable among them—who revelled in citing the millionaire's name in connection with the tragedy. Any rumour was fodder for the mill, although it was clear that he had absolutely nothing to do with the affair.

He remained a powerful figure in the Conservative party and in B.C.'s business world during the 1930s. During the Second World War he turned Hycroft over to the federal Department of Health and Pensions for $1 for use as a hospital. He moved to his Eagle Crest estate near Qualicum Beach on Vancouver Island, where he became a gentleman farmer, raising Angus cattle. McRae was 71 when his colourful life ended in Ottawa on June 26, 1946.

Hycroft remains one of Shaughnessy's most striking mansions, the property of the University Women's Club, which purchased the beautiful home from the federal government in 1962 after it had ceased to be a hospital and had been abandoned for two years. The front garden and fountain have been replaced by a parking area, but the towering sequoia still stands proudly. McRae's beloved Eagle Crest burned to the ground in 1969.

Lily Lefevre

If Alexander McRae was on the top rung of the ladder of success in the city in the 1920s, Lily Lefevre was his female counterpart. A striking, patrician woman, she had a cultured style and was equally at home in a splendid salon or a company board room. She ruled in elegance for 50 years, in later years residing at her magnificent home, Langaravine, near what is now the University of B.C. campus. A pioneer, her obituary when she died on October 17, 1938, headlined the fact that she "Arrived Here Before the Railway."

Like McRae, she was a native of Ontario, born in Brockville. She came west from Montreal in 1886 when her husband, Dr. John S. Lefevre, was appointed surgeon for the Pacific division of the new CPR. He was both doctor and investor, a founder of B.C. Telephone Company, with interests in a variety of other enterprises. As an employee of the CPR he had access to information about new city developments, which enabled him to invest in land in the right place at the right time. He purchased property on the far side of False Creek just before the first bridge was built across it. He was a member of the first city council of Vancouver and president of the Board of Trade. When he died in 1906, his widow took over his portfolio, and her business acumen added significantly to the considerable fortune she had been left.

She was prominent in Vancouver's cultural life as one of its leading hostesses. A philanthropist, she also was a poet and a patron of the arts. Her poetry was gentle if not memorable. She published a book of her work in 1895 and another in 1934. With her obituary, the *Province* carried these lines from her verse:

> When bathed in sunset splendour
> The snow-capped mountains rise
> Like some great altar soaring
> In greatness to the skies.

She was a founder of the art gallery in Vancouver and of the Vancouver chapter of the International Order of the Daughters of the Empire. Mrs. Lefevre was the elder Mrs.

Baker's sister and the aunt of the Baker brothers and their sister. Having no children of her own, she took the trio under her wing and taught them the social graces, giving them the opportunity to enjoy the finer things in life. Before her death in 1938, she presented a $5,000 scholarship and gold medal to the University of B.C. in memory of her husband.

Among the honorary pallbearers at Mrs. Lefevre's funeral was Alexander McRae. Together they represented in their different ways what success could be obtained and what contributions could be made in the young province of British Columbia, just as did Yip Sang, who came to Vancouver in 1880, organized Chinese labour for the CPR's Onderdonk section, became a businessman and exporter of B.C.'s goods, founded the Chinese Benevolent Association, and raised a remarkable family of achievers.

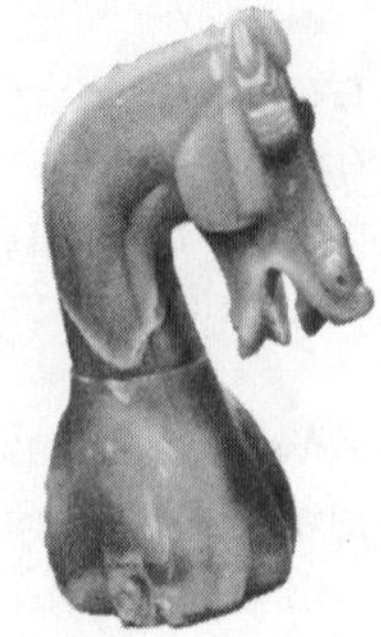

Acknowledgements

We are indebted to the following for their advice and assistance:
Helen Abbott, former *Vancouver Sun* reporter
Freda Bailey, University Women's Club Archives
Andy Joe, first Chinese lawyer called to the bar in Vancouver in 1953
Chuck Lew, fifth Chinese lawyer called to the bar in Vancouver in 1953
Vera Lucas, Victoria researcher
Sheena Macdonald, computer researcher
Zheng Zhang, UBC Asian Centre Library, for providing translations from the *Chinese Times*

Bibliography

Primary Sources

B.C. Legislative Library, Victoria
B.C. Provincial Archives, Victoria
National Archives, Ottawa
National Library, Ottawa
Vancouver City Archives, Vancouver
Vancouver Public Library, Vancouver
Victoria Public Library, Victoria

Books

Berton, Pierre. *The Last Spike*. Toronto: McClelland & Stewart, 1971.

Canadian Parliamentary Guides 1916–30.

Harris, Heather and Mary Sun. *The Chinese Canadians*. Toronto: Nelson, 1982.

MacDonald, Bruce. *Vancouver, A Visual History*. Vancouver: Talonbooks, 1992.

Moore, Vincent. *Angelo Branca: Gladiator of the Courts*. Vancouver: Douglas & McIntyre, 1981.

Morley, Alan. *From Milltown to Metropolis*. Vancouver: Mitchell Press, 1974.

Roy, Patricia E. *A White Man's Province*. Vancouver: UBC Press, 1989.

Sing Lim. *West Coast Chinese Boy*. Montreal: Tundra Books, 1979.

Starkins, Edward. *Who Shot Janet Smith?* Toronto: Macmillan, 1984.
Walker, Russell. *Politicians of a Pioneer Province.* Vancouver: Mitchell Press, 1969.
Who's Who in B.C. 1947-48.

Newspapers and periodicals

B.C. Monthly
The Beacon
Canadian Annual Review, 1925
The Chinese Times
The Labour Statesman
Nanaimo Free Press
The Saturday Tribune
Searchlight
Vancouver Province
Vancouver News Herald
Vancouver Star
Vancouver Sun
Victoria Colonist
Victoria Times
Victoria Times Colonist

Index

In previous books for Heritage House, **Betty O'Keefe** and **Ian Macdonald** have developed a knack for providing insight into Canadian social history while relating an engrossing, often dramatic story. ***The Mulligan Affair: Top Cop on the Take***, was shortlisted for the City of Vancouver Book Award and is on reading lists at UBC's School of Journalism. ***The Final Voyage of the Princess Sophia*** and ***The Sommers Scandal*** have been applauded by reviewers from Ottawa to Vancouver Island.

The Mulligan Affair

Top Cop on the Take

Ian Macdonald and Betty O'Keefe

ISBN 1-895811-45-7

5½ x 8½ • 160 pages

Softcover • $16.95

The Final Voyage of the Princess Sophia

Did they all have to die?

Betty O'Keefe and Ian Macdonald

ISBN 1-895811-64-3

5½ x 8½ • 192 pages

Softcover • $16.95

The Sommers Scandal

The Felling of Trees and Tree Lords

Betty O'Keefe and Ian Macdonald

ISBN 1-895811-96-1

5½ x 8½ • 192 pages

Softcover • $16.95

For more information on these books visit the publisher's website at www.heritagehouse.ca

The Authors

Betty O'Keefe was a *Vancouver Province* reporter for seven years in the 1950s. She worked in corporate communications for fifteen years and was commissioned to write two corporate biographies.

After stints at the *Victoria Colonist* and the *Vancouver Province,* Ian Macdonald joined the *Vancouver Sun* and was legislative reporter in Victoria for five years and then bureau chief in Ottawa from 1965 to 1970. He worked in media relations for the prime minister's office and was head of Transport Canada Information. He has written for magazines, radio, television, and film.

Since 1994 Macdonald and O'Keefe have collaborated on writing projects related to West Coast history. Published books include *The Klondike's 'Dear Little Nugget'* for Horsdal & Schubart through to 1999's best-seller *The Sommers Scandal. The Mulligan Affair: Top Cop on the Take,* their first book published by Heritage House in 1997, was nominated for the City of Vancouver Book Award. *The Final Voyage of the Princess Sophia* followed in 1998. With *Canadian Holy War* now between covers, Betty and Ian have begun research for a new book.